PANAVIA TORNADO

AVIATION SERIES

Panavia TORNADO

Andy Evans

The Crowood Press

Acknowledgements

My sincere thanks to all who aided in the preparation of this book. In particular I would like to would like to single out Gordon Bartley from BAe for his excellent support and enthusiasm, and to mention the following, in no order of preference: Flt Lt Mike Tomlinson, Wg Cdr Alan Threadgould, Flt Lt Caroline Hogg CRO RAF Coningsby, Flt Lt Maggie Pleasent CRO RAF Leeming, RAF Cottesmore, Gary Parsons of f4 Aviation, Shirley Grainger at W.Vinten, Paul J. Perron, Graham Causer, Dave Stock, Wg Cdr Stuart Black, Flt Lt Steve Morris, Flt Lt Ian Donovan of No.617 Squadron, Sgt Rick Brewell, Dale Donovan RAF Strike Command PR, Panavia Aviation and John Oliver at Rolls Royce.

First published in 1999 by
The Crowood Press Ltd
Ramsbury, Marlborough
Wiltshire SN8 2HR

British Library Cataloguing-in-Publication Data

A catalogue record for this book
is available from the British Library.

ISBN 1 86126 201 9

Designed and produced by Focus Publishing

Printed and bound in Great Britain by Bookcraft, Bath

Contents

Introduction

By today's exacting military standards the success of the Panavia Tornado is an historic achievement, and one that must make this tri-national programme one of the greatest feats of international military and political co-operation of the 20th century. Rather than being the proverbial 'camel' (otherwise known as a horse put together by a committee), the Tornado has proved itself to be a true thoroughbred, able to deliver 'as advertised' in all weathers. The latter is the cornerstone of the Tornado's performance, as there are painfully few aircraft in NATO that can function by night, by day, in fog, in rain or snow, and mount realistic offensive operations.

Although many would argue that the best way to ensure your aircraft can still fly if your runways are knocked out is to have a totally V/STOL force, designers and commanders have, up to now, resisted this at all costs, as is shown by the size of the worldwide Harrier force. Future aircraft will be endowed with such items as vectored thrust for improved STOL performance; Tornado was conferred with an excellent short field ability, by virtue of the power of its engines, which included thrust reversers, and the arrangment of its flaps and slats. It offers a compromise between traditional runways and STOL performance, and it must also be remembered that even the unique Harrier requires a take-off run to carry anything like a worthwhile payload.

Many aviation historians would doubtless say that the famous De Havilland Mosquito was the original Multi-Role Combat Aircraft, but the arrival of the jet age brought a plethora of new aircraft into the skies. Their designers clung to their 'traditional' one aircraft—one mission thinking, and therefore air forces found themseleves with specialized fighters, bombers and reconaissance aircraft. As budgets became tighter, many promising projects began to be discarded through financial or political pressures, and a number of countries began to see the sense in committing to bi-national or tri-national military projects, or alternatively were persuaded to 'buy American'. In Europe the growing Soviet threat postwar led Britain, Germany and Italy to agree to produce a single aircraft type that could fly a wide variety of combat missions, and yet still be tailored to meet the needs of the individual user nations.

So was born the MRCA – later Tornado – and a management company, Panavia Aviation, was created to oversee the project which was to be a swing-wing, low-level 'bomb truck', also capable of defence surpression, stand-off laser designation, anti-shipping and reconnaissance tasks, with further consideration for a dedicated interceptor variant. The programme was a triumph of co-operation, which incredibly faced few hitches and has produced perhaps the greatest aircraft of its type in the world today. This author's computer spell check has no knowledge of the word 'Panavia', and instead suggests 'Panacea', which the Tornado has ably demonstrated it is! Proven in battle as well as in keeping the peace, the Panavia Tornado has a singular history, and with Mid-Life Upgrade programmes in place, the aircraft will continue to play its part in European and in Middle Eastern defence policies well into the next century.

Andy Evans

CHAPTER ONE

From The Ashes

Background to MRCA Project

On 5 July 1967 Denis Healey, then the United Kingdon's Minister of Defence, announced that France had withdrawn from the Anglo-French Variable-Geometry (AFVG) aircraft project and that he was authorizing the British companies involved, British Aircraft Corporation (BAC) and Bristol Siddeley, to continue variable-geometry studies to an amended specification. This seemed to fly in the face of government policy, as the administration had for the previous ten years been denying any need for manned combat aircraft, and was at the time negotiating to buy fifty American F-111K 'swing-wingers' for the RAF!

BAC had, in fact, been one of the originators of variable-geometry technology, and the Tornado can trace its roots back to the fascinating world of the intriguingly-named 'polymorphic aircraft configuration studies' – in other words, aircraft that can change their shape in flight – pioneered at Weybridge by the renowned Sir Barnes Wallis, who had done more work on the subject in the decade following World War Two than anyone else. Later, his colleagues at Warton 'discovered' the advantages of having a wing that could spread out to a wide span with high-lift slats and flaps for a short take-off with heavy loads, be 'cleaned up' and then pivot back for supersonic flight. It was these studies that eventually resulted in the BAC P.45 design, a two-seat variable-geometry fighter-bomber upon which the Anglo-French Variable Geometry (AFVG) strike-attack aircraft was to be based. In 1958 the Warton team, then

working on Specification GOR.339, which led ultimately to the TSR.2 programme, studied variable sweep as a possible route to a true multi-role capability. Test rigs were built at both Warton and at Vickers' Weybridge factory, but when Vickers, English Electric and Bristol merged to form the nucleus of BAC in order to build TSR.2, they agreed that there were too many unknowns with variable geometry and TSR.2 was designed with a fixed wing.

Originally intended as an interceptor for France, the AFVG was a troubled project, born as the 'British-led' partner to the 'French-led' SEPECAT Jaguar, but more than anything as a consolation prize for BAC's not being given the lead in the Jaguar project. The reasons for making the AFVG a collaborative project still remain something of a mystery to many observers,

Test firing the IWKA Mauser canon. BAe

Prototype P.01 in its garish red and white colour scheme. BAe

as there was little commonality between the British and French requirements, although a bi-national design would have been easier and cheaper. Britain already had its P.45 airframe design, the RB.153 engine and the avionics from the (by now cancelled) TSR.2, ready and waiting for a suitable customer. As an aircraft destined for French service, but not blessed with the French having design leadership, the AFVG never stood much chance of being a success, since Dassault was continuing with its own swing-wing project, the Mirage G, and continued to insist that any collaborative aircraft be powered by the (Anglo-French) M45 engine.

There was also the French government, which did everything possible to delay and complicate the aircraft, constantly changing its specification and the numbers it required. At the same time, the French used their participation in the AFVG to squeeze the best possible terms out of the British for the on-going collaborative helicopter deals – which later became the Gazelle, Puma and Lynx – for which the French also managed to gain the leadership, and all this came alongside the baggage brought along by their 'joint ownership' of the Jaguar programme. Furthermore, as the United Kingdom was trying at the time to enter the Common

Market (as the European Union was then known), the British were obliged for political reasons to adopt a 'softly-softly' approach to the AFVG project.

Inevitably, the French pulled out of the project, but studies continued in the UK under such names as UKVG, VGCA, ACA (Advanced Combat Aircraft) and Future CA, with the M45 engine being replaced by the Rolls-Royce RB.153. BAC engineers were able to do enough testing to perfect two areas that were vital to building a swing-wing aeroplane. One was the wing pivot bearing and the highly stressed wing roots and centre-section box linking the pivots, all of which caused major problems on the F-111. The other was the high-lift slats and flaps which were essential if the full gains of variable geometry were to be realized. By mid-1968 BAC Warton had built and tested an excellent wing pivot using a Teflon bearing, which demonstrated the required safe life for fatigue-free service in the most demanding kind of flying, low-level transonic attack. Another and more comprehensive full-scale rig proved the centre wing box, not as a research tool but as a proposed production item built by hard tooling and subjected to 'production type' inspection.

Despite having already been 'stung' by a

collaborative deal, Britain was once again looking to work with its European allies on a multi-national programme, a deal that was made more plausible by the abandonment of the UK's so-called 'East of Suez' commitments, which resulted in the RAF's radius of action being significantly reduced. On 10 July 1967, a team from Warton visited the Munich headquarters of EWR-Sud, an aircraft-industry consortium formed in 1959 by Heinkel, Messerschmitt and Bolkow – later abbreviated to MBB with the association of Blohm, who included in their design team the famous Kurt Tank – to develop a Mach 2 V/STOL aircraft to a NATO requirement. EWR later became a subsidiary of the new giant Messerschmitt-Bolkow-Blohm (MBB), and were collaborating with the United States on an even more ambitious and complex Advanced Vertical Strike (AVS) aircraft. MBB teamed up with Fairchild Republic on this supersonic single-seat project which featured 'swing-out' lift engines in the forward fuselage.

BAC proposed German collaboration with UKVG or another P.45-derived swing-wing aircraft, with the Jaguar (to be made partly in Germany) as an interim aircraft. This proposal was eventually deemed unacceptable, in part because of heavy sales efforts by Northrop with its P.530 Cobra: Northrop had convinced the Luftwaffe that it would be possible to design a single multi-mission aircraft much simpler and lighter than AVS to replace its F-104 Starfighter and G.91 aircraft. In January 1968, Germany was joined by other major NATO F-104 users – Italy, Belgium and the Netherlands, with Canada taking part merely as an observer – for what was entitled the MRA 75 or Multi-Role Aircraft for 1975 (its proposed service entry date).

This effectively torpedoed a Jaguar/UKVG deal, but it also helped kill AVS. In the second half of 1967, the MBB engineers slowed down work on AVS and got down to non-jet-lift studies not dissimilar to those being undertaken at Warton. Engineers and diplomats from Munich and Bonn talked to all possible collaborators, but BAC seemed by far the best bet because of common objectives and timescale. MBB had, however, already begun work on the *Neue Kampfflugzeug* (NKF), which was to be a lightweight, single-seat, single-engined fighter-bomber. Although it was totally incompatible with the big, twin-engined,

two-seat UKVG, it did fulfil a requirement closer to the RAF's needs than had the *Armée de l'Air*'s requirement for the AFVG.

BAC seemed remarkably relaxed about who could have design leadership in any collaborative project, having shaped and driven the Anglo-French Jaguar despite not having full control. They were, however, nervous that if the inexperienced Germans led a project in more than name, the result could be disastrous. By this time the UKVG had faded into oblivion, to be replaced by the lighter Advanced Combat Aircraft, and the twin-BS143-engined 'Future Combat Aircraft' which was slightly smaller than UKVG, and was offered as a solution to the participants in MRA 75.

Their interest was encouraging, so much so that on 25 July 1968, Britain, Germany, Belgium, Canada, Italy and the Netherlands signed a memorandum of understanding to explore their requirements for a joint project, whilst Britain, Germany, Canada and the Netherlands agreed to fund a feasibility study. Belgium and Canada quickly dropped out of the project, since they required an aircraft

which was more interceptor-orientated, with high specific excess power. Therefore, in mid-December 1968, BAC of Britain, MBB of Germany and Fiat of Italy formed a joint company and drew up a formal tri-national aircraft requirement.

The MRCA Takes Shape

At this stage in the proceedings there were actually two rival designs. MBB's submission had a mid-set wing, outboard wing pivots, outboard ailerons and an all-moving tail. BAC's design, however, had a high-set wing with its pivots buried within the fuselage, full-span trailing-edge flaps, and tailerons and spoilers for roll control. A compromise solution was therefore adopted, incorporating MBB's outboard pivots and wing glove design with BAC's high-set wing. The German design had been intended to be powered by a single TF30 engine, which would have serious consequences in the event of engine failure, redundancy or battle damage to the aircraft. Therefore a further compromise was reached, and it was agreed

Prototype P.02. BAe

Prototype P.02 taking on fuel from a No.55 Squadron Victor tanker. BAe

that the aircraft would be fitted with two of the compact yet powerful RB.199 turbofans.

The result was a design that was a fair amalgam of all the parties' requirements and bore a very close resemblance to the original UKVG, and went on to become the basis for what would soon be known as the 'Multi-Role Combat Aircraft' (MRCA). The configuration was agreed at a meeting in Manching on 14 March 1969. The partners agreed that despite its higher cost the British-designed forward fuselage with a tandem seating arrangement and state-of-the-art avionics would be adopted, despite the German preference for a much cheaper single-seater with much more basic systems. The British design had F-104-esque semi-circular air intakes; the German design had simpler intakes above the wing root, and in order to maximize high supersonic performance, the Italians pressed for a more sophisticated raked intake with variable ramps, similar to that used on the Concorde; this was accepted. Another

interesting point was the agreement that the aircraft should carry internal guns, a fact that would have surely been declined had the project been undertaken ten years earlier when the 'gun' was seen as uneccessary in the light of 'all-missile' armed aircraft.

The RAF, having lost the TSR.2 and F-111K, was by this time desperate to replace their Canberras, which were fast becoming obsolete and needed to be replaced by 1970 at the latest. The cynical, however, suggested that MRCA stood for 'Must Refurbish Canberra Again'.

Panavia was officially formed as a joint industrial company on 26 March 1969, and shares were allocated on the basis, originally, of one-third each for BAe and MBB, and one-sixth each for Fiat and VFW-Fokker. (VFW-Fokker pulled out at an early stage when the Netherlands decided to buy the American F-16 instead, and the workshare was redistributed.) It was decided that the MRCA would have three assembly lines, in

Britain, Germany and Italy. At this stage there were still two distinct versions of the aircraft. The Panavia 100 was a single-seater optimized for interception and designed for the German, Italian and Dutch air forces; the Panavia 200 was a two-seat strike aircraft destined for the German Navy and the RAF and fitted with integral fuel tanks in the wings. The three governments set up a single customer, called NAMMO (NATO MRCA Management Organization) made up of the senior executives – uniformed and civilian – controlling the programme for each government. NAMMO policy decisions were undertaken by the organization's executive branch, NAMMA ('A' for Agency), with a large staff of specialists skilled in such matters as advanced aircraft technology, military operations, international contract law and various political considerations; NAMMA was accommodated in the same building as Panavia. Panavia was prime contractor for the entire Tornado programme and was tasked with the management of all potential suppliers and specifications for the fifty-odd major avionic items. NAMMA had the job of administering System Engineering GmbH, Easams at Camberley (UK), ESG (Germany) and SIA (Italy).

MRCA project definition was completed in April 1970 and the development and manufacture of proto-type aircraft was authorized later that year. The three governments authorized the industrial partners to prepare for production on 15 March 1973. The aircraft was of a very traditional construction, without the use of composite material technology: the MRCA was one of the last conventional light alloy fighters to be built, with the usual mix of machined forgings, chemically- and mechanically-milled integrally-stiffened skins and honeycomb-stabilized structures.

The Germans wanted to use an advanced Autonetics radar, while Britain preferred a European solution, or a cheaper radar from Texas Instruments. Control forces were another area of conflict, and a compromise had to be found between the British preference for light stick forces and the traditional American heavier controls which were preferred by the Germans. More serious than any actual technical problem, however, was a widespread campaign of criticism and misinformation. One accusation made in Germany and Italy was that the MRCA as proposed would not meet the requirement as originally stated. This was true, but ignored the fact that the requirement itself had developed, and that the MRCA would be a much more militarily useful aircraft. In a sarcastic reference to its multi-role capabilities, the aircraft gained the unkind German nickname of *eierlegende Wolhmilchsau* – egg-laying, wool-bearing, milk-giving pig! To others it was simply 'The English Aeroplane'. Every delay, every technical problem, every careless utterance was seized upon by the MRCA's detractors and used against the programme. Many believed that a campaign was being undertaken by a number of US aircraft companies, who saw the MRCA as a threat to their own potential European fighter sales.

Britain's role in the project included the provision and operation of two Buccaneer avionics test-beds, XT272 and XT285, which were converted by Marshalls of Cambridge, and XA903, an Avro Vulcan which would act as an RB.199-34R engine testbed. MBB was responsible for

the avionics integration and the flight control system, Aeritalia was given responsibility for the clearance of external stores, while Fokker would build the tail and the full-span trailing-edge flaps. The workshare was revised when the Netherlands withdrew from the project early on.

The early days of the MRCA programme were fraught with delays caused by the need to get agreement from three partners to find common solutions which were acceptable to all, and to work out workshare and methods by which unnecessary duplication of effort could be avoided. In order not to lose further time in the flight test programme, it was decided that the development effort would be shared by a relatively large number of prototypes, with a further batch of pre-production aircraft. It had originally been thought that seven prototypes would be sufficient, but the number grew to thirteen before a compromise of nine flying prototypes was reached. Construction of the prototypes began in November 1970. Politically, but not practically, there had to be three flight test centres – one per partner nation – but, as far as was possible, flight test tasks were not duplicated. Britain built and used four prototypes, Germany three and Italy two. However, this does not give a true reflection of the extent of the actual British leadership of the MRCA programme, with BAC operating only one more prototype than MBB. The MRCA was given the name 'Panther' in April 1969, an appellation which was short-lived, and subsequently became known universally as the 'Tornado'.

As a working basis the Tornado was described by Panavia thus:

An aircraft with continuously variable-geometry wings, with leading-edge sweep angles up to 67° maximum, on movable positions up to 63° when 2,250ltr drop tanks are carried. The aircraft will be classed as having 'modest overall dimensions and loading to minimize low-altitude gust response' and fitted with wing pylons that retain their stores alignment. Full-span double-slotted wings are to be fitted together with an inset rudder, actuated by controlled tandem hydraulic jacks. Full-span wing edge slats are to be included with two-up spoilers/lift dumpers and Krueger flaps on the leading-edge of each wing box. Door-type airbrakes will be fitted on each side of

the top of the fuselage, and the wing sweep will be hydraulically powered via a ballscrew mechanism (the aircraft can land safely with wings fully swept if the mechanism fails); triple-redundant Command Stability Augu-mentation System (CSAS) (see page 27), PFD and TFE terrain-following E-scope. The aircraft is to be basically of an all-metal (mostly aluminium with integrally stiffened skins, titanium alloy for through box and pivot attachments); FRP for dielectric panels and interface between the fixed portions of wings; Teflon-plated wing pivot and a rubber seal between the outer wings and fuselage. The radome will hinge sideways to starboard for access to radar, as will a slice of the fuselage immediately aft of nosecone for access to forward avionics bay and the radars. Hydraulically retractable tricycle forward-retracting undercarriage and a twin-wheel steerable nose are to be included, with the main wheel units retracting forward and upward into the fuselage. Emergency extension of the wheels is via nitrogen gas pressure. The complete landing gear and associated hydraulics is to be produced by Dowty (UK), with Dunlop providing aluminium alloy wheels and multi-disc brakes with low-pressure tyres and anti-skid units. Mainwheel tyres are to be Type VIII (24- or 26-ply); nosewheel tyres to be Type VIII (12-ply). A runway arrestor hook will also be fitted in the rear fuselage. Two Turbo-Union RB199-34R engines are to be fitted with bucket-type thrust reversers. Mk101 engines of early production aircraft will be nominally rated at 38.7kN (8,700lb st) dry. 66Kn (14,840lb st) with afterburning, downrated to 37.7kN (8,475 lb) for squadron service – 37.0kN, 8,320lb st dry for TTTE service life. Mk103 engines will be dry rated, nominally at 40Kn (9,100lb st) and will provide 71.5kN (16,075lb st) with afterburner.

The Test Bed Aircraft

Development of the Tornado was aided by the use of several other aircraft types as flying test beds for the various systems that had been developed for the new aircraft.

Vulcan

As briefly related above, it was decided to use an Avro Vulcan as an engine test bed and to check engine behaviour and gas-ingestion during gun firing under various flight conditions. The chosen aircraft was the XA903, the last Vulcan B.1 to remain in service, which had previously been used as the flying test bed for Concorde's engine, and thus already had suitable stressing and instrumentation for a large belly pod. Aeritalia and Marshalls jointly made a near representation of the left half of an MRCA body with a functioning variable inlet, dummy reverser, engine and gun. When gun firing began from Tornado P.06 it was mainly to confirm the Vulcan's results. XA903 was painted in a white anti-flash colour scheme, the simulated MRCA fuselage being in royal blue.

Lightning

IWKA Mauser-Werke at Obendorf had pioneered the revolver cannon during World War Two, and they developed a new gun for the Tornado, the 27mm Machinen Kanone, with a high muzzle velocity and firing either Diel or Dynamit Nobel electrically-ignited ammunition. Development of the gun was assisted by a Lightning F.2A leased by the MoD to IKWA Mauser on behalf of Panavia. Based at Warton and maintained and flown by BAC staff, it was used to prove the Mauser cannon. There was little difficulty in fitting the new gun on the left side of the Lightning's belly tank, previously occupied by a 30mm Aden gun. Air firing with live ammunition took place at West Freugh and Eskmeals in southern Scotland, and the cannon was one of the first major Tornado items to be cleared for production.

Buccaneer

Buccaneers XT272 and XT285 were equipped with the Tornado's radar and avionics systems. Described as CDMT Buccaneers, the aircraft were based at Warton from November 1974. Completely rebuilt by Marshalls of Cambridge, these CDMT 'Stage 3'-rigged aircraft flew all the larger items in the Tornado avionic systems; however, they were unable to simulate the Tornado's automated terrain-following and weapons delivery systems.

MRCA Prototypes

The first MRCA/Tornado prototype, P.01/D-9591, was structurally complete in the autumn of 1973 and was taken by road from the MBB factory at Ottobrunn to Manching on 12 November 1973, where it was assembled together with engines which had been cleared for ground running only. Airborne development had begun with the first testing of an early prototype RB.199 under the Vulcan in April 1973. It was planned to complete a 320-hour programme within an eighteen-month period, using successive engines under the Vulcan. Unfortunately, the Vulcan suffered unexpected structural and electrical trouble which greatly reduced its flying rate. This was extremely serious, as during the period between 1974–77 the engine was the pacing item in the Tornado flight programme. Therefore the Tornado's first flight was delayed while Panavia waited for flight-cleared engines to be delivered.

It was decided that the first aircraft should fly at Manching, and so the responsibility for the first general handling and performance measurement trials would fall into MBBs hands. However, as the German partner's main assignment concerned the the integration of the avionics and flight-control systems with aircraft P.04, a compromise was struck: P.01 would fly at Manching, but in the hands of a British pilot; the backseater would be a German. There was naturally intense competition to make the first flight, and R.P. 'Bee' Beamont would have been the obvious candidate for the role had he not been appointed Panavia Director of Flight Operations!

During delays throughout the first half of 1974, P.01 was continually updated to progressively higher technical standards. At the same time it was still a relatively basic aircraft, packed with trials instrumentation in place of operational avionics. The delays and technical hitches were soon forgotten when, on 14 August 1974 when BAC Military Aircraft Division Chief Test Pilot and Project Pilot MRCA Paul Millet and Nils Meister took P.01, callsign 'Luna-23', aloft. In dull and overcast weather they accelerated down the runway with wings at 26°, partial flap and full afterburner selected; rotating, they 'unstuck' cleanly and climbed away at progressively steeper angle, to stay inside the gear-down limit. Afterburner was gradually reduced until, with a Luftwaffe TF-104G watching from one side and a G-91T from the other, the aircraft settled into cruise at 10,000ft, still in take-off

configuration. Millett checked behaviour in a simulated approach, in case a quick return was necessary; then he cleaned P.01 up and checked handling in turns at successively higher speeds to 300kt. Arriving back at Manching, the flaps were again lowered to the take-off setting and the gear extended. Millett deliberately flew a missed approach, and landed on the second. Thrust reversers were used as well as jabs of wheel brake. Everything had gone perfectly. The thirty-minute flight had covered all of the planned test points, and there was no sign of a system failure or a fault indication. Millett and Meister made a second, fifty-minute, flight a week after the first, checking wing sweeps to 45°, single-engine flight, the effect of airbrakes and flight control with certain failure modes simulated. For the third flight, on 29 August, the two pilots changed places. On this third mission, Meister explored handling with the wings at all angles to 68°, with no trouble at all.

Increasingly P.01 became unrepresentative of the production Tornado and so, while later prototypes took over the measurement of aerodynamic factors such as drag and performance, P.01 concentrated on engine development. It did most of the proving of the reverse installation, previously developed on engine test-beds, and perfected directional stability on the runway at full reverse thrust; for this, modified buckets were used which 'attach' the airflow to the fin to keep the rudder effective. Additionally, in spring 1977, P.01 was fitted with a gantry on the rear fuselage housing a spin-recovery parachute. It was also given a hydrazine-fuelled 'Monofuel Emergency Power Unit' (MEPU), intended to allow emergency engine relights. It had been planned to re-engine P.01 with the full-thrust Dash-04 engines in mid-1977, but these took longer to develop and did not get into the air in P.01 until March 1978. These were the first full-thrust engines to fly, allowing clearance beyond Mach 1.92. In 1979 P.01, still in its original colour scheme, was busy with various engine, CSAS and other investigations.

The first British prototype P.02/XX946, assembled in England, made its maiden flight on 30 October 1974 from Warton, again flown by Paul Millet, this time with Pietro Paolo Trevisan in the back. This was the first aircraft with fully variable engine intakes, enabling it to work across the Tornado's entire speed range, and was later used for envelope expansion, engine development and preliminary in-flight refuelling trials. Uniquely, P.02 was fitted with small square-section fairings on the tips of its tailplanes which were 'flutter exciters', although these were later removed, leaving small blisters on the tailplane tips – another facet unique to this aircraft. P.02 was at first painted red and white like P.01, and was regarded as the workhorse of the prototype fleet; it certainly flew the most hours. Its main tasks were to explore the flight envelope, and carry out stalling, spinning and both the low-speed and extremely high-speed investigations.

The third Tornado to fly was another UK aircraft, P.03/XX947, which made its maiden flight on 5 August 1975, in the hands of BAC's chief test pilot, Dave Eagles, and Tim Ferguson. It was the first Tornado with dual controls and, as the aircraft destined for stalling and spinning

trials, was fitted with an emergency spin recovery 'chute and a Sundsirand hydrazine MEPU. XX947 was the first Tornado to be delivered in a camouflage colour scheme, although several other early aircraft were similarly repainted, and some later prototypes made their first flights in Panavia's garish red and white 'house colours'. It was also the first aircraft fitted with a nose radome, rather than a representatively shaped fairing.

One of the few serious incidents in the flight development programme befell P.03 on 4 October 1976. The aircraft made a landing in torrential rain on a runway covered in varying amounts of standing water. Pilot Tim Ferguson was unable to stop the aircraft sliding diagonally off the runway, striking the grass verge and coming to rest on the nosewheel, rear fuselage and wingtip. The result was the stiffening of the main leg mounting brackets, revision of reverser geometry to improve flow

over the rudder and preserve symmetric thrust, and the introduction of nosewheel steering augmentation for such extraordinary conditions. So this was actually a useful accident! Despite the back-up provided by the Buccaneers, P.04 was nevertheless a vital aircraft. It amassed virtually all the avionics data needed for the production go-ahead decision during a series of twelve flights in 1975–76. It was the first aircraft to integrate the forward radar, TFR, Doppler and other navigation and weapon-aiming systems through the digital autopilot and flight-control system, to fly the aircraft automatically. A huge effort was needed to make the mass of integrated equipment work properly. From late 1975 P.04 was regularly going out with a formidable list of tasks. It was also instrumental in finding hiccups in the software, improving the HUD symbology and perfecting the brightness and uniformity of the TV tab displays. By

Prototype P.03/XX947 fitted with a 'buddy-buddy' refuelling pod. BAe

Italian prototype P.05. BAe

1977 P.04 was often engaged in weapon trials, and it was the first to fly with the MW-1 anti-armour dispenser.

The early prototypes were limited to Mach 1.3 and 40,000ft by the lack of fully rated engines, but early flight trials still progressed relatively smoothly. One of the most serious problems encountered – almost the only aerodynamic problem encountered in the entire programme – was excessive base drag, with some directional instability at transonic speeds (Mach 0.9 to Mach 0.95) and a tendency to snake at about Mach 09. Warton handled most of this investigation, trying a large number of often seemingly trivial changes to the profiles of the spine and rear fuselage. Unlike the F-111 there was never a drag problem; it was just that the boundary layer was breaking away at the base of the fin, causing mild directional instability at high subsonic speed. This was eventually solved by the refinement of the fairing below the rudder filling the gap between the jet pipes and the bottom of the rudder), the addition of new vortex generators at the base of the fin, adjacent to the rudder leading edge, and later by using a redesigned rear fuselage, of slimmer form. These improvements considerably improved the airflow around the tail

unit and reduced drag, as well as solving the stability problem.

The fourth Tornado was P.04/D-9252 (later 98+05), which Hans Friedrich Rammensee and Nils Meister took into the air on 2 September 1975; this aircraft was fitted with an almost representative and integrated avionics system, and was used to prove the avionics system. The aircraft was also briefly 'tufted' for aerodynamic investigations. It was used for the low-level automatic terrain following radar, digital autopilot, navigation system and ground mapping radar testing, and was later assigned to work with the MW-1 dispenser.

Italy's first Tornado (P.05/X-586) was flown solo, its rear cockpit full of instrumentation, by Pietro Trevisan on 5 December 1975 and was the only prototype to have a really unlucky early history: its first flight was delayed some five months by the unavailability of suitable engines. In high-visibility white/red, it carried national markings unlike 01 and 02, and was a particularly attractive machine. Tasked with flutter and load measurement, it had completed just six flights when, in January 1976, it was severely damaged during a 'heavy landing', perhaps better described as a 'crash',

at Caselle, which was caused primarily by the over-sensitivity of the pitch channel. The aircraft's nose hit the ground with such force that major structural damage ensued; it was lucky that the accident happened at Caselle, as this made repair an economic option, but P.05 was not back in the sky until March 1978. This inevitably left a hole in the programme, but thanks to ready-made contingency plans, P.02 was able to take over P.05's flutter work, having instrumentation already installed. After a lengthy rebuild, P.05 was used mainly for weapons trials; it also carried the CASMU Skyshark stand-off dispenser weapon.

The sixth pre-production aircraft, P.06/XX948, was assembled at Warton and introduced a new rear fuselage of slightly slimmer profile to cure the problem of directional instability at transonic speed described above. XX948 was flown solo by Dave Eagles and was used for stores trials; it was also the first aircraft fitted with the 27mm Mauser guns. The next of the prototypes was a German aircraft, P.07/98+06, which was flown by Nils Meister on 30 March 1976, with Fritz Eckert in the back seat. This was the first aircraft with a complete avionics suite, and was therefore used for avionics trials.

By prototype P.07 the Tornado was beginning to mature, and the prototypes were emerging with changes resulting from flight testing. As far as possible its standard duplicated P.04 so that each could backup the other, but in fact P.07 introduced a near-production autopilot and spent a full year on intensive low flying over specially designated routes, most of them across the Black Forest, proving the most vital of all the aircraft's sub-systems – the one linking the TFR, radar altimeters, flight controls, CSAS, HUD and weapon aiming. Paul Millet flew prototype P.08/XX949 on 15 July 1976, with Ray Woolett in the rear cockpit. This aircraft was used for avionics and weapons aiming development trials, and was the second dual-control trainer. The final prototype P.09/X-587, an Italian aircraft, was almost joined by the first pre-production machine (P.11/98+01) when the pair made near-simultaneous first flights on 5 February 1977. Pietro Trevisan was accompanied

by Manlio Quarantelli for P.09's maiden flight. This prototype was used for flutter trials and clearance of external stores, as well as climatic trials and autopilot development. Amongst its other duties was the testing of the German reconnaissance pod, and the aircraft was eventually camouflaged, with prominent Dayglo stripes and a plethora of calibration markings. The tenth prototype was a static test airframe and never flew.

All of the aircraft carried extensive instrumentation and telemetry equipment, with some 460 instrumented points per aircraft, capable of transmitting up to 150 parameters simultaneously. Some features seen on the prototypes were short-lived or temporary, including extended, lengthened nose-mounted test instrumentation probes and forward-looking camera fairings which sometimes replaced the forward fin mounted RHAWS antenna fairing. All of the prototypes were upgraded repeatedly during their lives, demonstrating and proving new equipment and sys-

tems. Two of the prototype Tornados were lost in service. Britain's P.08 crashed during a simulated toss-bombing manoeuvre on 12 June 1979, killing Russ Pengelly and Squadron Leader John Gray. In April 1980 Germany's P.04 crashed during an air show practice, killing Ludwig Obermeier and Kurt Schreiber. The survivors flew on in the trials and development role into the 1980s, when they were withdrawn for a variety of ground instructional purposes.

Pre-Production Aircraft

The nine prototypes were followed by six pre-production aircraft. These were intended to be as close as possible to the initial production standard and introduced the definitive engine nozzle fairing. The fin dressing was also refined, with the seven vortex generators being reduced to six per side. The first of the pre-production aircraft, P.11, was flown

P.02 lights its afterburners. BAe

Pre-production aircraft P.12. BAe

for the first time on 5 February 1977, which was, as related above, earlier the same day as the ninth and final flying prototype. This was probably no coincidence, as it was widely reported that a tri-national agreement bound the partners fly a pre-production jet before all nine prototypes had got into the air. Certainly the British and German pre-production aircraft had been rolled out some months earlier.

P.11/98+01, a German twin-sticker, could be identified by the production-standard fin fillet. The first German-assembled two-pilot aircraft, it was originally intended to have gone to Germany's Official Test Centre (OTC) at Manching for final contractual performance tests, but was kept back by Panavia for the measurement of total aircraft drag. The second pre-production aircraft, P.12, was Britain's XZ630, assembled at Warton and the first Tornado delivered in tri-national markings, but with a British serial number. This aircraft had the Dash-03 engines, and became the first Tornado to be delivered to an

official test centre when it was flown from Warton to the Aircraft and Armament Experimental Establishment (A&AEE) at Boscombe Down on 3 February 1978, with BAC's Tim Ferguson and Roy Kenward at the helm.

The other four pre-production aircraft were very close to production standard. P.13/98+02, another German machine, was flown by Fritz Soos, with Rainer Henke in the rear cockpit, for its maiden flight on 10 January 1978, and was the first Tornado with a kinked tailplane leading edge. Britain's P.15/XZ631 first flew at Warton on 24 November 1978 in the hands of Jerry Lee and Jim Evans, and this aircraft was the first with a production rear fuselage and the first with the 'wet fin' intended for all RAF aircraft. The only Italian pre-production aircraft, P.14, flew on 26 March 1979 in the hands of Manlio Ouarantelli and Egidio Nappi; it introduced production wings. P.16/98+03 was the last to fly, with Armin Krauthann and Fritz Eckert; this aircraft had the definitive production fuselage, was the first aircraft assembled

on the MBB assembly line at Manching, and was also used to test the Kormoran anti-ship missile, along with the fourth prototype (98+05). It was later upgraded to full production standard though it, along with a handful of the German and Italian aircraft, was never issued to a front-line unit. The pre-production aircraft were also rebuilt with full production-standard wings.

Tornado Production

Production of the Tornado was divided into nine batches. The Tornado was developed in two basic versions: the Interdictor Strike (IDS) and the Air Defence Variant (ADV). The IDS can be further divided into four 'role-specific' groups: overland strike, electronic warfare, reconnaissance and maritime strike. The stories of the four IDS variants and the ADV will be described in detail in later chapters, after a description of the basic aircraft in Chapter 2. The batches in which they were produced were as follows:

Batch 1

This initial batch included twenty-three RAF IDS aircraft and twelve twin-stickers. The RAF serial numbers ran from ZA319–ZA330 and from ZA352–ZA362, and the aircraft were assigned to the TTTE at RAF Cottesmore where they have remained ever since, though a handful have moved on, mainly to development and trials duties. TTTE aircraft have not been retrofitted with LRMTS, and retain RB.199 Mk101 engines. They are down-rated (reportedly to 36kN/8,093lb) because the aircraft routinely fly without pylons, the thrust reduction ensuring lighter fatigue life usage. Batch 1 included seventeen German aircraft, including the fourteen trainers GT001–014, serialled from 43+01–43+17, and virtually all were assigned to the TTTE; they have also remained with that unit ever since. There were no Italian aircraft in Batch 1.

Batch 2

The 110 Batch 2 Tornados were assigned plane set numbers 044–153. There were fifty-five RAF IDS aircraft in Batch 2 (ZA540–564 and ZA585–614, including sixteen twin-stickers (ZA540, -541, -544, -548, -549,- 551, -552, -555, -562, -594, -595, -598, -599, -602, -604, and -612 (8T013–028). The RAF Batch 2 aircraft were initially assigned to the TWCU and to Nos15, 27 and 617 Squadrons. Batch 2 also included forty German aircraft GS004–G5030 and GT015–GT027, twenty-four for the Luftwaffe and sixteen for the Marineflieger. The German aircraft were shared between the TTTE, JBG 38 and MFG 1. Among the Marineflieger aircraft in Batch 2 were the first Tornados equipped with the Multiple Weapon Carrier System (MWCS), which added a centreline underfuselage pylon to the two shoulder stations to allow a wider range of stores, such as the Kormoran missiles, to be carried. The MWCS was subsequently fitted to all German and Italian Tornados, and the centreline pylon made its appearance on later RAF aircraft. Finally, Batch 2 included fifteen Italian aircraft: ten operational aircraft, MM7002–MM70111, and five twin-stickers IT001-IT005, MM55000-MM55004 The twin-stickers initially went to the TTTE and most of the operational aircraft went to 154° Gruppo.

Prototype P.01 taxies out for a ground testing sortie. Note the presence of the red mesh intake covers. BAe

Batch 3

This consisted of 164 aircraft, which were assigned plane set numbers 154–317. Sixty-eight of the Batch 3 aircraft were RAF IDS, including eight twin-stickers. These aircraft should have had ZB-series serials, but an administrative error allocated them elsewhere, and the aircraft therefore had to be given ZA serials actually 'lower' than the Batch 2 aircraft which preceded them. The Batch 3 aircraft also had a Marconi ARI18241/2 RWR in place of the original Elettronica ARI18241/1. These aircraft were mostly delivered to the RAF Germany's Laarbruch Wing, though the first eleven went to the TWCU, with a few going to the Marham Wing. The Laarbruch-based aircraft were subsequently re-engined with the RB.199 Mk103.

Batch 4

Tornado Batch 4 comprised 162 aircraft, allocated plane set numbers 318–479. Of these, eighteen were F.2 fighters and 144 were IDS. Fifty-three were RAF IDS aircraft (85111–155) including eight twin-stickers. They were serialled from ZD707–720, ZD738–749, ZD788–793, ZD808–812, ZD842–851 and ZD890–895; the twin-stickers were ZD711, -712, -713, -741, -742, -743, -812 and -842. All were powered from the start by the RB.199 Mk103. The RAF Batch 4 Tornados were produced primarily for RAF Germany's Brüggen Wing, the last being delivered on 30 September 1985. Batch 4 production for Germany totalled sixty-four aircraft, GS087–142 and the eight twin-stickers GT040–047. Italian Batch 4 production included aircraft IS034–IS060, with no twin-stickers.

Batch 5

Batch 5 consisted of 173 aircraft. It was planned to include twenty for the RAF, but only two of these were actually delivered, as GR.1As. The rest of the aircraft planned for Batch 5 were destined for Saudi Arabia. Batch 5 Tornado IDS aircraft carried a Mil Std 15538 digital databus, a 128k Litef Spirit III computer, and an ECM transmitter with chaff/flare dispensers coupled to the aircraft's RWR suite. Batch 5 also included fifty-two RAF fighters and seventy aircraft for Germany, with Italian Tornado production concluding with the final twenty-nine AMI aircraft. The German and Italian Batch 5 aircraft were able to operate the AGM-88 HARM, although the missile was harmonized only on delivery to the Marineflieger.

Batch 6

Batch 6 included sixty-eight IDS and twenty-four F.3 fighters for the RAF, and sixty-three IDS originally destined for Luftwaffe, with none for the Marineflieger. The fifteen Luftwaffe twin-stickers wore serials 45+60, 45+61, 45+62, 45+63, 70, 45+73, 45+77, 45+99, 46+03, 04, 46+05, 46+06, 46+07, 46+08, and 09. Twenty-four of the aircraft were, in fact, delivered to the Marineflieger's MFG 2. There were no Italian aircraft in Batch 6.

Batch 7

The 122 aircraft built as Batch 7 wore the set numbers 808–929. The production of Batch 7 airframes included twenty-seven IDS aircraft for the RAF, including six twin-stickers and fourteen built as reconaissance-configured GR.1As. The seven non-reconnaissance-configured operational aircraft went to the Brüggen-based squadrons. Panavia also delivered twenty-eight Saudi IDSs (including eight twin-stickers and six built to GR.1A standard) as part of Batch 7. Batch 7 also included twenty-four RAF F.3 fighters and another eight ADVs ordered by Oman, but diverted to the RAF as F.3s. Germany's thirty-five Tornado ECRs (see Chapter 3) used the final German identities, GS256–290, and were delivered as part of Batch 7. They wore serials running from 46+23–46+57. Again, there were no Italian aircraft in Batch 7.

Batch 8

Batch 8 was to have consisted of twenty-six aircraft for the RAF and thirty-five for the Luftwaffe, but they were subsequently cancelled.

Batch 9

Batch 9 consisted of forty-eight IDS aircraft for Saudi Arabia. This brought Tornado production to 978.

A No.12 Squadron Tornado GR.1B in North America. RAF

CHAPTER TWO

The Tornado Described

The Radar System

By far the largest and most important sensor aboard the Tornado is its radar. This unit is actually two radars, both made by Texas Instruments: a GM (ground mapping) radar and the TFR (terrain-following radar). The installation occupies the whole nose of the aircraft and is optimized for air-to-ground use, though full air-to-air facilities are also available. Earlier it was suggested that the Texas Instruments radar was chosen because it was cheaper and less advanced than the Autonetics set – however, it remains an excellent choice and more than capable of the tasks set it. The RAF was at the time one of the acknowleged experts in all-weather attack avionics, and they were determined to fit the Tornado with the best possible systems for its roles. One of the main features apart from the radar system was to be a high degree of computerized fault detection, and to satisfy this the aircraft was fitted with a comprehensive 'Built-In Test Equipment' (BITE) system with a number of easily accessible 'Line Replacement Units' (LRUs) if a failing module was detected. An LRU is a single box which can be pulled out and replaced in a few seconds by a ground crewman.

The radars can operate in a number of modes. 'Ground Standby' allows continuous operation at low power to save current and permit adequate cooling with ground fans; it is normally selected by a switch on one of the main landing gears. 'Standby' provides full power to everything except the transmitter high-voltage circuits, and can normally only be selected in the air. 'Test' is a special mode with a dummy load, the BITE auto-matically detecting 94 per cent of all possible faults and isolating 88.6 per cent to a single LRU.

The most common airborne mode is 'Ground Mapping', and this in turn is available in any of four sub-modes, each usable from ground level to the stratosphere. 'Ground-Map Spoiled' is the normal mode, giving a general picture of the terrain ahead, with the navigator able to control scan angle and rate. Though certain radar information can be fed to the pilot's HUD or – more rarely – his moving-map display, the normal presentation is onto one of the navigator's CRTs. Where necessary the radar picture can update the display and specific, accurate radar 'fixes' can be made. In the 'Ground-Map Pencil' mode the radar sends out a narrow 'pencil' beam for various mapping or tracking purposes. 'Ground-Map Wide' gives a one-bar azimuth pattern with the navigator free to select the antenna tilt angle and scan

A navigator enters his route into the CPGS via the computer keyboard. Author

rate. 'Ground-Map Narrow' scans a narrow one-bar azimuth sector, usually related to a drift-stabilized centre.

'On Boresight Contour Mapping' eliminates all objects below the stabilized horizontal plane through the aircraft, and supplies video signals from everything that penetrates above this plane, such as a mountain peak, radio mast or tall trees. 'Height Find' is a versatile mode in which tilt angle to an identified surface target is measured, giving a new input to the computer for height computations. A range line appears on the display which the navigator can align over the target.

In the 'Air to Ground Ranging' mode the antenna is pointed by azimuth/elevation commands from the computer, thereafter performing acquisition, range lock-on and tracking automatically against either ground clutter or discrete targets. The output is digital data giving slant range, range-rate (that is, rate of change of range, vital for weapon aiming), azimuth/elevation pointing angles and a signal to the operator that range tracking has been accomplished. 'Lock-on' is a mode in which the computer commands the antenna to point in the right direction, and feeds the radar with the predicted range data, the radar subsequently locking on to the surface target to feed the computer with all range and angle tracking data for weapon aiming. In this mode the antenna does not respond to azimuth/elevation commands from the computer, but to guard against possible lock-on to the wrong target it does accept a 'lock-on reject' signal that makes it break lock and re-enter the acquisition phase.

The 'Air to Air Tracking' mode is rather similar. When hostile aircraft, or a friendly in-flight refuelling tanker, are in the vicinity, the computer provides pointing commands, and the radar 'looks' in the direction indicated and initiates a range search. After range lock-on the mode switches to angle tracking, sending the data to accept a 'lock-on reject' signal, causing it to break lock and re-enter the acquisition phase. Otherwise, nothing will deflect it; if lock-on is interrupted due to signal fading or hostile ECM the radar keeps outputting tracking data from the last-known parameters until tracking is resumed.

The final mode for the main radar is 'Beacon', in which it interrogates friendly aircraft, ground or surface-ship bea-

Squadron Leader Robbie Stewart draws up his route map. Author

cons, and displays the replies as alphanumeric codes in the correct positions on the combined display. This gives the identity of each beacon and its bearing and distance from the aircraft. Ground-mapping video is displayed simultaneously. This provides either ground 'fixes' or aim points, or assists rendezvous with friendly aircraft or ships.

The TFR is under the main radar and its phased array antenna has the vital duty of ensuring that, no matter how close to the ground the Tornado flies, it never hits anything. The polarization of the signals is circular, to minimize weather problems. The two-lobe monopulse beam makes a two-bar scan between 8° left and 8° right of the forward centre-line and between the elevations of −20° and +10°. In a banked turn this scan is at first opened up linearly; for faster turn rates it is switched to a figure-of eight scan with total azimuth of some 15°, the scan being steered into the turn by up to 7° so that the aircraft can 'see' where it is going (which is no longer straight ahead). Full

power for TFR is obtained only in the air; on the ground the set is held to the 'Ground-Standby' mode by a switch on the nose leg, though this can be manually overridden to give the 'Standby' mode with the radar under full power but inhibited from firing until 'Test' or 'TFR' are selected. The Automatic Terrain Following (ATF) subsystem is too complex to describe in full within these pages – suffice it to say it provides a major advancement on any F-111 variant, and is in many ways superior to that developed for the Rockwell B-1 Lancer.

Like other TFRs, the unit fitted to the Tornado maintains an imaginary 'ski-toe' shape below and ahead of the aircraft, and makes this ride along and over obstacles. The shape and position of the ski-toe is controlled by the chosen clearance height, ground speed and ride comfort. The sudden intrusion of anything into the ski-toe causes an immediate auto-matic manoeuvre by the aircraft, and the TFR computer works out whether it is best to pull up or go around an obstacle.

The TFR and main radar share their own computer – quite separate from the main computer – which handles such tasks as management of the gimbals (antenna bearings) and scan limits, scan mode, displays and, in the case of the TFR, the complex calculations to maintain safe ground clearance.

Also fitted is a radar altimeter built into the underside of the aircraft to provide an accurate digital height read-out at low levels. This is not fed direct to the back-seater, but is so important to the pilot that it can appear on two of his displays, and sometimes on three. Another secondary radar is the Doppler, which continuously measures ground speed along four slanting beams reflected from the surface. This provides digital along-track and across-track velocity data for the main computer. The Doppler is one of the two prime navigation systems, the other being the Inertial Navigation System (INS) which has its own computer to convert accelerations into velocities and distances. A reversionary navigation capability is provided by the Secondary Attitude and Heading Reference (SAHR) with a twin-gyro platform and a magnetic detector which monitors the attitude and heading, but is not normally called upon if other systems work correctly.

Other Sensors

The most basic of the aircraft's other sensors is the pitot-static system, which measures dynamic pressure to provide the basis for calculated true airspeed. In the Tornado such calculation is one of the duties of the Air-Data Computer (ADC), which has its own stored programmes to feed the avionics with accurate digital data on the atmospheric environment. Another is the laser rangefinder, which can measure accurate range to a target at the low 'grazing angles' associated with 'under the radar' attacks which would defeat rangefinding by most radars. The laser can also determine the range to a fixed point more accurately than the radar, because of its very much shorter wave length, and it can also operate in a passive search mode to locate targets designated by a separate laser fired from another aircraft or by friendly troops on the ground.

CPGS Planning

In both variants of the aircraft the flight plan can be recorded by the crew whilst on the ground using a Cassette Preparation Ground Station (CPGS). This consists of a computer keyboard, a screen and a special map table. The navigator places the cross hairs of his hand hand-held cursor over each target or way-point, pressing the button to 'enter' each into tpoint automatically as the cursor button screen. The information is then loaded onto a standard cassette tape and inserted into the aircraft's

Tornado 'exposed'. Author

The navigator's cockpit. BAe

autopilot, and if necessary the tape could 'fly the mission'.

Mission Management

Any Tornado mission is usually managed by the navigator. With his systems in 'Planning Mode', one of his TV tabs (as the television-type displays in the cockpit are known) is first made to fit the mission territory, inserting latitude and longitude lines. Waypoints then appear as A, B, C and so on, and the targets as small triangles marked with an X. After take-off, the system continuously receives information from the sensors, which the navigator studies and occasionally uses to update the system. As the Tornado travels down the track to the first waypoint its position is displayed by a small circle moving along the fixed track line. When the mission is over land the navigator will have inserted the position of all identifiable landmarks, or fix points, which appear as 1, 2, 3 and so on. As the small 'aircraft-circle' approaches each fix point, the navigator keeps a sharp look out for it, and usually tells the pilot, who has a better view ahead. The exact position of each fix point helps refine the accuracy of the navigation, so that each fix point or waypoint should be reached more precisely. The normal method of navigation is for the computer to steer the aircraft according to the stored flight plan and the combined inputs from the INS and Doppler. The two inputs are combined in a method known as a 'Kalman-filter' software routine to give the most accurate dead-reckoning position, normally suffering from errors less than half those of the INS alone.

Normally the mission is flown with one TV tab in the 'Nav Format' and the other spelling out various kinds of helpful information. The Nav Format is not the same as Planning Mode, though the latter can

RB.199s at full power propel a Tornado GR.1A of No.II(AC) Squadron along Laarbruch's runway. Author

be restored at the touch of a key. The Nav Format is based on aircraft's present position, shown as a small fixed circle at the centre, around which is a 'circle of 95 per cent certainty', and a much larger range circle with a boxed 'N' on it to show the direction of true north. Superimposed on this is a vertical line passing through the 12 o'clock position showing the current track, which is read off a scale at the top of the screen. Therefore, changing heading causes the scale to slide past the track line, while the boxed 'N' moves smoothly around the range circle. Planned Track (PLTK) is spelt out digitally, with parallel lines scaled a fixed distance apart to show cross-track error (if any), as well as the next waypoint, the next track beyond the waypoint and many other things as well. Blocks of data in the upper corners show (left) distance in nautical miles to the next fix point and to the next waypoint, and (right) the system time (which may or may not also be the precise time of day), the time to the next waypoint and the time the aircraft is early or late. This only scratches the surface of the naviga-

tion process, and this book is hardly intended to be a technical manual! Between the tab-displays is the big combined display on which present position is seen at the centre of a detailed coloured 'topographical map' and a detailed radar display. The moving radar video picture is overlaid onto the moving map, and any discrepancy helps the study the situation as shown by the INS and Doppler.

Cockpit

Flying the Tornado close to the speed of sound at tree-top level demands the full attention of the crew. Having two crew makes the tasks of operating the radar, updating the navigation and monitoring threats more manageable. The crew are strapped into their Martin Baker Mk10A 'zero-zero' ejector seats inside a spacious and ergonomic cockpit which is remarkably quiet for such a class of aircraft. In the front seat the pilot has his traditional controls, as well as his HUD, moving-map display, terrain-following E-scope and

radar warning equipment directly in front of him. In the rear cockpit two identical CRT displays with integral keyboards for communication with the main computer as well as for navigation and mission planning dominate the forward view. Between them is the navigator's combined mapping radar and moving-map display; below these is a hand controller which is used for designating and updating navigation/ weapon aiming data in conjunction with the radar/map display.

The RB.199 Engine

During 1967 an intensive study by the former Bristol Siddeley (now Rolls-Royce) team at Patchway in Bristol developed an afterburning turbofan that reached a performance far beyond that which had been intended to power AFVG. They also deliberated over the Rolls-Royce-developed technology of using three separate rotating spools: low- (LP), intermediate- (IP) and high-pressure (HP). Pioneered originally in the RB.211 civil engine, this

Close-up of the afterburner 'cans' on a German Tornado IDS. Author

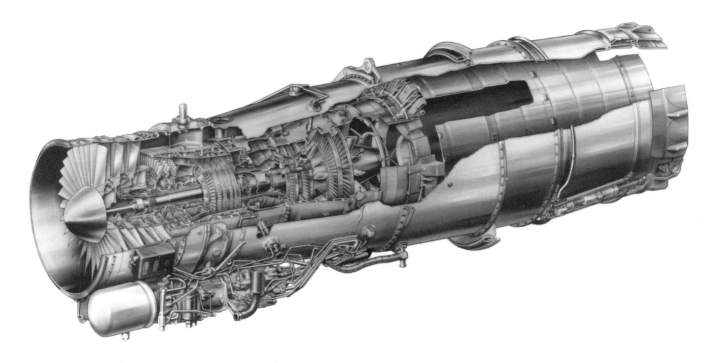

Cutaway of the RB.199. BAe

design appeared to make the engine more complex, but in fact made it smaller and shorter, and reduced the number of parts. Each of the three spools could run at its own best speed without the need for extensive variable blading, and fewer stages were therefore needed to achieve the desired pressure ratio. The new powerplant was called the RB.199.

In March 1969, as the MRCA was defined and Panavia was formed, an engine competition was held. Pratt & Whitney did their utmost to promote the various advanced developments of their TF30, including the new JTF22 and the 'paper' JTF16, but none quite matched the requirement; the company was also handicapped by US security, and eventually withdrew. General Electric perhaps tried harder, with the GE1/10; however, the RB.199 was so demonstrably superior that on 5 September 1969 the RB.199-34R was selected, and on 30 September an international consortium was formed to produce it.

The consortium was called Turbo-Union Ltd, Rolls-Royce of Britain and Motoren und Turbine Union München (MTU) of Germany each taking a 40 per cent share and Fiat of Italy taking 20 per cent. Turbo-Union's head office was at

Bristol, with another office in Munich next to Panavia. The production allocation was as follows: Rolls-Royce produced the inlet, LP case, fan, combustion system, HP turbine complete, turbine casings, afterburner and fuel control system; MTU the IP and HP compressors, intermediate casing, accessory drive and gearbox, by-pass duct (outer engine casing), IP turbine and drive-shaft, and reverser; and Fiat the LP turbine complete, LP drive-shaft, exhaust diffuser, rear jet-pipe and variable nozzle. Unlike the Tornado airframe the RB.199 was designed to use all the latest technology. The three-stage fan, which was aerodynamically derived from the much larger fan of the Rolls-Royce Pegasus engine, is assembled by precision Electron-Beam Welding (EBW), and the fan stators are also all welded. The EBW construction saves weight compared to the traditional insertion of separate blades, and also reduces vibration. Replacement of damaged blades by cutting and welding has been demonstrated. The IP compressor rotor, with three stages, is also an EBW structure, and is driven by a single-stage air-cooled turbine. There were no variable stators, the only airflow trimming control being an IP blow-off.

The six-stage HP compressor was driven by a single-stage air-cooled turbine as advanced as any in the world at the time, with entry gas temperature of over 1,327°C at full power. This shaft also powered the accessories, which were located on the underside of the engine for easy access once installed. The combustion chamber was of the annular type with vaporizing burners and gives outstanding fuel economy for long-range interdiction, as well as very high thrust for short take-offs, Mach 2 performance and combat manoeuvring. Most unusually, the engines were linked via gearboxes to a cross-drive which is automatically engaged should the engine speeds differ by more than a specified limit, than either engine can drive all secondary power supplies.

The importance of the programme prompted the use of a Vulcan flying test-bed with a representation of the left half of an MRCA body (see p.11), and while this installation was being built, prototype engines began to appear to the RB.199-01 standard, and the first made a successful bench run at Patchway on 27 September 1971. Further prototypes ran at Bristol, Munich and Turin during the following year, and on 19 April 1973 the chief test pilot of Rolls-Royce, John Pollitt, under contract to Turbo-Union, began flight development in the Vulcan, whilst simulated Mach 2 flight was investigated in a supersonic test cell at the National Gas Turbine Establishment at Pyestock.

The performance targets that were agreed for the Dash-01 engine fell well short of the intended production figures, and between 1971–76 Turbo-Union transformed engine performance through a series of development engines, culminating in the Dash-04 which was virtually the same as the production powerplant. The first major improvement, the Dash-02, achieved increased thrusts at all regimes with no increase in gas temperature, chiefly by opening out the annulus area between the IP and LP turbine stator blades to give a greater core airflow. This was an important engine and a few were still flying in 1979. The Dash-03 introduced broader fan blades to cure a flutter problem at high rpm in one part of the

flight envelope, and other changes to give higher thrust; these engines entered the flight programme in March 1977. In 1978 the Dash-03 powered most Tornado prototypes, but the main engine on the test bed was the Dash-04, with even more refinements. RB.199 Mk103 engines power the later Tornado IDS aircraft, although some Mk101 engines, to the initial production standard of slightly lower thrust, are still in service. The Tornado ADV uses the Mk104 engine which has Full Authority Digital Electronic Control (FADEC) and an extended jet pipe for improved reheat efficiency, giving added thrust and reduced specific fuel consumption in reheat. All of the current production engines have FADEC. RB.199 Mk105 engines, which are similar to Mk103 but have a higher pressure ratio fan and increased thrust, power the Tornado Electronic Combat and Reconnaissance (ECR) aircraft for Germany (see Chapter 4).

Flight Systems

The Tornado was the first production military aircraft to feature an all-electrical, triplexed 'fly-by-wire' flight control system, with electrical and mechanical back-up systems. The tailerons are actuated differentially for roll control and synchronously for pitch control. At low-to-moderate wing sweep angles the wing spoilers provide additional roll control power. Yaw control is provided by a conventional rudder. In its normal mode the system operates through the Command Stability Augmentation System (CSAS). This consists of three sets of triplicated-rate gyros and two computers: one for pitch and one for roll/yaw computations. The aircraft's present angular acceleration in each axis is compared to the rate of turn demanded through the the pilot's controls or the autopilot in a control loop known as the Manoeuvre/Demand (MD) loop, and any difference results in the

RB.199 being prepared for fitting into a Tornado F.3. BAe

appropriate correcting command going to the control surfaces.

Aircraft speed and height (dynamic-pressure) from the Air-Data Computer, wing sweep, airbrake and spoiler position data are also taken into account by the CSAS. This ensures that optimum control response is obtained throughout the flight envelope in all configurations. In the main operating mode, with the MD loop in operation, the fly-by-wire system automatically compensates for gusts disturbing the aircraft's flight path, and gives the same crisp handling characteristics regardless of external load carried. The CSAS incorporates a failure logic which continuously monitors and consolidates the triplex electrical signals to meet the failure survival requirements and to avoid nuisance disconnects due to tolerance build-ups or normal system transients.

When multiple system failures are detected, mode reversion is first to direct electrical signalling, instead of the MD loops. Subsequent, additional, failures will cause the engagement of the normally de-clutched mechanical back-up system, which provides an adequate 'get-home' capability. To prevent loss of control or spin entry at high angles of incidence, the Tornado is provided with a Spin Prevention and Incidence Limiting System (SPILS) This system reduces the roll-and-yaw command authority available to the pilot at high incidence angles by taking the rudder pedal and roll stick position signals from the CSAS and scheduling each of them as a function of incidence. It augments the pitch stiffness to provide a more precise incidence control, effectively limiting attainable incidence angles by feeding the incidence signals back to the pitch channel of the CSAS, so that a critical value is not exceeded. SPILS comprises the computer and control panel mounted on the left-hand console in the pilot's cockpit.

The Autopilot and Flight Director System (AFDS) provides automatic flight control of the aircraft, reducing the pilot's workload and increasing the all-weather effectiveness of the weapons system. The two AFDS processors compute autopilot command signals, which are routed to the CSAS, and flight director command signals, which are routed for display to the HUD and to the Attitude Director Indicator (ADI). The following modes are provided: Basic Mode (attitude and heading hold); Heading Acquire; Track Acquire; Altitude Hold; Mach Hold; Radar Height Hold; Terrain Following; Auto Throttle; and Approach. To ensure flight safety, the AFDS continuously monitors and compares the INS attitude information with that of the SAHR. Should the data from these two sensors differ by more than a pre-set amount, the autopilot will automatically disengage, with the appropriate warning indications. An instinctive cut-out facility on the control column enables the pilot to quickly disengage the autopilot.

Defensive Systems

Tornados from the three partner nations differ considerably in their ECM fit. RAF aircraft carry a BOZ-107 chaff and flare dispenser pod on their starboard outer wing pylons and a Sky Shadow ECM pod on the port outer wing pylon, whilst German aircraft carry a BOZ-101 to port with a Cerberus II, III or IV ECM pod to starboard. More recently some German aircraft have been seen using the US-produced AN/ALQ-119 instead of the usual Cerberus, especially in sorties over Bosnia. Marineflieger Tornados carry Ajax ECM pods instead of Cerberus, whilst Italian aircraft use the BOZ-102 along with the with Cerberus pod, or alternatively with the Elettronica EL/73 ECM pod. Over Bosnia, Italian Tornados carried a BOZ pod under each wing, presumably one loaded with chaff and one with flares. British, German and Italian aircraft are also able to carry the AIM-9 Sidewinder AAM on the inner faces of their inner wing pylons.

The Tornado also carries carries an extensive Defensive Aids Sub System (DASS), which provides warnings to the crew and which can neutralize or severely decrease the effectiveness of air-to-air interceptors, surface-to-air missiles and anti-aircraft artillery. It consists of the following major components: threat warning receivers and displays; active ECM; and chaff and flare dispensers – chaff and flares can be dispensed simultaneously or as an alternative to active ECM. The threat warning receivers can be programmed before the flight with the characteristics of expected threats. On the Italian variant, the AECM equipment is an internally-mounted self-protection jammer, enabling the carriage of a chaff/flare dispenser pod on each outboard pylon. The expendables capacity is therefore doubled. The (IT) advanced (GE enhanced) radar warning equipment is able to operate in a highly dense signal environment. It can intercept, identify and display enemy emissions, including command guidance RF signals, and allows automatic active or passive countermeasure actions.

The highest-priority identified threats can be presented via synthetic symbology on the dedicated displays, or on the TV tab/CEDAM. The ARWE provides a functional interface to cue threat data for HARM operation in self-protect mode or unplanned attack with threat library load via the avionics bus with the Mission Data Transfer System (MDTS). The two aerials/RF heads are located in the leading and trailing edges of the fin, providing rear azimuth coverage of 180°. These aids, combined with Tornado's small size and high-speed terrain following ability, minimize the acquisition capability of enemy radars. This gives Tornado a very high degree of survivability, even in the most hostile environments.

CHAPTER THREE

Tornado IDS

Tornado production was authorized on 10 March 1976, with a planned start date of 1 July, some time before the first of the pre-production aircraft had been flown. It was estimated that the first batch of twenty aircraft for the UK, sixteen for Germany and four for Italy would take around eighteen months to complete.

For the RAF, the basic IDS (Interdictor/Strike)version was to be known as the Tornado GR.1, (Ground Attack/Reconnaissance Mark 1) whilst Germany, Italy and – later on – Saudi Arabia chose to retain the IDS designation. The main differences between British, German and Italian IDS aircraft lie in the individual user nation's choice of avionics equipment, which are described in later sections. Uniquely, all RAF GR.1s have an extra 121gal fuel tank in their tail fins, giving the aircraft an additional internal fuel capacity of 285gal (5842ltr), an advantage exploited on the British TTTE aircraft, which gained additional endurance over the German and Italian machines. However, these have since been de-activated (in preparation for Gulf War service, as a precaution in case of AAA or small arms hits).

The Tornado GR.1 and IDS bombers look externally identical, though new batches introduced improvements and important modifications. To the casual observer, perhaps the best method of defining the various Tornado batches is by their external fit: later RAF aircraft are fitted with a Laser Rangefinder and Marked Target Seeker (LRMTS) in an external fairing, and the later German aircraft can carry HARM anti-radar missiles. However, this can be deceiving: some early-batch aircraft have 2-4 been retro-fitted with equipment normally associated with later batches. To the more serious-minded, serial numbers and squadron markings are perhaps the best batch indicators.

Tornado IDS cutaway diagram. BAe

Bolt-on IFR probes were introduced on some of the RAF machines: although not a common sight on the Germany-based aircraft, they were useful for the UK-stationed Tornados, giving them additional range to strike targets in Europe should this become necessary. An interesting aside was the RAF's interest in fitting low-intensity night formation-flying lights, such as can be seen on US-built aircraft. One Tornado was outfitted for trials in Germany, but the idea was short-lived.

Weapons Systems

As can be expected with their wide range of tasks, the individual air arms use a wide range of weaponry on their Tornados. In the strike role, RAF Tornados were to carry the indigenously designed and produced WE.177B free-fall nuclear bomb,

previously found on the RAF's Vulcan bombers. WE.177B was to be withdrawn in 2005, to be replaced by the Royal Navy's Trident missiles, but this withdrawal was subsequently brought forward, and the last RAF WE.177Bs were retired in a low-key event at RAF Marham in mid-1998. This use of nuclear bombs marked a major difference from Italian 2- and German Tornados, which can carry the US B61 – on which the WE.177 was based – but these weapons are operated under a 'dual key' system, with the USA/NATO in control, rather than the individual nations.

The main conventional weapons used by RAF Tornados are the Mks1–12 500lb free-fall or parachute-retarded bombs, the latter fitted with a Hunting Mk118 retarding tail. The Mk 13–22 1,000lb bombs are of the 'medium case' high-explosive bomb type, and this weapon can be used either

The RAF tested low-intensity night formation lights during the early 1990s as a way to aid night formation flying. via Mike Tomlinson

The RAF's Mk13–22 1,000lb bombs can be fitted with a Hunting Mk117 parachute retarding tail for low-level use, as is demonstrated here. BAe

'slick' for delivery from medium level or for lofting attacks; for low-level use, the same weapon can be fitted with a Hunting Mk117 parachute-retarding tail. For precision use the bomb can be fitted with Paveway II/III guidance kits, with a new nose which incorporates a laser sensor and control fins, plus a new tail fitted with pop-out stabilizing fins. This brings the basic 1,000lb bomb up to the standard of the US GBU-16. The Tornado force was unable to self-designate targets for its LGBs for many years, and in times of conflict this role would have fallen to the older Buccaneers using their AN/AVQ-23E Pave Spike pods – as it did in the Gulf War. This system has since been replaced by the GEC TIALD pod, described on page 112.

RAF Tornados also carry a range of specialized weapons such as the Hunting BL755 cluster bomb, iin both original and 'improved' forms. A weapon unique to the RAF Tornado is the Hunting JP233 bomblet dispenser, used primarily in the anti-airfield role. In peacetime, Tornados more often simply carry ML Aviation CBLS 200 practice bomb carriers, fitted with 3kg 'flash and smoke bean-tin' bombs made by Portsmouth Aviation, which accurately simulate the ballistic characteristics of a normal bomb.

Luftwaffe Tornados also use a wide range of weapons, including some items left over from the F-104G Starfighter days. The aircraft can carry a variety of US Mk80-type bombs, either 'slick' or retarded, the Hunting BL755 CBU and, as related above, nuclear weapons. In the same vein as the RAF and its JP233, Luftwaffe Tornados carry the ungainly-looking MBB/Diehl MW-1 dispenser, detailed on page 55. Another unusual store very occasionally carried by the Luftwaffe Tornados is the Dornier Aerial Target System, used for gunnery training.

The weapon aiming and delivery system provides the Tornado with the ability to carry out attacks in all weather conditions, by day or night, with a previously unknown level of accuracy. The following modes of operation are available: planned targets; straight-pass attack with retarded bombs or dispenser weapons, with direct or offset-point aiming; dive attack, bombs; loft attack, bombs; air-to-surface missiles; air-to-ground guns; unplanned targets (targets of opportunity); bombs, using Continuously-Computed Impact Point (CCIP); and bombs, using CCIP plus laser target seeker.

For planned targets the co-ordinates are part of the mission plan and are stored in the MC. For targets where, for tactical or topographical reasons, direct acquisition is to be avoided, up to three offset points in the target vicinity can be pre-programmed and used for aiming with no loss in accuracy. MC-predicted system target or offset location appears to the navigator as a marker cross on the radar screen, or to the pilot on the HUD. Using the hand controllers for a final update, either crew member can adjust his display marker or lock the ranging sensor, radar or laser, onto the target to feed accurate three-dimensional co-ordinates, as well as range and angle data, to the weapon release software in the MC. The system's flexibility allows a quick, one-button blind/visual or offset/target changeover to use the best possible target position update routine. Targets of opportunity use the CCIP symbology with manual release.

Due to the low 'grazing' angles of sensors pointing at a target from low altitudes, precise relative height is required to minimize along-track errors on the ground. The laser ranger together with the updated height from the navigation system are the primary means

Tornado GR.1 front and rear cockpit. BAe

of establishing the precise height above the target. Alternatives are the Texas Instruments radar in elevation mode, the radar altimeter or baro-inertial height, the latter together with 2- memorized target elevation. At medium altitudes, the GMR is used for height finding as well as baro-inertial height.

The MC uses the stored ballistic characteristics of the selected weapon, the exact target relative position and the aircraft's velocity, attitude and drift data to determine precisely the weapon release point

The Stores Management System (SMS) is a duplex system containing two processors at each channel. It controls the selection, arming, release and firing of all weapons and stores carried on the air-

craft. The system is pre-flight-checked by the BITE system. The navigator can programme up to five attack packages on his control panel. The type of weapon, release quantity, release modes and intervals and fuzing modes can all be pre-programmed. Any of these packages can then be called to instant readiness at the press of a single button. The SMS accepts release cues from the MC and, in the event of a computer failure, substitutes its own release cues. The use of reprogrammable memories in the SMS provides tactical flexibility, and only software changes are required to integrate new weapons.

The Tornado is fitted with three underfuselage and four wing pylons for the carriage of over nine tons of

external loads. The inboard wing pylon, the fuselage centerline pylon and the centre points of the fuselage shoulder pylons contain heavy-duty Ejector Release Units (ERUs) to accommodate large fuel tanks and other heavy stores, with suspension lugs set either 14in or 30in apart. Light-duty ERUs on the outboard wing and the fuselage shoulder pylons accept all stores with the standard 14in lugs. Automatic sway-bracing incorporated in all ERUs speeds up re-arming and role changing, leading to quick turnaround times. Twin and triple store carriers can be fitted if required.

RAF Tornado IDS

The UK has taken delivery of 398 Tornados, including 173 ADVs. Three were refurbished prototypes and eighteen were of the early (F.2) ADV type that was rapidly superseded by the F.3.

The IDS aircraft were destined to form eleven front-line strike/attack/reconnaissance squadrons, with eight based in Germany. Two reconnaissance units, Nos II (AC) and 13 Squadrons, were also formed. The first unit to operate the Tornado was No.9 Squadron, which received its first aircraft, ZA586, in January 1982 and officially re-formed on the type the following June at RAF Honington, with Wg Cdr Peter Gooding

Specification – Tornado IDS	
Weights:	
empty	30,800lb (13,950kg)
maximum take-off	61,700lb (28,000kg)
Dimensions:	
wingspan swept	28ft 2in (8.6m)
forward	45ft 7in (13.9m)
length	54ft 10in (16.7m)
height	19ft 8in (6m)
Performance:	Maximum speed Mach 2.2
Fuel capacity: maximum internal	1,920gal (7,270ltr)
maximum external	1,981gal (7,500ltr)

A birdstrike on the nose of this GR.1 resulted in quite a bit of bent metal. In this instance the errant bird was whipped over the canopy, thus avoiding being ingested into the engines! Author

being the first OC of an operational Tornado squadron. The squadron was a former Vulcan B.2 unit, as was No.617 Squadron which reformed on Tornados in May 1983 at Marham, along with No.27 Squadron, which reappeared in August 1983. In addition to these front-line units, a handful of Tornados were assigned to the Tornado Operational Evaluation Unit at Boscombe Down.

With the full complement of three home-based squadrons successfully established, units in RAF Germany began to re-equip with the Tornado, higher priority being given to the squadrons which had been operating the Buccaneer in the overland role. The first to do so was No.15 Squadron, which reformed on the Tornado at Laarbruch in October 1983. This unit had previously operated the Buccaneer, and was followed by RAFG's other Buccaneer unit, No.16 Squadron, in February 1984. No.20 Squadron, previously a Jaguar squadron based at Brüggen, re-equipped with the Tornado in June 1984, also at Laarbruch. No.31 Squadron, formerly a Jaguar unit, stood-up at Brüggen in November 1984, whilst two more RAFG

squadrons converted to the Tornado from the Jaguar during 1985, these being No.17 and No.14, with the final depature of the Jaguars being made during October. These RAFG Tornado units formed part of the 2nd Allied Tactical Air Force (ATAF), which also contained air elements from Belgium, the Netherlands, West Germany and the United States.

RAF Tornado Strike Units

No.9 Squadron

Per noctem volamus – 'We fly by Night'

In its early days No.9 was involved in air–ground wireless trials, and from the 1920s served as a bomber unit. A former Vulcan squadron, No.9 disbanded on 29 April 1982 to re-form as the world's first front-line Tornado squadron when it re-emerged at Honington on 1 June 1982. The squadron participated in a Green Flag exercise in March 1985, although it had taken some months to become combat-ready. The squadron moved to RAF Germany on 1 October 1986, in the process swapping its original aircraft for new LRMTS-equipped aircraft from Batch 4. It celebrated by winning the prestigious Salmond Trophy – awarded to RAFG squadrons for bombing and navigation accuracy – in the same year. The squadron was nominated to become the first user of the ALARM missile, and began receiving ALARM-capable aircraft even while the missile itself was still being tested, with the squadron's strength increasing from twelve to eighteen at the same time. During the Gulf War, No.9 Squadron provided eight of its ALARM-capable aircraft for use in Operation *Desert Storm*, but they were destined to be flown by aircrew from No.20 Squadron, while No.9's pilots and navigators flew conventional bombing missions with the Tabuk- and Muharraq-based detachments.

No.14 Squadron

'I spread my wings and keep my promise'

No.14 Squadron was the first RFC unit deployed to Egypt in World War One, remaining in the area until 1945. More recently, it was the last squadron of the

JP233 in action. Laying down and detonating two types of weapon simultaneously makes it very difficult for enemy engineers to effect repairs. BAe

Brüggen Wing to form, but the first to be equipped with JP233. Aircraft for No.14 (Designate) Squadron began to arrive in April 1985, with the squadron celebrating its 75th anniversary on 3 February 1990, and it was No.14 Squadron's CO who led the first Tornado deployment to the Gulf during Operation *Desert Shield*. In late 1993, No.14 Squadron received the bulk of the RAF's TIALD-capable aircraft from No.617 Squadron using the code range 'BA'–'BZ'.

No.15 Squadron

'Aim Sure'

This squadron served on the Western Front as a reconnaissance unit in World War One before converting to the bomber role, with which it has been associated ever since. As the first RAF Germany Tornado unit, No.15 began receiving Tornados at RAF Laarbruch on 5 July 1983, officially forming on 1 November 1983 and being declared operational to NATO on 1 July 1984. The squadron had a nuclear strike commitment until this was taken over by the Royal Navy. No.15 was one of three Laarbruch casualties in the post-Gulf War cutbacks, and the squadron flew home to the UK for disbandment on 31 December 1991. Disbandment was, however, short-lived as the unit's 'number-plate' re-appeared on the aircraft of the Tornado OCU at Lossiemouth, this becoming No.15 (Reserve) Squadron. During its time at Laarbruch, No.15

Squadron used the code range 'EA'–'EZ'; the aircraft coded 'F' is by tradition named 'MacRobert's Reply', after one one the unit's wartime Stirlings.

16 Squadron

Operta Aperta – 'Hidden things are revealed'

During the inter-war years No.16 served as a

No.9 Squadron's Bat emblem. Author

No.14 Squadron's emblem. Author

Tri-National Tornado Training

BELOW: **German, Italian and British Tornados share the Cottesmore flight-line, though German training will move to Holloman AFB in Germany in 1999.** Author

ABOVE: **Pilot and instructor head out for a training sortie. Note the use of the International Orange flying suits.** Author

LEFT: **Pilot and instructor strap in ready for pre-take off checks.** Author

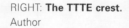

RIGHT: **The TTTE crest.** Author

A tri-national agreement, similar to the one which established the original Panavia Tornado programme, set up a joint training programme for the three nations and four air arms involved. The objective was to have all aircrew trained up to squadron level, though this aim was dashed when Germany pulled out of the proposed common weapons and tactical training phase, which has therefore always been a national responsibility. Based at an RAF Cottesmore in Leicestershire since 1975, the Tri-National Tornado Training Establishment or TTTE ('triple-T-E') saw its first personnel begin to arrive from April 1978. Although it remains a component of the RAF's No.1 Group under an RAF station commander, the unit is truly multi-national, with senior positions being rotated between the British, German and Italian officers with aircraft from all users being based at the site. Aircraft began to arrive on 1 July 1980 and the first instructors (nine pilots and six navigators) trained on the Service Instructor Training Courses at Manching from 5 May 1980. They in turn trained additional instructors at

Cottesmore before No.1 Course arrived on 5 January 1981.

The unit built up to an initial establishment of twenty-two German, twenty-one RAF and seven Italian aircraft, conforming to the 42.5 per cent, 40 per cent and 17.5 per cent funding spilt between the nations. Instructors were provided in the same ratio. The standard Main Course lasts thirteen weeks, with a nine-week flying phase providing thirty-five flying hours for pilots and twenty-eight for navigators. The first eight hours are flown with instructors, before crews team up. By the end of the course, crews can fly an academic attack sortie, with automatic TFR. The TTTE also provides shorter Instrument Rating Examiner courses, Senior Officer's familiarization courses and Competence to Instruct courses for TTTE instructor pilots and navigators.

Instructors and students are divided into three squadrons (A, B, and C), irrespective of nationality, and there is a separate Standards Squadron. Aircraft are nominally assigned to one of the four squadrons but are actually

pooled, so a British student, for example, might well find himself with a German instructor in an Italian aircraft. A reduction in the need for new aircrew led to a reduction in the unit establishment in 1989, to eighteen German, sixteen RAF and five Italian aircraft. The 200th TTTE main course graduated on 19 February 1994. TTTE tail numbers were pre-fixed with 'B' for British, 'G' for German and 'I' for Italian, with 'BR' (British Reconnaissance) codes being briefly used by recce-earmarked aircraft assigned to the unit while waiting for their GR.1A conversion. In 1997 it was announced that the TTTE would disband in 1999, with the Germans moving their training programme to the USA. RAF crews will be trained by an expanded No.15(R) Sqn at Lossiemouth. RAF Tornados assigned to the TTTE differ from the German and Italian IDSs by virtue of their fin fuel tank, which gives them better endurance. TTTE aircraft are always flown 'slick', that is, without 2-11 pylons or stores, again making them more aerodynamic and therefore more fuel efficient.

All three nations are represented in this shot, led by B-50 from A Squadron, with G-39 from B Squadron and I-43 from the Standards Squadron, and it would not be unusual for a British pilot to be flying a German Tornado with an Italian student! BAe

reconnaissance unit, remaining in Germany post-war. It became RAF Germany's second Tornado unit on 1 March 1984, having received its first aircraft on 13 December 1983. It was based alongside No.15 Squadron at Laarbruch, and also converted from the Buccaneer. No.16 Squadron commemorated its 75th anniversary by painting one of its aircraft overall black, with a huge yellow 'Saint' on its tail fin.

No.17 Squadron

Excellere Contende – 'Strive to Excel'

No.17 Squadron initially served in Macedonia in World War One, establishing itself as one of the RAF's premier fighter units. It forms part of the Brüggen Wing, sharing the commitment to provide aircraft and aircrew for Operation *Jural*, the British element of Operation *Southern Watch* (see page 75). The squadron uses the code range 'CA'–'CZ' along with its highly imaginative zigzag markings and mailed fist emblem. No.17 Squadron is due to disband in 2002 when the Brüggen Wing returns to the UK.

No.20 Squadron

Facta non Verba – 'Deeds not words'

One of the RFC's top-scoring units in World War One, No.20 Squadron went on to fight in India and Burma in World War Two. It had been a Jaguar unit at Brüggen and it disbanded there on 29 June 1984, reforming as a Tornado squadron at Laarbruch on the same day. No.20 Squadron was another unit which fell victim to the defence cuts imposed after the 'Options for Change' defence review. No.20 officially disbanded in May 1992, re-emerging in a new guise that September, its historic numberplate being saved from extinction and re-allocated to the Harrier OCU, which became No.20 (Reserve) Squadron.

No.27 Squadron

Quam Cellerrine Ad Astra – 'With all speed to the stars'

No.27. Squadron served in France as a day

bomber unit in World War One, moving to India post-war for policing duties. Although there were widely-held expectations that No.101 Squadron would be the RAF's third Tornado unit, having previously been the first with Canberras and one of the initial Vulcan units. Instead, No.101 found itself with the less glamorous role of in-flight re-fuelling, using VC-10 tankers. No.27 Squadron was the next most senior of the disbanding Vulcan squadrons, and was therefore chosen to be the third Tornado unit. The Vulcan squadron disbanded on 31 March 1982, and the new No.27 Squadron was officially formed on 12 August 1983. No.27 Squadron's aircrew converted to the maritime role and moved to RAF Lossiemouth where they replaced the Buccaneers of No.12 Squadron, taking over that unit's historic identity, and using the code range 'FA'–'FZ'. No.27 Squadron's own numberplate was re-allocated to the Puma and Chinook helicopter OCU at RAF Odiham.

31 Squadron

In Caelum Indicum Primus – 'First in Indian Skies'

Formed in India in World War One, this unit remained there on policing duties until World War Two, when it served with distinction in the Burma campaign. The 'Gold Stars', as No.31 Squadron is known, became the first unit to convert to the Jaguar at Brüggen and officially changed over to the Tornado on 1 November 1984, receiving its first aircraft on 3 June. Following the Gulf War, No.31 Squadron became the second

TTTE Main Student Training Course (9–12 weeks, dependant on weather)		
Flying	Pilot	Navigator
Familiarization	2	1
Lay-down/ toss bombing	5	5
Dive bombing	5	4
Progress check	1	1
Night flying	4	3
Air combat	4	3
Operational phase	5	5
	26	22

No.17 Squadron's reduced size nose marking. Author

No.17 Squadron's mailed fist tail badge. Author

ZA470/FL when with No.16 Squadron. Author

ABOVE: **Tornado GR.1 ZA546/JB of No.27 Squadron, a former Vulcan unit which has operated the type since 1983.**

BELOW: **A Tornado GR.1 of No.27 Squadron at RAF Marham.**

ZD461/DK, No.31 Squadron's anniversary ship. Author

ALARM-capable Tornado unit. Its aircraft carry the codes 'DA'–'DZ'.

TWCU – No.45 and 15 (Reserve) Squadrons

As related earlier, plans for a 'Tri-National Tornado Weapons Conversion Unit' were abandoned. RAF trainees were therefore sent from the TTTE to the purely British Tornado Weapons Conversion Unit at RAF Honington, which was formed from 1 August 1980, with the first training course beginning on 12 January 1982. TWCU 'geared-up' to allow new squadrons to form or convert every six months. TWCU was originally staffed by instructors drawn from Buccaneer,

Phantom and Jaguar squadrons, none of whom had operational experience on the Tornado. By 1984, however, the first front-line Tornado aircrew were being posted back to the TWCU as instructors. As Tornado instructors with direct operational experience on the aircraft, they could give the unit the potential to serve as an additional front-line squadron in time of crisis or war, and as a so-called 'shadow squadron' during peacetime. By 1984 the squadron had twenty pilot instructors, fourteen navigator instructors, and four pilots and four navigators who ran the simulator.

The No.45 Squadron numberplate was allocated as the Reserve Squadron identity of the TWCU in 1984. This would

have been used had the unit ever been transferred to SACEUR control in times of war. No.45 Squadron was allocated the wartime tailcodes 'LA'–'LZ', but they were rarely seen, except during the Gulf War when at least two aircraft had these codes applied. The No.45 Squadron identity was dropped on 31 March 1992, with a formal disbandment as the TWCU 'shadow'. No.45 Squadron's identity was transferred to the Multi-Engine Training Squadron of No.XX FTS, re-forming as such on 1 July 1993. TWCU formally adopted the new shadow identity of No.15 (Reserve) Squadron on 1 April 1992 and moved from Honington to Lossiemouth on the 1st of November 1993.

Beneath the fuselage of each of the

TWCU Tornado is fitted either one or two CBLS 200 pods, holding up to four miniature bombs of either 3kg or 14kg size. (The actual masses differ from the nominal weights, at 3.39k and 14.57kg, respectively.) These resemble full-size bombs in their trajectories following release.

The 3kg practice bomb behaves like parachute-retarded 1,000lb bomb or BL755 cluster bomb, and may be fitted with different sizes of circular drag-plate. Forward throw is typically 2,000ft when released from 500ft at 550kt in a 10° dive. The longer, thinner 14kg matches the 1,000lb 'slick' bomb, and for toss bombing a 1,500ft release in a 30° climb at 550kt will see the weapon travel four miles (6.7km). When simulating the JP233 dispenser system, the 3kg bomb is used as an approximation, the pilot's HUD showing 3kg ballistics so that the accuracy of aiming can be assessed even though the bomb will fall the 'wrong' place. On hitting the ground, practice bombs emit a puff of smoke so the range controller can plot their fall and report the results. The Tornado's two 27mm cannon are loaded with ball ammunition for air-to-ground strafing practise.

A staff of 170 cares for TWCU's Tornados under the direction of a Senior Engineering Officer and two Junior Engineering Officers. Two shifts are worked, five days per week, Monday to Friday and each aircraft generates some 30–35 flying hours per month. Aircraft strength is some twenty Tornados evenly divided between standard strike versions and dual-control trainers which, it should be stressed, are fully combat-capable. Even allowing for update programmes, that means a broad spread of aircraft standards to be accommodated. All the unit's Batch 1 and 2 aircraft have been retrofitted with lasers under the forward fuselage, whilst during 1990 the whole fleet was fitted with refuelling probes during primary servicing (which is

effected every 125 flying hours). Most also gained the 128K main computer capacity brought in with Batch 5 and a few have progressed to 224K as an interim step towards 256K. With the Batch 4 aircraft the Mk103 version of the RB.199 was introduced, but all TWCU aircraft are standardized on the Mk101. These are de-rated by 225lb st (102kgp) to 37.7kN dry thrust (8,475lb st/3,844kgp) to conserve turbine life. Being a modular powerplant, RB.199 has no single time between overhauls, but a typical time between removals is 90–120 hours, including FOD damage and birdstrikes. Aircraft total flying hours begin at 1,500 for the youngest, the TWCU fleet leader being ZA557, which arrived from 27 Squadron in mid-1989 having just clocked 2,000. By October 1990, the last of the RAF's Tornado GR.1s had been through the 'SFI' structural improvement programme at St Athan, allowing the interval between major overhauls (under-

In its No.45 Squadron guise, a TWCU Tornado sits on the Honington hardstand. With the disbandment of the Laarbruch Tornado wing, however, No.45 Squadron was succeded by No.15(Reserve), and the unit moved to Lossiemouth. Author

A 'clean' ZA599 on a TWCU training sortie, designed in this instance for the navigator's benefit. Author

taken at the same location) to be extended from 1,600 to 2,000 hours. The first female fast-jet pilot to graduate from Cottesmore was Flt Lt Jo Salter, who went on to fly the GR.1B with No.617 Squadron.

Strike Attack Operational Evaluation Unit (SAOEU)

Following the formation of the first three UK-based Tornado squadrons, RAF Strike Command established a specialist trials unit to expedite the development of tactics and operating procedures for the Tornado strike and reconnaissance force. The Tornado Operational Evaluation Unit – TOEU – formed as a lodger unit at Boscombe Down on 1 September 1984 and reported jointly to the Central Tactics and Trials Organisation at HQ RAF Strike Command, and to the A&AEE. The unit was actually initially destined to operate from Marham, to which its first aircraft (ZA393) was delivered on 11 November 1982, and four Tornados

assigned to the TOEU remained in storage at the base; one of these was assigned to another unit before it could be used. Finally, the TOEU was formed at Boscombe under Wg Cdr John Lumsden on 1 September 1983. Markings comprise a red, dark grey and light blue circle on the fin containing three swords in a 'Y' pattern, this being an adaptation of the CTTO badge. Single code letters are carried at the rear tip of the fin, being 'T', 'O', 'E' and 'U' f'or the four aircraft.

Initially the TOEU was planned to have a two-year existence, conducting trials under the four main categories of weapon system accuracy measurement; electronic warfare; terrain following system; and tactics. This involved a deployment at Elgin AFB, USA between August and November 1984 as well as flights from other bases in the UK, including those close to weapon ranges. Up to the time of its planned disbandment, the TOEU had developed operating procedures for laser-guided bombs, optimum methods for delivering

the JP233 airfield attack weapon, improvements in thc electronic warfare suite and development of passive night-flying operations using night vision goggles and a forward looking infra-red sensor. A further year of trials was thcn authorized, keeping the unit active until September 1986 with further operational weapon delivery assessments, ECM/EW development and a live drop of JP233 in the US. By January 1986, when Wg Cdr 'Raz' Ball was appointed CO, thirty-eight tasks had been received by the unit.

The unit gained permanent status and on 5 October 1987 was retitled as the SAOEU, receiving Harrier GR.5s in 1988 and later acquiring a Jaguar as well. The unit was incorporated into the Air Warfare Centre when it was formed on 1 July 1993. The main change was to the unit insignia, with a blue chevron containing a disc with the letters AWC replacing the old insignia of three swords radiating out to form a 'Y' shape, superimposed on a roundel. This badge was itself replaced by a winged sword within the same blue chevron.

RAE/DERA

Even before it became part of the Defence Research Agency (now the Defence Evaluation and Research Agency), the Royal Aircraft Establishment was a Tornado operator. The RAE acquired its first Tornado in mid-1983, in the shape of ZA326, the eighth production Tornado GR.1 and the first Tornado assigned to pure research – as opposed to development of the Tornado weapon system specifically – which was subsequently damaged by an APU fire at Warton on 31 July 1980. The aircraft was repaired, repainted in the RAE's 'raspberry-ripple' high-visibility colour scheme of gloss Signal Red BSC381C/427, white and Oxford Blue BS381C/105 with white serial numbers and red cheat line, and was assigned to the Flight Systems Department at Thurleigh, near Bedford. It is currently in use with the DRA's Experimental Flying Squadron at Boscombe Down. ZA326 has been a DRA/RAE stalwart, and is still employed on numerous trials programmes including the RAPTOR reconnaissance pod evaluations.

Tornado Air Servicing Flight

All major Tornado bases have an Aircraft Servicing Flight (ASF) for second-line servicing of resident aircraft. The ASF conducts inspections of aircraft newly delivered to the base and undertakes servicing tasks which are beyond the means of a squadron, but not complex enough for outside help to be called in. Another role is to hold spare aircraft until they are required, and it was in this connection that ZA614 was delivered to Honington in August 1982 as a common aircraft for the resident units (No.9 Squadron and the TWCU). The aircraft was marked on the fin with an ingeniously devised badge containing the letters of 'Tornado ASF', the last three of which were in the shape of a Tornado aircraft. The word 'Tornado' was in yellow and the aircraft in red. In December 1982 ZA614 was allocated to No.9 Squadron as 'Q', but did not transfer. Instead, it was reserved for the TOEU and began operating with that unit on its formation in September 1983.

Aircraft Servicing Support

Third-level support of the Tornado force is provided at the St Athan maintenance unit, although the base is no longer known as an MU. The principal unit in the station is the Engineering Complex, within which the Aircraft Engineering Wing (AEW) is responsible for supporting several types of aircraft. The AEW components include No.10 Squadron, which is specifically assigned to the Tornado. Production deliveries were made initially from BAe at Warton to the appropriate operating base, but from December 1982 onwards most aircraft went through No.10 Squadron for acceptance checks and holding prior to issue. The first arrival was ZA394, the ninety-third from UK production. No.10 Squadron was also responsible for major overhauls, but it is the AEW's No.1 Squadron which handles re-painting. In November 1985 St Athan delivered (or re-delivered) its hundredth Tornado to an operational unit (ZD851 to No.31 Squadron), the total being made up of sixty-eight acceptances from the

ZA326, the eighth production Tornado GR.1 in its 'raspberry ripple' high-visibility colour scheme. DERA via Mike Tomlinson

manufacturer, twenty-three modifications and nine overhauls. The first Tornado ADV was received for familiarization on 10 January 1986 when F.2 ZD933 flew in from No.29 OCU at Coningsby.

Low-Level Training in Canada

As the Tornado's original *raison d'être* was to attack under the radar, great importance was, and still is, placed on low-level training. For the units based in Germany this has proved to be a major problem as no low flying is allowed in the country, and the available slots at UK ranges are always at a premium. In response to this problem the RAF increased its commitment to undertake a greater percentage of the low flying sorties at more 'suitable' locations. In October 1983 No.9 Squadron made the first Tornado deployment to CFB Goose Bay in Labrador, Canada for training, and was followed by other units. Rather than shuttle aircraft over the Atlantic, it was decided to base a number of Tornados at Goose Bay for an extended period, during which they would be flown by crews from several squadrons.

Accordingly, on 20–21 February 1986, nine Tornados wearing the insignia of Nos9, 27 and 617 Squadrons were flown

out with Victor tanker support. On arrival one of their first duties was to take part in a Green Flag exercise attended by Nos20, 31 and 617 Squadrons at Nellis AFB in the United States, and it was not until April that No.31 Squadron personnel flew out to Canada by transport aircraft to begin training. Aircrew of No.17 Squadron took over on 10 May, followed by No.617 on 21 June. These aircraft were then flown home during July, but not before nine more from Nos15, 16 and 20 Squadrons had been ferried from Marham to Goose Bay, on 9 July. No.15 Squadron crews began using this batch for training on 1 August, followed by Nos16, 20 and 17. After taking part in a Red Flag exercise at Nellis, the second batch of aircraft returned to the UK.

The majority of this training now takes place at Goose Bay, the RAF deploying varying types and numbers of its aircraft to this remote airfield each year. For 1998 the first deployment came under the title of *Western Vortex '98*. On 31 March, eight GR.1s set off for Goose Bay from RAF Brüggen, in Germany, flown by aircrew of No.31 Squadron with the support of two VC-10 C.1Ks of No.10 Squadron and a solitary VC-10 K.2 from No.101 Sqn, in an operation that the RAF call a Storm Trail. At

Goose Bay RAF flying activity is steadily increasing, and as a result, the unit has expanded to meet the task.

Among the main assets at Goose Bay are the large hangars that are available to visiting aircraft. These giant hangars not only provide more than average cover and workspace, but also house the operations, administration and briefing facilities. During winter they also provide much-needed shelter from the elements, as temperatures often fall to around −30°C. The flying season runs from April to October, when approximately 1,300 sorties will be flown. The eight Tornados deployed to Goose Bay during 1998 will stay in North America for the whole flying season: they will also be flown to such locations as Nellis AFB, Eielson AFB and CFB Cold Lake for various exercises.

RAF Camouflage

When they entered service, the RAF Tornados carried the standard 'overland' Dark Sea Grey BSC381C/638 and Dark Green BS381C/641 wraparound camouflage scheme, though the Gulf War saw the aircraft involved being overpainted in the so-called 'Pink Panther' desert sand

Seen here over the Canadian forests in the late evening sun, a No.14 Squadron GR.1 (note the maple leaf 'zap' on the tail) and one from No.17 Squadron head home to Goose Bay from a low-flying exercise. Paul Bolland

'NightFox' Tornado

ABOVE: **Tornado GR.1A ZA706/E carries the unofficial name 'NightFox', following on the heels of the 'NightCat' Jaguar and the 'NightBird' Harrier, all of which pioneered that type's introduction to after-dark flying techniques.** Author

BELOW:**Close-up on the underfuselage FLIR pod fitted to 'Nightfox'.** Author

Tornado GR.1A ZA706/E carries the name 'NightFox', which alludes to its role in evaluating sensors intended for the RAF's Tornado GR.4 upgrade. 'NightFox' was equipped with a FLIR sensor in an underfuselage pod which, unlike the internal fit on the GR.4 which has its 'eye' in an under-nose fairing, was carried on one of the shoulder stations. The pod was a one-off built by the DRA at Farnborough, the shell being constructed by Cranfield Aviation, with the internal parts coming from the already-proven Harrier GR.7 programme. The aircraft's cockpits were NVG-capable, and the SAOEU's Special Projects Team installed an F.3 sticktop with changed functionality to enable better manipulation of the FLIR system. Also fitted were a pair of 'Hindenburger' fuel tanks, stillin their F.3 paintwork, thus extending the aircraft's endurance.

A No.2(AC) GR.1A in Arctic garb for the NATO *Cold Winter* exercises held in Norway, where this style of paintwork is ideal in the snowy conditions. Author

ARTF scheme. Since the mid-1990s a new scheme of all-over Medium Grey LIR (Low Infra-Red) paint was applied, starting with the 'overwater' Tornado GR.1Bs (see Chapter 4). Winter camouflage has also been trialled on a few aircraft, most notably to the GR.1As of Nos II (AC) and 13 Squadrons for their role in the NATO Cold Winter exercises held in Norway. This particular scheme mirrored the ARTF scheme applied to the Jaguar and Harrier aircraft that had previously been involved in the same areas.

Marking Time

During the late 1990s, with the RAF's Tornado force being committed more and more frequently to 'live' conflicts, it became neccessary to tone-down the squadron markings carried on the aircraft, not only for reported health and safety

reasons but also to make them easier to remove in order to 'sanitize' the aircraft for combat. Where possible, markings were located on removable panels for easy changing if the aircraft was rotated to another unit. At the time of writing, only the Germany-based strike units and the UK-based F.3s have adopted such schemes, although the first of No.13 Squadron's new Tornado GR.4s were also noted with a new toned-down style of insignia. The other UK-based squadrons, Nos2, 12, 15(R) and 617, have yet to fall into line, but as these aircraft are used for reconnaissance and maritime strike, they seem less likely to be interchanged, so the need for the adoption of easier-to-apply/remove markings is not so great.

In Germany, No.9 Squadron has seen the famous fin-mounted bat emblem increase in brightness to a more 'malachite' green and moved to the forward

fuselage, within a smaller yellow/green bar replacing the nose chevron. The unit's code has also been moved to the rear edge of the fin tip, reduced in size and changed to white, as opposed to the previous black outlined in white.

No.31 Sqn has followed suit with its bright green/yellow chevron being replaced by a green/yellow checkerboard bar in an identical place to that of No.9 Sqn, with the unit's yellow star superimposed upon it. However, the original larger version is retained on the fin.

No.14 Sqn had always used a smaller nose insignia, so the alterations here comprise some slight relocation to fall into line with other units, and the adoption of the white tail code on the trailing edge of the fin.

No.17 Sqn has retained its black/white zigzag nose chevron, although in a much reduced form, and once again this has been applied on the same forward nose

No.31 Squadron's usually flamboyant gold star can now be seen in a reduced form, applied to the side of the aircraft's nose. Gary Parsons f4 Aviation

FBW controls; provision for the GEC TIALD laser designator; and stub pylons on the outboard face of each underwing pylon, to be dedicated to the carriage of ALARM anti-radar missiles. It was also hoped to incorporate provision for huge 592gal (2691ltr) auxiliary fuel tanks.

A development and investment contract for the MLU was issued to Panavia on 16 March 1989, under which three aircraft would be converted to serve as prototypes. They were XZ631, ZD708 and ZG773. XZ631 was chosen to serve as PINST for most of the systems, whilst the other two prototypes were converted to full GR.4 standard. A number of other aircraft were also used in support of the programme, including the SAOEU's ZG706. Indeed, it was the Boscombe Down-based SAOEU which pioneered the GR.4 FLIR, flying an underfuselage podded version in order to 'write the rule book' on Tornado/FLIR operations.

The RAF had hoped to order twenty-six new-build Tornado GR.4s in Batch 8, and planned to follow that with 126 conversions from existing GR. 1s and GR.1As. The budget for the upgrade was estimated at around £1 billion, with each conversion taking ten months and twenty aircraft being upgraded simultaneously. It was planned that the first seventy aircraft would be converted by BAe, with the next fifteen being produced by joint BAe/RAF working parties at RAF St Athan.

As defence cuts began to bite following the collapse of the Soviet Union, the extent of the upgrade was progressively reduced. The new-build Batch 8 aircraft were cancelled on 18 June 1990, and it became apparent that the number of conversions would also be reduced. The MLU also ran into some development problems, while constantly moving 'goalposts' caused even greater delays. By 1993 the entire project was running eighteen months behind schedule, and the Treasury pressed for its cancellation. With the reduced Waraw Pact threat, it became increasingly difficult to justify the upgrade, which had been designed to allow the aircraft to continue to penetrate Warsaw Pact defences at low level. Instead, the budget was reduced to £750 million and the number of aircraft to be converted was further decreased. This reduction was accompanied by the deletion of some of the MLU's major elements, including the abandonment of the major structural mod-

panel as the other squadrons'. The tail code has been changed to white and repositioned towards the top rear of the fin.

Toward the future – Tornado GR.4

With the Cold War at its peak, the RAF drew up a requirement, SR(A) 417, for an upgrade to its Tornado GR.1 fleet to enhance their ability to penetrate hostile airspace, to make increased use of more accurate weapons from greater stand-off ranges, and for them to be able to make electronic 'emission-less' covert incursions into enemy territory. When first mooted, the extent of the Tornado MLU, or GR.4, upgrade modifications was ostentatious to say the least. There were rumblings that the fuselage would be stretched to provide extra space for avion-

ics, and that new, 'low observable' air intakes would be fitted. The canopy would receive a thin gold coating to reduce radar cross-section and proposals were put forward to fit the aircraft with the 20,230lb st (90.0kN) Eurojet EJ200 engines designed for the Eurofighter 2000, or with the RB.199 Mk105 fitted to German Tornado ECRs (see page 00), with FADEC units incorporated. The principal external change was to be a new fairing under the port forward fuselage to house a FLIR system, to be complemented by NVGs as standard equipment.

Other features originally outlined for the GR.4 included a new Ferranti wide-angle holographic HUD; a new Smiths Industries MFD HDD for the pilot; a Marconi Zeus RWR to replace the existing Sky Guardian equipment; a new GEC stores management system; digital

Prairie Vortex

'It's vulnerable, heavy and expensive. I just don't think it's a good 'plane.'

So said Richard DeLauer, Under-Secretary of Defense for Research and Engineering in the US Department of Defense, in an off-the-record chat with the editorial staff of the *Washington Times* at the end of October 1984. Mr DeLauer chose his moment well – the very moment that RAF Tornados, competing against the best USAF crews that could be fielded in the annual Strategic Air Command Bombing Competition, made an almost clean sweep! Eligible to compete in three categories, the Tornado crews took first place in two and second in the other – as well as a second, a third and a sixth place in the three events. The contest is widely regarded as one of the most realistic of exercises, and the success of the Tornados is the more remarkable considering that the RAF's Tornado GR.1s are low-level inter-dictor strike aircraft, while much of the SAC competition is flown at high level, and also that this was the Tornado's first appearance in Giant Voice, as SAC codenames the event.

HQ Strike Command decided in July 1983 that No.617 Squadron would provide two teams of two crews each to participate in the SAC competition with the support of the Victor tankers of No.55 Squadron. Although there was a phase in Giant Voice for the tanker support elements, the RAF declined to enter the Victors, as they were required to support the Tornados during their competition sorties. Once the RAF decision to participate had been taken, plans were made to bring eight Tornados up to the required standard, in order to fly six to the United States. This would ensure that at least four aircraft were always available for the competition sorties. Among the modifications required were a data-dump facility for tone-release scoring; increased waypoint/fixpoint numbers in the Ferranti Digital Inertial Navigation System; a stores-management modification to allow stores jettison on take-off; inclusion of an AFDS display on the HUD for use during low-level operations, and improvements to the RWR and ECM pod to cope with the EW element of the competition.

After each work-up sortie at Marham, every Tornado was carefully scrutinized to ensure maximum knowledge of systems and serviceability, with a full debrief conducted between aircrew and chief tradesmen. Each major system was scored out of ten for accuracy and effectiveness, and the results fed into the squadron's computer. Thus an instant record of individual aircraft performance was available at any stage.

The Victors, too, received their share of fine tuning, with particular attention being given to the avionics, and an IFF interrogator was installed to ensure an accurate rendezvous with the Tornados. As Sqn Ldr Pete Dunlop pointed out, 'The Victors couldn't win the competition for us, but they could have lost it for us.'

At least two air-to-air refuellings (AARs) were required for each competition sortie, so close co-operation between the Victors and Tornados was essential. The location of both squadrons at Marham ensured face-to-face debriefs. With aircraft modifications underway, selection of the aircrew began. All squadron aircrew were considered eligible: flying skill and 'big match temperament' were required of the pilots, while the navigators were selected for their radar background and skill, plus competence in the full spectrum of the Tornado's equipment. The Victor crews were constituted for the duration of training and the competition. By May, six crews had been selected for the first in-theatre detachment to Ellsworth AFB, South Dakota. They completed identical work-up routines, and the final selection was made, as required by SAC, in September. The chosen crews were:Team A: Sqn Ldr Pete Dick Dunlop; Flt Lt Dick Middleton; Flt Lt Iain

Hunter; Flt Lt Dermot Dolan.Team B: Flt Lt Steve Legg; Flt Lt John McDonald; Sqn Ldr Vic Bussereau; Sqn Ldr Alan Dyer-Perry.

During late April/early May, three Tornados and two Victors detached to Ellsworth AFB, as Prairie Vortex I (the RAF code-name for its participation in the SAC contest), to gain in-theatre experience of USAF operations. Specifically, their job was to investigate operations over the United States, to fly representative sorties over routes and targets, and to collect first-hand intelligence and target data. The detachment was successful – all the planned sorties were flown – with the much-needed mapping and radar data collected. Operating out of a USAF base into an FAA-controlled sky presented its own problems, but plans to deal with this were formulated in the light of the experience. The final three months of the UK work-up started to bring the elements of training together. June was devoted to 'academic' radar offset bombing and tone-release techniques over the Spadeadam range by day and night, with the limited number of modified aircraft available. Further aircraft were used for trials with the reprogrammed Marconi Sky Shadow ECM pod, and all aircrew became current in AAR techniques. Half-route simulations of 3–31/2-hour duration were flown during July, including one AAR bracket. Practice bombs were dropped over West Freugh and the results analyzed. AAR techniques were refined and ECM pod trials continued. By August, full route simulations of 5–6 hours were being flown, using Spadeadam, West Freugh, Holbeach and Wainfleet ranges by day and night. Despite carrying 330gal external fuel tanks, the Tornados required at least two AAR brackets per sortie. The technique worked successfully during the detachments, and brought the Victor and Tornado together by day or night, in VMC or IMC, without ground radar assistance. At the rendezvous (RV) point, the Victor was required to be Xnm (Xkm) ahead of the Tornado: using the Victor's IFF interrogator to ensure long range accuracy, the Tornado's ground-mapping radar, TACAN and stopwatch timing, the tanker and receiver approached one another at different heights, timed to arrive at the datum points.

In mid-August, an advance party left for Ellsworth AFB to prepare for the main party of six Tornados and three Victors, which departed the UK on 29 August. This gave the detachment, code-named Prairie Vortex II, the whole of September to complete its in-theatre training. The work carried out by Sqn Ldr Huckins and the advance party, and the subsequent preparation of route and target combat mission folders tailored to each crew, was to pay dividends. The competition was split into two phases, with each crew flying one live-bomb drop sortie, and one radar-offset simulated tone-bomb release by day and night. To ensure launching a competition sortie within the XX-minute 'window', two aircraft were always taxied to the end of the runway, while ground parties stood by to correct any last-minute problems, in touch with the aircrew and squadron operations room by portable radio. The first-phase sorties, flown on 3–4 October, involved a high-level transit of two hours to the Red Flag ranges over Nellis AFB with AAR support; a thirty-minute run across the ECM range with jamming and fighter harassment from Canadian CF-101 Voodoos directed by an E-3A Sentry (without success!) to drop two bombs on targets using one offset; followed by climb-out, AAR and return to base. The Tornados were launched on time and performed successfully, although one problem occurred on a Sky Shadow ECM pod which, fortunately, did not result in the Tornado in question being 'killed'.

The next week began with what should have been the night sortie of phase two but, because of the squadron's order in the take-off stream this became the day sortie. After the high-level sector with AAR and one tone-bomb release, the flight came down to low level where the terrain-following radar of Tornado was used to advantage. During this sector, four more tone-releases were made. The action was further complicated by the need to climb to to 8,000ft for a second refuelling between the second and third bomb run. The time from bomb release to this RV datum was a mere three minutes! A high-level return to base completed the six-hour sortie. As Flt Lt Dick Middleton said, 'It was long periods of inactivity interspersed with short bursts of hyper-activity'.

Take-off timings were again met and successful sorties flown, although computer malfunction caused a wild score for one member of Team A. The second sorties, nominally the daylight one, became nocturnal for the Tornados after an 1830hr take-off slot. The route and requirements were identical to the previous sortie, but flown in reverse. The aircraft launched

on time and in good order, but one member of Team B suffered radar failure in flight, while another ECM pod played up. The detachment returned to the UK on 3 October, while the results from all sorties were being analyzed, but was back at Barksdale AFB a week later for the announcement of results, competition de-brief and (as it turned out) the prize-giving and subsequent celebrations. Despite the complex nature of the tasks, the Tornado demonstrated timing accuracies of +/–2 seconds during a six-hour sortie with a less than 30ft weapons aiming error at low-level, and successful ECM jamming against threats. The units gained both first and second places for both the Le May and Meyer Trophies, but its 97.2 per cent score was just beaten by a US team in the Mathis Trophy. Making Richard DeLauer, it was felt, a prime candidate for a little word-eating contest!

ifications. On 4 May 1993, it was further announced that the GEC Spartan and covert radar altimeter had been dropped from the upgrade.

The first GR.4 (XZ631) was not ready to make the type's much delayed first flight on 29 May 1993, so the second aircraft (ZD708) was used instead. Apart from a huge 'GR.4' logo on the fin, the aircraft had a forward-facing test camera in the leading edge of the fin RWR fairing and a new FLIR fairing below the nose, offset to port adjacent to the usual LRMTS fairing. The FLIR fairing was flown in mock-up form by the Boscome Down FJTS on a GR.1A before being released to service.

The Tornado GR.4 programme was accompanied by separate requirements for new stand-off precision-guided munitions, intended for use by the new variant and subsequently by the new Eurofighter. SR(A) 1244 called for a new nuclear weapon, but was abandoned along with the aircraft's existing nuclear role. SR(A) 1238 was also drawn up to find a stand-off anti-armour weapon, initially as a dispenser system, but filled in the end by the Matra/BAe Brimstone munition, whilst SR(A) 1240 called for a short-range radiation missile. A final weapons requirement, SR(A) 1242, called for a

low-level bomb: Britain became the first European customer for the Texas Instruments Paveway III when it was ordered in July 1994, in preference to Marconi's rocket-boosted Lancelot, which offered greater stand-off range, but at a much greater price tag.

The initial update programme fell victim to defence cuts and was shelved until after the Gulf War, when it was resurrected as MLU 93. Eventually, following the government's Front Line First defence review, BAe received a £640 million order on 14 July 1994 for the conversion of just eighty aircraft, with an option to convert sixty-two more during

Front and rear cockpit of the Tornado GR.4; compare this to the standard GR.1 shown on page 31. BAe

A mock-up of the FLIR fairing fitted to a GR.1A of the Boscombe Down-based FJTS, installed to trial the aerodynamic shape of the fit. Author

2000–2002 – a total of 142 aircraft. Under the Options for Change and Front Line First defence reviews the number of front-line Tornado GR.1 squadrons was reduced to eight. This led to disparate standards of software and modifications throughout the Tornado force, with each aircraft being suitable only for its particular role and no other. This was referred to by the engineers as 'fleets within fleets'. The MLU was therefore designed to regain commonality across the force, with only the GR.4A aircraft being different from all the others. By this time the scope of the upgrade had narrowed even further, and covered only the installation of a digital map display; GPS; an enhanced weapons control system; a new wide-angle holographic HUD allowing standard HUD symbology to be overlaid on the FLIR image; a video recorder; the pilot's MFD HDD; and a new fixed FLIR sensor. The FLIR can be used by either crew member to update the navigation kit or attack a target. This was a very much downgraded upgrade than that which had originally been planned.

Reflecting the Tornado's role of low-level night attack, the cockpit has also been made fully night vision goggle (NVG) compatible in addition to the FLIR sensor. This has meant replacing all the original equipment lighting with NVG-compatible bulbs, and the introduction of green floodlighting for ambient cockpit lighting. On the central warning panel, the old red captions, which denoted a major aircraft problem, became yellow and the amber captions became green. To turn the aircraft from non-NVG into NVG mode involves just one switch, which extinguishes the normal lighting and activates the NVG bulbs, whereas the GR.1 relies on dimming the normal lighting as much as possible to allow the use of NVGs. While this is a reasonable short-term solution, the fact that the NVGs amplify ambient light by a factor of about 10,000 means that reflections around the cockpit often degrade the view of the outside world. All the GR.4 aircraft are fitted with NVG auto separation built into the seats, so in the event of ejection the goggles are blown clear of the helmet, reducing the danger of severe neck injury. This also gives the capability to take off from a

The 'prototype' GR.4, ZD708, cranks up its undercarriage. BAe

A brace of GR.4s formate for the camera, and from this angle it is hard to tell them from the standard GR.1 – apart from the huge 'GR.4' on the tail! BAe

blacked-out airfield, climb to height for a medium-level transit, and stow the goggles until they are needed for the low-level portion of the mission.

The weapons system has also been completely overhauled, and a Mil Std 1553 databus fitted, in order for GR.4 to fully integrate with current avionics and weapons. This is coupled with a 1760 weapons bus that will allow the aircraft to communicate with the next generation of 'smart' weapons, such as the Storm Shadow stand-off missile and the Brimstone anti-armour weapon, and pass them updates until they are released from the aircraft.

In September 1996, a Tornado GR.1A 'spoofed' as a GR.4 for static display at the Farnborough SBAC show. The aircraft, ZA401, had big GR.4 logos applied, but was otherwise unmodified. The choice of a reconnaissance GR.1A was not entirely inappropriate, despite the first aircraft to

be upgraded being a GR.1, which arrived at Warton on 1 April 1996 after a brief period at RAF St Athan; the second aircraft was a GR.1A, ZA371, which arrived on 3 June 1996. It seems likely that a high proportion of the upgraded aircraft will become GR.4As. The first Tornado GR.4 to actually enter squadron service was grey-clad ZD847/AA, which was deliverd to No.9 Squadron in Germany on 11 May 1998.

Tornado 2000

Tornado 2000 was a proposed successor to the RAF's GR.4 which would be optimized for low-level, high-speed, long-range penetration, and able to carry stand-off weapons. The aircraft would feature a longer fuselage which would contain greater fuel capacity and have a stealthy 'faceted' nose section to minimize

its radar cross-section. However, Tornado 200 would remain a 'paper project' and was never built.

On Display – 'Black Beauty'

Traditionally the RAF's dedicated Tornado flying display was undertaken by one of the front-line units or by TWCU/No.15(R) Squadron. However, during the 1995 air-show season, the job was transferred to the TTTE at RAF Cottesmore. The UK crew chosen for the year were pilot Flt Lt Mike 'Tart' Allton from the base's Standards Squadron and navigator Flt Lt Mike Harland from A Squadron. Both airmen were vastly experienced, Allton being ex-Nos14 and 31 Squadrons from Germany and Harland being ex-No.617 Squadron, following five years as a navigation instructor at RAF Finningley.

The crew found out quite late that they were to be the display crew: most stations having a display are up to speed by November/December time, but Allton and Harland did not receive the 'nod' until after Christmas, which was unfortunate because Mike Harland was just recovering from an operation! Mike Allton therefore went up to Lossiemouth to talk to the previous year's pilot, Sqn Ldr Mark Roberts and flew with him, returning home totally overloaded and wondering what he had let himself in for! Drawing therefore on their own operating experience, past displays, former display crews and the 'rule book', the duo pulled together their sequence for presentation to the AOC on 1 February and, after some minor modifications, they began their work up soon after. Mike Allton recalls:

The Strike Tornado isn't really designed for flinging about the sky. The biggest thing we had going for us was that the Tornado was noisy, and we intended to capitalize on that feature! The jet looked at its most impressive going 'very loud, very low, very fast', and we built on that concept, with, of course, a slow-speed pass to show that we can operate in that mode! We also added an inverted pass, trying to keep the whole thing as tight as we could. During the first few practices we just about managed to stay within the same county, but we were soon able to keep it within the airfield boundary! The low pass was at 100ft, 150kt, plugging the 'burners in at the end, turning hard away from the crowd and entering a slow climb, hanging on the 'carrots' as we went, a manoeuvre which looks very impressive from the ground, as it seems we were going almost vertical.

While Mike Allton concentrated on flying the aircraft, Mike Harland in the back seat ensured that all went smoothly:

I spent a lot of time talking to Mike about heights, speeds, time frames and the effect the wind may be having on our display, plus backing-up the next manoeuvre, especially if the Met report was none too sharp. Our three weather-orientated programmes had their similarities, and it was important that we didn't start off flying one programme and accidentally slip into another!

Our arrival was planned to be slightly behind the crowd and out of sight, engaging the 'burners as we turned onto the display line, and banking over to give the spectators a good plan view of the aircraft. The exit was equally noisy as we wound-up with a lazy

The real thing. The GR.4 FLIR fairing on an operational GR.1A of No.13 Squadron, looking much more purposful in camouflage colours! Gary Parsons f4 Aviation

The display jet for the year, ZA560, was taken on loan from No.15(R) Squadron, and chosen because of its good fatigue life. In order to obtain a striking visual presence it was painted in an overall gloss black finish and adorned with the TTTE crest on the fuselage, the flags of the three participating nations across the RWR and the Rutland coat of arms on the tail. (Cottesmore is jokingly referred to as home of the 'Rutland Air Force' – a pun on the RAF's initials, as Rutland, within whose borders the base lies, is Britain's smallest county!) The aircraft was sprayed up at Cottesmore, the painters setting up shop in the station's pre-fabricated 'Rubb-Hanger'. Working two twelve-hour shifts, the jet took two weeks to complete, in less than ideal conditions. The first attempt 'orange-peeled' and had to be removed, but the second try was an unqualified success, achieving a high gloss finish. The markings were stickers which were painstakingly applied, and the crew had to take the aircraft supersonic to ensure that they continued to adhere to the surface!

ZA560, one of the RAF's all-blacks, and although it has TTTE markings, the aircraft was actually borrowed from No.617 Squadron for the season! Author

Flt Lt Mike Harland (left) and Flt Lt Mike Allton (right). Author

accelerating wing-over into a 100ft, 600kt pass pulling 7g into the vertical, sweeping the wings back to 45°, and giving the illusion that the jet was continuing to accelerate as we climbed away.

The role of Tornado display remained with the TTTE crews for the years 1995–96; included in the 1996 display crew was Squadron Leader Robbie Stewart, who had been a prisoner of Iraq during the Gulf War after ejecting from his stricken aircraft.

Luftwaffe IDS

The Luftwaffe began the 1970s with five *Jagdbombergeschwaderen* (fighter-bomber wings), two *Jagdgeschwaderen* (fighter wings), two *Aufklärungs-geschwaderen* (reconnaissance wings) and a *Waffenschule* (weapons school) equipped with the F-104G Starfighter, and four *Leichtenkampfgeschwaderen* (light combat wings) with Fiat G9ls. All needed replacement by the mid-1970s, along with two Marineflieger F-104 units. The G91s were originally to have been replaced by the VAK-191 (a vertical take-off aircraft eventually cancelled due to funding difficulties) but that still left a requirement for some 700 Tornados to replace the F-104s one for one. It soon became clear that the Tornado would not be available until the early 1980s, and it

was decided that some wings would have to be re-equipped before then. The two RF-104G equipped reconnaissance wings were the most pressing priority, followed by the air defence-tasked JG 71 and JG 74, especially after Germany accepted the UK version of Tornado as a long-range all-weather interdictor. With the RF-4E already selected as an RF-104G replacement, the standard F-4E fighter seemed to offer some advantages as an interceptor replacement for the F-104G, and also offered sufficient air-to-ground capability to allow the formation of two ground-attack wings, one of which had previously operated F-104s and one Fiat G91s. The decision to re-equip these five Starfighter wings with Phantoms led to further reductions in the Tornado buy from its original 700-aircraft level, first to 420, then to 322. Economic considerations resulted in Tornado deliveries being delayed. Despite plans to increase production from forty-six to sixty-three aircraft per year between 1981 and 1983, deliveries actually fell: forty-four

From all-black to all-grey as demonstrated by ZA321/B-58, the 1996 display ship, looking superb in this non-standard colour scheme. RAF Cottesmore

were delivered in 1981 and 1982, and only forty-two in 1983. The Luftwaffe's original four front-line Tornado wings were based in the central and southern parts of Germany with the conversion unit, JBG 38, in the far north at Jever. Plans to reform JBG 37 at Husum in 1995 with new Tornados were abandoned when Germany cancelled its planned Batch 8 order for thirty-five IDS aircraft. Two Tornados are also on charge with *Technischeschule der Luftwaffe* 1 at Kaufbeuren, and are used for technical training of ground crew and engineering personnel. The RAF Germany Tornados were partnered within 2ATAF by Luftwaffe Tornados of JBG 31 at Norvenich. The Tornados of JBG 32 operate as part of 4ATAF, partnered by JBG 33 at Buchel. On 1 April 1994, the

The Luftwaffe uses the BOZ-101 chaff and flare pod on their aircraft, whereas the RAF use the Mk103. Author

Luftwaffe set up a new command structure. *Luftwaffen Führungskommando Sud* consisted of 1 Division HO Karlsrühe controlling JBG 32 and JBG 34, and 2 Division HO Birkenfeld controlling JBG 33. *Luftwaffen Führungskommando Nord* consisted of 3 Division and 4 Division HO Aurich which controlled JBG 31 and JBG 38. The end of the Cold War and the consequent arms limitation treaties imposed ceilings on the numbers of combat aircraft that could be operated, and Germany decided to reduce the number of F-4s in service, rather than getting rid of Tornados. Thus, the last wing of RF-4Es were retired and a new wing of Tornados was formed from aircraft that had been rendered surplus to Marineflieger requirements. Tornado numbers were also reduced, some being diverted to Holloman AFB in America for training purposes, whilst others were placed in long-term storage at the MADC, at Davis-Monthan AFB in Arizona.

Luftwaffe Strike Tornado Units

Jagdbombergeschwader 31 'Boelcke'

JBG 31 received the 100th production German IDS on 24 August 1983. Five years on, in 1988, this aircraft was decorated to celebrate JBG 31's 30th anniversary. As the first German Tornado Wing, JBG 31 set many milestones. In May 1986, an aircraft from JBG 31 (with another from JBG 38) deployed across the Atlantic, buddy-refuelling from two pod-equipped JBG 31 Tornados. The unit has achieved many firsts, including the initial Luftwaffe participation in Red Flag. JBG 31's two squadrons, 311 and 312, have badges depicting two mules for 311, and a wolf's head, three crowns and a sword for 312.

Jagdbombergeschwader 32

It had always been intended that the German front-line units would convert to the Tornado in numerical order. Original plans called for JBG 32 to convert in mid-1982, but the unit did not fly its last Starfighter mission until 18 April 1984. The wing received its first aircraft on 27 July 1984 and officially reformed on 1 August. Uniquely among German Tornado wings, JBG 32 has never had a nuclear strike commitment, but has always been closely associated with ECM and EW training. The wing's third Staffel operated Hansa Jets in the ECM training role, and the wing also parented the joint civil/military *Gemeinesame Flugvermess-ungsstelle GMFS Fachbereich IVI*, with its calibration

BAe 748s and 125s. JBG 32 became the Luftwaffe's second Tornado ECR operator from June 1991, receiving the final Tornado ECRs produced, after the first eighteen went to 382 Staffel at Jever. It had originally been predicted that JBG 32's first batch of Tornado ECRs would equip 323 Staffel, displacing that unit's ECM training Hansa Jets. In fact, they were delivered to 321 Staffel, whose standard IDS aircraft were redistributed to other units. JBG 32 formally became the Luftwaffe's only ECR unit on 1 July 1994, when 322 Staffel re-equipped with the Tornado ECRs previously used JBG 38.

Jagdbombergeschwader 33

Original plans called for JBG 33 to convert to the Tornado in late 1982 or early 1983, but the unit did not relinquish its last F-104Gs until after a final sortie on 30 May 1985. The first Tornado was delivered to Buchel in August 1985, and the unit had received its full complement by August 1986.

Jagdbombergeschwader 34 'Allgau'

The conversion of JBG 34 to the Tornado was originally scheduled for late 1983, but badly over-ran, since it became the last German unit to transition to the aircraft, following the second Marineflieger wing,

An all-grey Tornado ECR tucks up its wheels for a *Deny Flight* mission over Bosnia. Panavia

MFG 2. The wing did not fly its last F-104 mission until 16 October 1987, and the eventual arrival of the Tornado marked a massive leap in capability. JBG 34 was subsequently declared operational on the Tornado and based at Memmingen in the south of Germany. Its badge shows two stylized aircraft overflying mountains, with the NATO star in the top corner.

Jagdbombergeschwader38 'Friesland'

JBG 38 was the first Luftwaffe Tornado unit to form, as its primary role was much the same as that assigned to the RAF's TWCU: weapons and tactical training for aircrew going on to front-line units. It was initially an offshoot of *Luftwaffenversorgungsregiment 1* (see below). At one time it was expected that the unit would take over the designation and traditions of what had been the Starfighter tactical weapons training unit, *Waffenschule 10*, but instead the unit gained a new designation, being classified as a *Jagdbombergeschwader*.

Newly trained crews from the TTTE at Cottesmore undergo a 30-flying-hour programme with JBG 38, learning how to use the Tornado as a weapons system, dropping practice bombs and practising delivery techniques for various weapons, as well as receiving some ACM training. Tornado QWI instructor's courses are undertaken by JBG 38 for the Luftwaffe and Marineflieger, and the unit also runs EW training for all fast-jet types in the

Luftwaffe inventory. The unit has occasionally used naval aircraft on loan from MFG 2. JBG 38 gained a second, operational *Staffel* (squadron), 382 Staffel, in 1989, and this unit was the first to equip with the new ECR variant (see Chapter 4), its aircraft beginning to arrive at Jever in 1990. 382 Staffel was, however, destined to be short lived as an ECR unit, and transferred its aircraft to JBG 32 during October 1994, receiving standard IDS aircraft in return.

Aufklärungsgeschwader 51 'Immelmann'

A former RF-4E user, AKG-51 is described fully on page 111.

Luftwaffenversorgungsregiment 1

LsVersRgt.1 at Erding was the maintenance unit responsible for the acceptance checking of Luftwaffe Tornados, and an initial weapons training unit was set up as an offshoot of this unit. This was described as the *Waffenausbildungs Komponente* – weapons training component – or WaKo, and the unit received its first aircraft on 9 November 1981, formally commissioning on 16 February. WaKo became JBG 38 on 26 August 1985, by which time some twenty-four Tornados were on charge, and eight more were accepted in subsequent years. Most of crews of the first operational German Tornado unit, the Navy's MFG 1, were trained at the TTTE and by WaKo.

Deutsches Ausbildungsgeschwader/ German Training Command

A Tornado squadron, under the title 'Holloman I' stood up as part of the German Air Force Training Command at Holloman AFB, New Mexico, on 1 May 1996, after the Luftwaffe spent $44.3 million improving facilities at the American base. The unit had an initial establishment of twelve Tornados, which were operated alongside twenty-four F-4Es. The Luftwaffe expected the unit to clock up 2,500 Tornado sorties per annum. The unit will train Tornado instructors, three crews per course, two courses per year. It will also host three-week detachments by eight crews from each Luftwaffe Tornado wing, whose training is hampered by poor weather and a lack of low-level training in Germany. *Deutsches Ausbildungsgeschwader USA* is the official title of the Holloman unit, and another 30 'Holloman II', will be added in 1999. The enlarged unit is expected to eventually take over basic Tornado type conversion training from the TTTE and the tactical training from JBG 38. Tornados assigned to the unit wear a new unit badge based on the New Mexico State flag.

Wehrtechnische Dienstelle für Luftfahrtzeuge 61

WTD 61 is the German test and evaluation centre, known until 1987 as Erprobungsstelle (ESt) 61. Based at Manching, the unit has been heavily

JBG 31 tail emblem. Author

JBG 32 tail emblem. Author

An example of the original Luftwaffe camouflage scheme – Black, Yellow Olive, Basalt Grey and Silver Grey. Author

involved in the Tornado development programme from the very earliest days, conducting its initial tests on the prototypes and performing the acceptance and initial operational evaluation trials of the new aircraft. Since then, the unit has been the prime agency for the integration and testing of all new German Tornado aircraft development, including a wide range of weapon systems and armament trials, and work is undertaken on behalf of both the Luftwaffe and Marineflieger. Principle early programmes were the integration of the MW-1 munitions dispenser and Kormoran anti-ship missile. In the late 1980s the main programme was the upgrade of earlier aircraft to Batch 5 standards with Mil Std 1553 databus and HARM capability. From 1988 WTD 61 was heavily involved in the ECR programme, accepting the first production aircraft on behalf of the Luftwaffe in 1990. In February 1993 the unit accepted the first of the definitive ECR aircraft that were fitted with ELS equipment. Currently WTD 61 is still running at a hectic pace with new Tornado systems and armament trials, which includes testing the Apache and KEPD 350 stand-off weapons, and the Aramis anti-radiation missile. Other tests are aimed at facets of the KWS/KWE upgrade programmes, which include Mil Std 1760 weapons interface, enhanced EW, laser designation pods, steerable FLIR and terrain-referenced navigation systems.

Luftwaffe Camouflage

Originally the Luftwaffe IDS aircraft were painted in a four-colour paint scheme consisting of Black, Yellow Olive RAL6014

MW-1 Munitions Dispenser

Although US-owned nuclear weapons are available to the German air forces, the main Tornado weapons are conventional. These include the rather ungainly-looking MW-1 sub-munitions dispenser, used for anti-armour and anti-airfield missions, which has been operational since 1984. Similar in concept to the RAF's JP233, the MBB-built MW-1 fits beneath the underfuselage and is a single unit, unlike the two-piece JP233. The MW-1 (Meluzweckawaffe No.1) carries 112 sub-munitions, which are ejected laterally to cover a wide dispersal area. It comes in two versions. In its anti-armour guise it is designated as MW-1/HZG-1 for *Hauptzielgruppe* – or Main Target Group – 1 and contains a mixture of KB44 armour-piercing, MIFF anti-tank and MUSA fragmentation munitions; whereas in its MW-1/HZG-2 guise for use against airfields, its contains StaBo runway cratering, MUSPA area denial, MIFF and MUSA bomblets. The sub-muitions are manufactured by Raketen Technik Gesellschaft and come in six varieties, of which the MW-1 can carry up to maximum of 224, although the more common loading would be 200. With all its various submunitions dispensed the MW-1 would be jettisoned, as to continue to carry the weapon would impose too high a drag factor on the escaping Tornado, despite the fact that the pod constitutes over 10 per cent of the single unit cost.

Specification – MW-1
Width:	4ft 11.06in (1.5m)
Height:	2ft 3.5in (0.7m)
Length:	17ft 4.66in (5.3m)
Weight:	8,818lb (4,000kg)

The MW-1 dispenser, a rather ungainly-looking weapon system, but nevertheless an effective one. BAe

and Basalt Grey RAL7012 disruptive upper surfaces, and Silver Grey RAL7001 undersides. This was later revised to a three-tone wraparound scheme of Dark Green, Medium Green and Dark Grey.

German IDS upgrade

German Tornados have received a succession of modifications and modernizations since the late 1980s. Early aircraft were brought up to virtual Batch 5 standards under the Tornado First Upgrade, and this programme saw the installation of a Mil Std 15538 databus, a new stores management system, improved EW capability, HARM compatibility, a mission data transfer system and DECUs for the engines. The Luftwaffe Tornados assigned to the strike/attack role will receive a further multi-step MLU (the first stage of which was known as KWS, or *Kampfwertanpassungsprogramm*) in the form of a combat efficiency enhancement programme from Benz Aerospace. This initially incorporates a new main computer and a Mil Std 1760 digital databus,

which are intended to allow the subsequent integration of a variety of new systems. The original 'Assembler' software package is transformed into an 'ADA' software package in the first step of the upgrade, which is known as the *Neue Avionikstruktur*. It is envisaged that later modifications will initially include a FLIR, a new laser INS with integers and improved cockpit displays. Under the KWE (*Kampfwerterhaltungsprogramm*) combat efficiency upgrade programme the aircraft will also receive a new defensive computer, with a new missile warning system, improved RHAWS and better ECM.

Italian IDS – Southern Flank Strikers

The Italian Air Force, the *Aeronautica Militare Italia*, had set its requirement at 100 Tornado IDS. The first of the AMI's aircraft was pre-series airframe X-588, and this was followed by ninety-nine from subsequent production batches. Unusually, Italy assigns separate serial

blocks to its dual-control aircraft, even though they retain full combat capabilities. After X-588 had been re-numbered MM7001, the production IDSs emerged as MM7002 to 7008, and the twin-stick aircraft as MM55000 to 55011. The AMI's structure consists of *Stormos* – Wings; *Gruppos* – Squadrons; and *Squadriglie* – Flights.

Deliveries to the AMI's units began on 3 March 1981, when MM7001 was flown to Pratica di Mare to be used by the *Reparto Sperimentale Volo* (RSV) (Experimental Flight Department) and received the code RS-10. The RSV, otherwise known as 311° Gruppo, comprises of 535a and 536a Squadriglie. The second production aircraft, MM7003, was temporarily assigned for maintenance familiarization and was delivered to Camerai-Novara on 17 April 1982 to allow the 1° Centro Manutenzione Principlae to prepare for its task of training ground personnel to undertake level three overhauls and repairs. Of the 100 Tornados bought by the AMI, only fifty-four were assigned to front-line units, the remaining thirty-six being held in

German IDS tanking from a USAFE KC-135. Author

reserve or in service with the TTTE at RAF Cottesmore.

Italian Tornados share a large proportion of their combat equipment with their German counterparts. Self-defence equipment beneath the wings comprises a Philips BOZ-100 chaff/flare dispenser, AEG Cerberus II jamming pod and AIM-9L Sidewinder AAMs. Offensive armament includes the MW-1 dispenser, of which 100 have been bought in anti-airfield (90) and anti-armoured vehicle form. The Italian firm Selenia is licence-

building Hughes AGM-65D Maverick ASMs used by several other European air forces, whilst 156° Gruppo is also armed with MBB Kormoran AShMs for its anti-shipping role. This weapon, it may be recalled, is also used by the German Navy, as is the MBB-Aeritalia centreline reconnaissance pod, twenty of which are assigned to 155° Gruppo for photography by traditional, TV and infra-red linescan means.

'Clip-on' retractable refuelling probes were used by Italian Tornados during the

Gulf War and also when RAF VC-10s refuelled them on their first overseas deployment in June 1987 for Exercise Sentry Wolverine at Selfridges ANGEL, Michigan. Also still in prospect is the Italian-developed CAMS Skyshark sub-munitions dispenser, dropping trials for which began in 1987. Intended as a complement to the MW-1, Skyshark will give the marginal added protection of gliding stand-off flight to the target, although a later variant is intended to be powered. A further order was placed for fifteen of the

The Tornados of 36° Stormo wear a diving eagle fin badge superimposed on a yellow lightning flash. Author

ECR Tornados developed by Germany, and an MLU is planned for AMI Tornados, Panavia having submitted a study of the AMI's requirements. The fighter/bomber/recce role within the AMI comprises of a mixed force of Tornado and AMX aircraft. The Tornados are currently undergoing an upgrade programme which has included the SMS-90 stores management system enabling the aircraft to deliver PGMs, and the AMI has purchased a number of Paveway II kits to convert its Mk83 1000lb bombs into GBU-16s.

Italian Tornado Units

6° Stormo 'Alfredo Fuseca'

154° Gruppo uses the devil badge of its parent Stormo. The Gruppo consists of 390a, 391a, 395a and 396a Squadriglie, and was the AMI's first Tornado squadron, receiving the first aircraft, which were delivered to Ghedi, in 1982. The Gruppo subsequently acted as Italy's Tornado OCU, training aircrew return-ing from the TTTE at RAF Cottesmore. 154° Gruppo operates the lion's share of the AMI's dual-control Tornados, apart from two with each of the front-line units.

A new Gruppo, 155°, was formed in January 1985 with 361a, 364a, 365a and 378a Squadriglie. Its aircraft wear three blue pennants on their tail fins in place of 154° Gruppo's red chevron, but with the same red devil Stormo badge. 155° Gruppo carries its panther's head badge on the engine intakes. The squadron was transferred to the command of the newly reactivated 50° Stormo on 1 December 1989, and moved to Piacenza the following year. The Stormo later provid-ed aircraft and crews for the Italian con-tingent in the Gulf War.

6° Stormo gained a new second squadron in 1993, in the shape of 102° Gruppo from 5° Stormo which will under-take a reconnaissance role, and was once slated to receive the new ATARS recon-naissance pod. The new unit wears the 6° Stormo devil badge on the fins of its air-craft, with the Gruppo's flying-suited Donald Duck badge in a black triangle on the engine intakes. The Gruppo consists of 209a, 212a, 239a and 244a Squadriglie. Underslung equipment routinely carried by the Ghedi-based Tornados includes the new Thomson-CSF CLDP laser designator and the MBB/Aeritalia reconnaissance pod. The Stormo became the first AMI unit in action over Bosnia on 2 September 1995, when its aircraft conducted an armed patrol over the region. On 7 September aircraft from the same unit bombed Serbian targets using Mk83 bombs free-fall. 154° Gruppo Tornados have also used the MBB/Aeritalia recon-naissance pod over Bosnia, and have reportedly also the used 'buddy' inflight-refuelling techniques during these operations.

36° Stormo 'Helmut Seidl'

36° Stormo's 156° Gruppo converted to the Tornado during 1984, returning to Gioia del Colle in May 1984 and becom-ing operational with their new jets in the August of that year. The Tornados of 36° Stormo wear a diving eagle fin badge superimposed on a yellow lightning flash. The 156° Gruppo lynx's head badge is carried on the engine intakes, while the

Typical AMI Tornado IDS camouflage.
Author

stylized initials 'HS' for 'Helmut Seidl' are occasionally applied to the base of the fin. The Gruppo consists of 381a, 382a, 83a and 384a Squadriglie. The unit's primary task is that of maritime strike and interdiction, and it is therefore the main user of the MBB AS34 Kormoran anti-shipping missile. 36° Stormo also flew combat sorties over Bosnia, and recently flew missions in support of ground forces involved in Operation *Joint Endeavour*. For these missions the aircraft been reported to have carried a pair of GBU-16 Paveway II LGBs, and operated alongside other Tornados carrying the Thomson-CSF CLDP pod.

The 36° Stormo's second squadron, 12° Gruppo, continued to operate the F-104 Starfighter in an air defence role until 1995, when it re-equipped with Tornado F. 3s leased from the RAF, and is more fully described on page 150.

50° Stormo 'Giorgio Graffer'

50° Stormo was reconstituted at San Damiano-Piacenza on 1 November 1988. 155° Gruppo moved from Ghedi to Piacenza on 23 July 1990, transferring from 6° Stormo to the new 50° Stormo.

An Italian pilot prepares to 'wind up' his Tornado. Tom Ross

A clean Saudi Tornado IDS, in its very colourful desert camouflage. Author

The winged sword of the 50° Stormo badge is usually superimposed on the Gruppo's familiar three blue triangular pennants which flow back from the fin leading edge, and Gruppo identity is further emblazoned by the panther's head badge on each intake. 155° Stormo are the AMI's SEAD specialists, becoming dedicated to the role on 1 April 1994. The squadron received HARM missiles in December 1994.

53° Stormo

The AMI's second Tornado ADV unit; it is fully described on page 150.

Autonomous Flight Detachment AMI

These aircraft flew 226 missions in the Gulf War when deployed to Al Dhafra in 1991. The missions are described on page 70.

Reparto Sperimentale di Volo – 311°

The AMI's research, evaluation and development unit is the RSV based at Pratica di Mare, which also has the identity of 311o Gruppo, with 535 a and 536 a Squadriglie included in its designation.

AMI Camouflage

Italian Tornados carry a three-tone camouflage scheme of NATO Dark Green BS381C/641, NATO Dark Grey BS381C/638 and Silver.

'Birds of Peace' – The Al Yamamah Programme

At the time of writing, Saudi Arabia remains the sole export customer currently flying the Tornado. In September 1985, the massive £4,000 million Al Yamamah I – Bird of Peace – deal was signed by the Saudi and UK governments, covering the supply to Saudi Arabia of forty-eight IDS and twenty-four ADV Tornados, along with thirty Hawks, two radar-training Jetstreams and thirty BAe-built Pilatus PC-9s. Saudi Arabia had previously bought BAC Strikemasters and Lightnings, but was far more used to buying US equipment, to which a massive fleet of F-5s and other American types bears witness. The Tornado faced stiff competition from the F-15, which was however forced to struggle against some strange constraints, including a US refusal to supply conformal fuel tanks or multiple ejector racks –

prompted by the Israeli government – and a further demand that stipulated the aircraft could not be based at Tabuk, the most northern Saudi airfield, which most threatened Israel. In the end, though, the attack-configured F-15 was seen to be too much of an unknown quantity, and as the Tornado IDS had reached a level of proven maturity the British option looked the more attractive. Saudi aircrew flew Tornado evaluation sorties from RAF Honington in 1984 and the arms deal was announced the following year.

Once Saudi Arabia had signed for the Tornado it wanted early deliveries, so eighteen RAF and two German GR.1s were diverted to the RSAF from Batch 5 orders, and all twenty-four ADVs were diverted from the RAF's Batch 6. Some RAF places at TTTE were given to Saudi crews, who began training there in October 1985, and deliveries to 7 Squadron RSAF (formerly operators of the Northrop F-5E) at Dhahran began with 701–704 (ex-ZD997, ZD998, ZE114 and ZE115) on 26–27 March 1986. They were followed by 705 and 706 in April, whilst the remainder were serialled 757–770. Trainers were 704–706, 759, 768 and 769, of which the two last-mentioned were scratch-built by BAe. The initial deliveries of Saudi Tornados allowed the formation of two IDS and one

ADV squadrons, and although delayed on several different occasions, the eventual second Saudi Tornado permitted the formation of two more squadrons.

The remaining twenty-eight IDS aircraft were built in Batch 7, along with the replacement aircraft for those the RAF had diverted from Batch 5; these began appearing in February 1988, the first being serialled 771.

The IDS aircraft were reportedly delivered with Sea Eagle AShMs, JP233 airfield attack weapons and ALARMs. Fourteen of the Saudi aircraft were twin-stick trainers, and the last six Saudi Tornado IDSs were delivered in GR.1A configuration, partially replacing recce-configured F-5Es. The Saudi aircraft also had the RAF-style tail fin fuel tanks incorporated.

Batch 5 Saudi Tornado IDS
8S157
ZD997 CS001 751 8S158
ZD998 CS002 752 8S159
ZE114 CS003 753 8T45
ZE115 CT001 754 8S161
ZE117 CS004 757 8S162
ZEllB CS00575B 8S163
ZE119 CS006 760 8T46
ZE120 CT002 755 8S164
ZE121 CS007 761 8S165
ZE122 CS008 762 8S166
ZE123 CS009 763 8S167
ZE124 CS010 764 8T47
ZE125 CT003 756 8S168
2E126 CS011 765 8S169
ZE144 CS012 766 BS170
ZE145 CS013 767 BS171
ZE146 CS014 770 8T48
ZE147 CT00 4759

Batch 7 Saudi Tornado IDS
8T49 None CT005 768 8T50
None CT006 769

The aircraft were painted with SWAM (Surface Wave Absorbent Material), and RAM (Radar Absorbent Material) was applied to the engine intake area. SWAM is applied like paint, though it is much denser (more like car underseal)

and so heavy that it takes two men to lift a five-litre tin. RAM was applied in steel-backed tiles, necessitating the removal of the engines to allow them to be bonded to the intakes adjacent to the first stage of the fan. The optional bolt-on retractable inflight-refuelling probe were also fitted.

The Batch 7 aircraft were serialled CT007–014 (trainers) and CS015–034. The twin-stickers were serialed 771, 772, 773, 774, 6620, 6621, 6622, and 6623; the operational aircraft carrying the serials 6610–6619 and 6624–6633. The final six, 6628–33, were in GR.1A configuration. Al Yamamah II, agreed on 1 July 1988, originally covered a further twelve IDS and thirty-six ADVs; however, the contract was cancelled in July 1990, and subsequently amended to total forty-eight of the IDS version, with the F.3 purchase being dropped as the Saudis were now in possession of a great many American F-15s.

Batch 9 Saudi Tornado IDS
CT015 7501 ZH905
CT016 7502 ZH906
CT017 7503 ZH907
CT018 8301 ZH9O8
CT019 8302 ZH909
CT020 8303 ZH910
CT021   ZH911
CT022   ZH912
CT023   ZH913
CT024   ZH914
CS035   ZH915
GR.1A equivalent
ZH916 to ZH952

The first batch of Saudi ADVs (described separately) took part in Operations *Desert Shield* and *Desert Storm*, sharing the burden of mounting pre-war defensive CAPs with Saudi F-15s, RAF Tornados and other Coalition fighters. Once war had begun, the Saudi IDS squadrons became involved, with the ADVs mounting both offensive and defensive CAPs, though they did not have the opportunity to engage the enemy.

All Saudi Tornados wear small squadron badges on their tail fins, below the national flag, aft of their serial which is presented in English numerals and Arabic script. The IDS' unusual scheme of sand, brown and green has proved very effective over the sparsely vegetated desert.

Saudi Squadrons

No.7 Squadron

In between October 1985 and early 1987, Saudi aircrew trained in four courses, which were conducted by a dedicated Saudi training team within the TTTE, before joining the TWCU. No.7 Squadron then assumed responsibility for the conversion training of Saudi Tornado IDS aircrews. When the first Saudi aircraft were delivered in March 1986, its first four crews had just graduated from the TWCU. Four more graduated in May 1986, and these eight formed the backbone of No.7 Squadron, to act as instructors for subsequent aircrew. The squadron took all twenty Batch 5 Tornados, which included eight twin-stickers, the high proportion of trainers reflecting the squadron's secondary role as a weapons conversion and tactical training unit.

No.29 Squadron

Based at Dhahran, No.29 Squadron is equipped with ADVs and its complement includes four twin-stickers.

No.32 Squadron

The second Tornado ADV squadron, initially co-located with No.29 at Dhahran, No.32 received its first aircraft on 14 November 1989. However, its aircraft and crews were later absorbed by No.29 Squadron, remaining as a small cadre within that unit.

No.66 Squadron

Formed under the auspices of No.7 Squadron, No.66 was in the process of forming when the Gulf conflict occured.

No.75 Squadron

No.75 Squadron will be the first Saudi Tornado squadron with the new Batch 9 aircraft, and will be based at Dhahran.

No.83 Squadron

The second Saudi 'Batch 9' squadron to be formed, No.83 will possibly have a dedicated reconnaissance role.

Tornados at War – Operation *Granby*

For the RAF, *Desert Storm* could be truly described as the 'Tornados' war'. Representing three-quarters of the British air attack force at the opening of hostilities, the GR.1 strikers undertook assaults on Iraq's war machine, hitting its airfields, weapon storage sites and communications, gaining in the process gaining an enviable reputation for accuracy and bravery. Despite early misfortunes – when disproportionate losses resulted in the Tornado receiving more flak from the UK media than the enemy – the aircraft emerged from the conflict with its reputation immeasurably strengthened. In addition to bombing, the aircraft hastily, yet successfully, introduced to service to as-yet untried systems then still under devel-opment: the ALARM anti-radar missile and the TIALD laser designator, and also flew reconnaissance missions.

Following the announcement that Jaguars and Tornado F.3 fighters were on their way to the Gulf, on 23 August 1990 it was further announced that a squadron of 'mud (or perhaps 'sand' in this instance) movers' with their Tornado GR.1s would leave their German bases and head for the Gulf. The former RAF Muharraq – now Bahrain International Airport – was first to receive GR.1s when a dozen aircraft left Brüggen, on 27 August 1990. A second squadron of Laarbruch-based aircraft, but with mainly Marham crews, began arriving there on 19 September, but repositioned to Tabuk, in far north-western Saudi Arabia, from 8 October onwards. Finally, it was decided to complement the interceptor Tornado F.3s at Dhahran in north-eastern Saudi Arabia with a further twelve Brüggen air-craft, the first of which arrived on 3 January 1991. The reconnaisance element, provided by Laarbruch, was of six GR.1As ferried to Dhahran between 14–16 January.

At Muharraq, Gp Capt David Henderson was in command of the RAF detachment and No.15 Squadron, led by Wg Cdr John Broadbent was the leading squadron, although crews for the fifteen GR.1s on the base were provided by Nos 9, 17, 20, 31 and 617 Squadrons. Tabuk's RAF station commander was Gp Capt Bill Hedges, and his leading squadron was No16, under the leadership of Wg Cdr Travers Smith, assisted by a large section of No20 Squadron and other crews from Nos2, 9 and 14, plus Nos13 and 617 later on. On station at Tabuk were fifteen Tornados, of which seven were equipped to carry ALARM missiles as an alterna-

Raiding Party. Armed with JP233s, a formation of four GR.1s hit their refuelling bracket with a No.55 Squadron Victor tanker before heading at low level to their target. BAe

Using the specially-designed loading trolley, this groundcrew uses muscle power to move the rear section of a JP233 into position underneath ZA707/BK prior to an evening sortie. Note the larger Hindenburger wing tanks borrowed from the F.3 community and the nearly-complete load of flare cartridges inside the BOZ-107 dispenser. RAF

tive to the usual bomb load. Dhahran had fifteen GR.1s and six recce GR.1As, and its RAF component came under the command of Gp Capt Cliff Spink who, unlike his two fellow base commanders, was an air defence rather than ground attack flyer. Also at Dahrahn, No.31 Squadron led by Wg Cdr Jerry Witts was reinforced by personnel from Nos 9, 14 and 17, plus Nos 2 and 13 from the reconnaissance world.

Each base made eight aircraft constantly available in two flights of four, with the remaining aircraft being held in reserve or undergoing servicing. There was no danger of crew fatigue, as each Tornado had three crews working a shift system to provide ample time for rest. A shift pattern was introduced a few days before expiry of the UN ultimatum on 15 January, so that crew sleep patterns were adjusted to the regime before hostilities began. Engineers used a two-day lull in activity to bring each aircraft up to its peak of serviceability. Crews reported in approximately five hours before take-off, worked for eight hours and remained awake for a further four hours or so thereafter, so that they

The rear of the JP233 is hoisted into position on one of the two underfuselage shoulder pylons.

would have risen just before the start of their next duty period.

Plans for the first RAF combat missions were launched. For the Tornado force this meant being equipped with two JP233s, two Sidewinder AAMs and two large drop-tanks, giving a take-off weight of 30 tonnes. Jerry Witts of No.31 Sqn led four aircraft from Dhahran and John Broadbent led out eight similarly equipped aircraft from Bahrain, all bound for Tallil airfield in south-east Iraq. Taking the defences by complete surprise, the Tornados scattered their JP233s over the base's parallel runways and associated taxiways, then made for home without loss, gliding back into their bases from out of the dawn sky.

One of the pilots, Flt Lt Ian Langen, recalled in a TV interview after landing:

It's absolutely terrifying. There's no other word for it. You're frightened of failure; you're fright-

ened of dying. You're flying as low as you dare but high enough to get the weapons off. You put the aircraft as low as you can over the target – just to get away as fast as you can.

His navigator, Flt Lt Gerry Gegg, added, 'All you could see were just a mass of white explosions around you.'

Another navigator, climbing from his cockpit asked, 'Have they given up yet?' For many Tornado pilots, this was their first taste of flying the aircraft with with two JP233 pods, and to their dismay they discovered that their hitherto docile mounts began to fly, as one pilot commented, 'like pigs'!

The second attack wave of the day was not so fortunate. Four Tornados from Muharraq were sent to Shaibah, close to the city of Basra, for a daylight lofting attack of 1,000lb bombs. Flt Lts 'John' Nicholl and John Peters of No.15 Sqn, flying ZD791, were hit by AAA, causing

one of their Sidewinders missiles to explode, forcing them to eject. Although their 'bang-out' was successful, the pair were captured and were next seen, having obviously been mistreated, on Iraqi TV in a repulsive, ill-conceived and counter-productive propaganda stunt.

Shaibah's 'jinx' would strike again that night when the Marham contingent from Muharraq sent four aircraft there and four more to Ubaydah bin al Jarrah, all of them armed with JP233. The Jarrah formation took off at midnight, the Shaibah wave two hours later, their shorter journey demanding only one pre-attack refuelling from a VC-10. To keep the defending radars off the air, Tabuk-based Tornado GR.1s with the new ALARM anti-radar missile were patrolling the area. Any radio communications which the Iraqis attempted were jammed by USAF EF-111A Ravens and their carrier-based equivalent, the EA-6B Prowler.

'Debbie, Emma, Helen and Nicki', wait underneath their Muharraq 'sun' shelters for their next call to action. Steve Morris

Loaded with two LGBs, one of Muharraq's aircraft taxies out. Steve Morris

As the Tornados sped towards Shaibah at 550kt, they relied only on the radar altimeter to keep them 200ft above the desert, and a map to locate the electricity pylons to the north and east of the field. There remained only the densely-packed short-range AAA guns and SAMs to be dealt with, and the USAF was distracting these in fine style. A mere twenty seconds before TOT, F111Fs bombed an oil refinery just one mile north of the Tornados' track, creating an explosion, the immensity of which appears to have surprised friends almost as much as foes. All weapons were released satisfactorily as the gunners were still gathering their wits, but three minutes later ZA392, flown by No.27's commander, Wg Cdr Nigel Elsdon, was seen to crash into the ground having been hit by a SAM, killing both the pilot and his navigator, Flt Lt 'Max' Collier. The remaining three landed back at base after 1 hour 55 minutes in the air.

The Jarrah raid also had its share of heart-stopping moments. Having taken

on fuel at above 10,000ft, the Tornados dropped to 300ft, crossing the Iraqi border and steadily descended to 200ft during a black and uneventful low-level flight of thirty minutes over the desert. The target was sighted in a blaze of anti-aircraft activity a full five minutes before the

attack went in, the softening-up force having also woken up the defenders. Flying parallel to the runway, the formation was in 'card four', the leading pair two miles apart, the trailing pair thirty seconds flying time behind them. Turning towards the airfield, the spacing was

Right: ZD809 'Awesome Annie' shows of her warload. Two LGBs on the shoulder stations, two Hindenburger fuel tanks, two Sidewinders, and the BOZ and Sky Shadow ECM support. Steve Morris

ZA447/EA 'Mig Eater', surrounded by support equipment, is prepared for annother sortie into Iraq. Mick Lee

closed up to one mile and the interval to fifteen seconds, then further tightened to ten. With one minute to go, Fg Off Ingle and Flt Lt McKearnan in ZD744 felt a bump and thought they had been hit, but the aircraft continued to fly, albeit reluctantly. At 550kt the Tornados swept over the runway, Nos1 and 2 dropping their JP233s at one-fifth and three-fifths distance along its length whilst the others unloaded their wares at the two-fifths and four-fifths points. Flt Lt Paul McKearnan:

> Running in ... running in ... committing ... it's going ... 550kt ... keep going ... there go the cannisters ... lets's go left ... 240 keep running ... that's the airfield ... no problems ... chaffing ... nothing on the RHWR ... keep running ... keep running ... looking good ... ok ... it's all behind us now, lets get back down.

After turning for home, Ingle was having difficulty flying his aircraft and could not maintain control above 350kt. Eventually finding the tanker, he could only maintain formation by adopting 45-degree wing sweep, but managed to complete the journey to Muharraq without further incident. Inspection later showed that a birdstrike had removed a large section of the port wing's leading edge, so the aircraft was patched up and flown back to Brüggen for repair. A mere three days later, it was re-delivered to the Gulf and

went on to complete thirty-five missions, most of them from Tabuk.

The following night, 18–19 January, four Muharraq Tornados armed with JP233 visited Tallil air base. They were preceded one minute earlier by other Tornados lofting thousand-pounders, fuzed for an airburst 15ft above the ground. This served only to stir up a hornet's nest and, after releasing their bombs some three miles from the base, Flt Lts Dave Waddington and Robbie Stewart of No.27 Squadron in ZA396 were hit 'in the face' by a Roland SAM which they had tried unsuccessfully to out-manoeuvre. Pilot Waddington was knocked unconscious by the explosion from the missile, with Stuart using the command ejection system to catapult both men clear the stricken aircraft. Their ejection-related injuries were treated well in an Iraqi hospital, and they returned to friendly territory after the end of the war.

At Tabuk, Wg Cdr Travers Smith, CO of 16 Sqn, was first away in ZA473 at 021 on 17 January, leading three more Tornados towards Al Asad airfield, which was given the 'JP233 treatment' despite one of the aircraft returning early with technical trouble. A second wave also visited Al Taqaddum the same night, whilst eight JP233 bombers returned to Al Asad.

A tactic tried against H-3 airfield early on 18 January was to send four ALARM

aircraft some time before the main raid and accompany three JP233 Tornados with another four 'ALARM'ists'. Despite having ALARM in their inventory, the Tornados found the Flak so intense that they were forced to abandon their attack and therefore reluctantly brought their JP233s home. Use of 1,000Ib bombs began at Tabuk when H-2 airfield was attacked on the evening of 18 February; these weapons were used in conjunction with the ALARM aircraft in defence suppression, whilst four more GR.1s made Tabuk's last use of JP233.

When a change of tactics became public on 21 January, there were unofficial reports that the losses being encountered by the JP233-armed aircraft were unacceptable; and having kept the Iraqi airfields closed in the opening stages of the war, the time had now arrived to abandon the near-suicidal low-level missions, and switch to a safer operating altitude. With up to twenty AAA sites, airfields were a formidable target, but in fact only one of the three aircraft lost by the Tornado Force had been carrying JP233, and even that crashed well after leaving the target area. The Tornado units' JP233 missions gave way to loft attacks with free-fall bombs, but a lofting attack by eight Tabuk Tornados with 1,000lb bombs on Ar Rutbah radar site claimed the lives of Sqn Ldrs Garry Lennox and Paul Weeks from No.16 Sqn in ZA467 during the early hours of 22 January. The following day, Dhahran lost its only Tornado of the war, ZA403, when Pilot Off Simon Burgess, the youngest RAF pilot in the conflict, and Sqn Ldr Bob Ankerson of No.17 Squadron suffered the premature explosion of one of their own bombs.

Tactics Change

By 23 January, five aircraft had been lost in combat: the Tornado force, representing just 4 per cent cent of the Coalition air strength, had suffered 26 per cent of the casualties. Sqn Ldr Peter Battson and Wg Cdr Mike Heath of No.20 Squadron, who had been interviewed by a TV crew just prior to take-off from Tabuk in ZD893on the evening of 20 January, had deliberately 'ditched' the aircraft when it suffered a control restriction, and were subsequently seen on TV in a field hospital with a few cuts and bruises, very philosophical about their 'adventure'. It was the Tornados at Muharraq that had been hit the hardest. On the second and subsequent nights of the campaign, Iraqi guns continued to blaze at random, except that their operators had now learned to fire almost horizontally, so greatly increasing the danger to low-flying aircraft. General Norman Schwarzkopf, the Coalition commander, was asked to comment on the sacrifices made by the Tornado crews; he remarked, 'Their contribution has been absolutely superb. I am damn glad they are with us.'

AVM Bill Wratten, the most senior RAF officer in the Gulf, also said in an interview, ' I will say that we have been extremely unlucky – and bad luck does not last for ever.'

Happily, this proved to be true. Switching to medium altitude and using free-fall bombs, the Tornado GR.1 losses receded drastically, though the aircraft did not take kindly to medium level attacks. Optimized for precision delivery of weapons from low level, it required new techniques of bombing to be introduced. Not least of these was revised software for the weapons computer which was unable to cope with corrections it was now faced with. As a means of improving accuracy, dive-bombing was tried. Starting from

24,000ft, the Tornado was rolled on to its back (to maintain positive g) and dived at 30 degrees while the pilot acquired the target in his HUD. Pull-out was achieved at about 16,000ft – still above SA-8 SAMs and most of the light flak – the aircraft's computer determining the correct moment of weapon release.

Airfield targets were becoming mixed with petro-chemical plants, fuel and ammunition storage, barracks and radar sites during the closing days of January, with Tabuk sending a six-ship up to drop thirty bombs on the Rufhah Fuwad Scud missile test site on the 30th. Muharraq aircraft caused a satisfying fire at Al Azziriyah oil refinery on the night of 1/2 February, but it was obvious that precision-guided weapons were the only means of efficient attack if the Tornado force was to remain at medium level.

The two TIALD laser designation pods (described elsewhere) were being rushed through trials for Gulf deployment, but something was needed immediately. On the morning of 23 January, RAF Lossiemouth was detailed to send six Buccaneers to the Gulf 'with all haste', to undertake laser designation duties with their Pave Spike pods. They arrived on

the 26 the and the first Tornado/Buccaneer/Pave Spike mission was flown on 2 February, against the Al Samawah road bridge over the River Euphrates, when two Buccaneers and four Tornados armed with LGBs successfully struck home. The seeker heads of the CPU-123 guidance kits for the LGBs took up a lot of space, so only three bombs could be carried, two in parallel at the forward point under the fuselage and the third at the rear centre.

By 8 February, twelve Buccaneers were in theatre and flying for both the Dhahran and Muharraq bomber forces. The campaign to sever Baghdad's communications with Kuwait slowed after 11 February, when airfields again came under attack. This time, however, individual HASs were hit with precision, for which it was soon established that two bombs per Tornado per shelter was sufficient. A mission comprised a Buccaneer and two Tornados in the lead, plus a similar formation a minute or so behind. When four Buccaneers and eight Tornados were first tried against Al Taqaddum airfield on the morning of 14 February, the mission became unduly complex. Despite variations in heights and approaches, the, defenders were able to knock down ZD717 with two SA-2 SAMs whilst the crew was preoccupied with the attack. Flt Lt Rupert Clark of No.15 Squadron later recalled:

> The first one got us as we were trying to evade and then the second one also hit. The whole cockpit was shattered. The instruments were gone, as were both engines. We tried to glide for a minute or two, but the controls froze up and then I ejected.

Flt Lt Steve Hicks, his navigator, was sadly killed in the incident. Double-sized raids were not tried again.

Out to the west, Tabuk had to wait longer for its laser designators to arrive. There was a short, but intensive campaign against ammunition dumps, petrol refineries and power stations during early February, ending with seven aircraft dropping thirty-five bombs on an artillery plant at Habbanniyah on the 10th. Later the same morning the TIALD designation pod was used for the first time, fast becoming the only means by which Tabuk-based aircraft released their bombs.

With the exception of occasional bridge like the ones at Falloujah, Ar Ramadi and

Desert aircrew. Flt Lts Steve Morris (left) and Al 'Byf' Byford pose beside ZA456/M 'Mel' after a mission on 4 February 1991. Steve Morris

'Who ya gonna call – HAS Busters!' Steve Morris

Asl Samawah, it was Iraqi airfields which received the attention of the Tabuk TIALD force until the end of hostilities. Two TIALDs and four bombers had literally a lucky break when they approached H-3 Southwest airfield on 17 February. Tasked with attacking shelters at the east and west ends of the runway, during the first pass, the air base was obscured by cloud which was seen to be clearing from the west, so the six Tornados made a ten-minute circuit. During their second pass, shelters at the western end were hit, but the eastern element was still frustrated. Another ten-minute circuit by the six-ship to give the cloud a little more time, and the opposite corner received its postponed strike.

Having led the first Tornado mission from Tabuk, Wg Cdr Travers Smith was also 'in' on the last raid, when four bombers and two TIALD carriers took off to attack Habbanniyah air base on 27 February. Unfortunately, No.16's Boss had to return early with an unserviceable aircraft and so was not among the three which attacked at approximately 22.30hr dropping the final RAF bombs in *Desert Storm*. The Buccaneer-led force in the east ended the same day's work in the late afternoon by attacking Skayka Mayhar

airfield. Six more Pave Spike missions planned for the 28th were cancelled at 0300 local time because the first would have taken place after the ceasefire came into effect. Muharraq had already loaded Tornados with a new weapon, the American CBU-87 cluster bomb used previously by Jaguars, in preparation for missions on the 28th, but the first delivery by four aircraft on to a SAM site, augmented by two Buccaneers and four LGB Tornados was timed just ten minutes after the cease-fire, at 0810 local, and was subsequently cancelled.

Of the three Tornado GR.1 detachments, Tabuk flew 650 sorties, of which 545 attacked their targets. The base expended thirty-two JP233s in twenty-three sorties (five missions); 123 ALARM missiles in fifty-two sorties (twenty-four missions), 1,451 free-fall bombs in 288 sorties (thirty-five missions); and 360 laser-guided bombs in 192 sorties supported by ninety-five TIALD sorties (forty-eight missions). Dhahran flew 567 sorties, comprising 439 interdiction (dropping fourteen JP233 containers and free-fall bombs), 305 to release LGBs and also reconnaissance. Muharraq housed a dozen Jaguars dropping conventional bombs

and twelve Buccaneers which delivered a small number of LGBs, the base's Tornados contributing approximately 1,700 free-fall bombs, 340 LGBs and fifty JP233s to the Coalition effort. Dhahran's conscientious statisticians additionally deduced that its aircraft had expended 310 infra-red flares and 21,330 bundles of chaff whilst consuming 3,830 tons of fuel, including 2,200 tons taken from aerial tankers.

Markings

As mentioned earlier the Tornados all wore the 'Desert Sand' colour scheme, retaining the black anti-glare panel atop the nose. The scheme extended to the pylons, wing-tanks and self defence pods, and was broken only by the natural metal areas around the Mauser cannon. As could be anticipated, aircraft markings were at a premium. All of the Tornados carried an identifying tail code, either in white outline, solid black or black with a thin white border, containing either a single- or two-letter code, depending on the operating base. Individual aircraft serial numbers were white, positioned on the rear fuselage. The only other markings, apart from the red and white ejection seat triangles, were white 'Rescue' arrows on the forward fuselage and pale pink/blue roundels above the port and below the starboard wings, but this was not standard on all aircraft.

Modifications

Modifications to the aircraft came under the umbrella of Gulf Updates, commonly known as Phase One, which were undertaken at RAF St Athan and at a number of front-line stations. There were twenty-three possible planned modifications and nineteen new modifications known officially as Special Trials Fits. Few aircraft incorporated all the modifications and STFs, with eighteen and thirteen modifications being typical. The possibility of battle damage led to the incorporation of a long-planned modification to the

Tornado's fin-mounted fuel tank, with a nitrogen purging system being fitted to remove any fuel vapour once the tank was empty. The modifications also included uprated RB.199 Mk103 engines. Sand ingestion caused a glass-like coating to form on the turbine blades, and to counter this a number of modifications were made to the engine. Single-crystal turbine blades (chemically milled) were added which gave them a longer life, and greater reliability. To solve the problems caused by sand build-up, cooling holes were made in the blades' leading/trailing edges. If these holes became blocked, the blades overheated and disintegrated, and as a result the main corrective action taken was to use a high-pressure lance firing a water/air mix into the turbines to clear the cooling holes.

Since the RAF aircraft would be operat-

ing as part of a force dominated by the USAF, all Tornado GR Mk.1s deployed to the Gulf had their Cossor SSR3100 MkX IFF equipment removed and replaced by a MkXII Mode 4 set. The aircraft were also provided with Have Quick secure voice radios and some carried a hand-held GPS receiver. Radar Absorbent Material (RAM) was also added to the engine intakes and the leading edges of the wings, tail planes and weapons pylons, but was less apparent than on the F.3, as it was concealed beneath the 'Trimite' Desert Sand colour.

Due to the percieved lack of tanker support, fifteen Sergeant Fletcher 28-300 refuelling pods were aquired from Germany's Marineflieger, and nine dual control Tornado GR.1s modified to use them in a 'buddy-buddy' tanker role. Modified under STF 238, the conversion

'Happy New Year from'Gazza's Gonads' aka Team 8'. Steve Morris

'With love from the *Fox and Hounds,* Marham'. Steve Morris

was undertaken at St Athan and the first aircraft to be so modified, ZA410, rolled out on 13 January 1991. As it turned out the aircraft were not required, and they remained in reserve.

Most of the aircraft began to sport 'nose art', courtesy of the ground crews. These ranged from the humerous to the risqué, and did not always meet with the approval of senior officers: many of the characters' names from the hit BBC comedy series *Blackadder* were applied to the aircraft, but it was felt that one or two may have had anti-authoritarian connotations, and they were quickly removed! Some pilots also took a dim view, claiming that it was their historical right to decide what, if any, art-work should be applied to their aircraft. That said, the graphics added a new dimension and a lighter side to the con-flict, and sent the aircraft spotter fraterni-ty into a frenzy of activity! The 'shark

mouth' also put in an appearance, giving the Tornados to which they were applied a suitably aggressive look. According to one groundcrewman, it started with the application of a 'low-visibilty' set of teeth, painted on from touch-up paint. The idea grew, and before long full-colour teeth, mouth and eyes were adorning the air-craft. Each base also had its perculiarities, such as Dhahran applying palm trees as mission symbols, and Muharraq having 'Snoopy Airways' as one of its flight's identifying marks.

A reduction of the RAF presence start-ed almost immediately after Iraq had con-ceded defeat. Evacuation of Tabuk and Dhahran began on 11 March, but a dozen Tornado GR.ls were maintained at Muharraq for a few months.

AMI Tornados – Operation *Locusta*

On 25 September 1990, as part of the growing multi-national Coalition ranged against Saddam Hussein, the Aeronatutica Militare Italiana deployed a number of its Tornado IDS strike aircraft to the Gulf region as part of Operation *Locusta* ('Locust'). The aircraft, drawn from 6° Stormo's 154° Gruppo, 36° Stormo's 156° Gruppo and the newly established 50° Stormo's 155° Gruppo, flew out from the Gioia del Colle base of the 36° Stormo, stopping over at Luxor in Egypt before heading on to the Gulf. In

STF-383 Aircraft					
ZD812	ZA365	ZA367	ZA410	ZA411	ZD712
ZD714	ZD741	ZD743			

all, twelve IFR probe-fitted Tornado IDS aircraft were rotated between Gioia del Colle and their forward operating base of Al Dhafra, near Abu Dhabi in the United Arab Emirates, between September 1990 and March 1991, where their initial task was to protect Italian military shipping and enforce the UN embargo against Iraq. Later, as part of *Desert Storm* operations, they undertook counter-air attacks on Iraqi airfields. Initially on station at Al Dhafra were eight IDS aircraft, these being replaced in November by a fresh batch of eight, with a further two being added to their number in December 1990, bringing the fighting force to ten aircraft.

The composite unit based at Al Dhafra went into action as a bombing force on the first night of the *Desert Storm* campaign with, it must be said, mixed fortunes. There were mitigating factors that worked against the Locusta Tornados in as much as they lacked the neccessary skills for night in-flight refuelling; they were not fitted with the RAF/Saudi GR.1-style laser rangefinder; there were no aircraft available to designate targets for PGMs; and weapons like JP233 and the CBU were not part of the Italian inventory – although reports at the time indicated the in-theatre purchase of Mk20 Rockeye CBUs from the US for area denial operations. This left the 'Locusts' with the option of carrying Mk82 'Snakeye' or slick Mk83 bombs.

On their first sortie during the night of 17 January 1991, out of the eight aircraft employed, only one was successful in receiving fuel from a USAF tanker en route, due to severe turbulence and inexperience in the use of the KC-135's drogue, with a seventh aircraft turning back before tanker contact due to a mechanical problem. Whilst the unrefuelled aircraft aborted the mission, the crew of the eighth Tornado – MM7074, from the 155° Stormo, piloted by Flight Captain Major Mario Bichirloni, and his backseater Captain Maurizio Cocciolone – bravely, or perhaps foolishly, decided to continue with the mission, regardless of being alone! The Tornado did actually strike its target (as was proved by the later recovery of the CVR), but the aircraft was shot down by enemy fire during its escape. The crew ejected successfully and were held captive for the remainder of the conflict. This particular sortie had the

honour of marking the first involvement by Italian forces where bombs had been dropped in anger since World War Two, and was happily also the AMI's only loss during the war. It was later reported by a senior officer that, '...the crews performed to the highest standards, given the limited choice and less than optimal weapons available, and the extreme range of the mission...'

Following the disastrous tanker experience, the AMI altered their refuelling practices by fitting some of their aircraft

with the more familiar (to them) Sergeant Fletcher 28-300 underfuselage 'buddy-buddy' refuelling packs. The aircraft then began operating in formations of eight, four acting as 'tankers' and four fully armed as 'bombers'. Therefore a mission would involve three in-flight refuelling stages: two from 'buddy' Tornados and one from a USAF KC-135 just prior to the low-level phase of the mission.

Typically, the 'Locust' Tornados carried either four or five bombs, four in two tandem pairs on the underfuselage shoulder

ABOVE: **Nikki**. Steve Morris

BELOW: **ZD 745/BM Black Magic (previously Melchie)**. Author

ZD744/BD Buddha. Author

ZD719/AD Check Six! Author

One of Muharraq's 'Snoopy Airways'. Steve Morris

ABOVE: **ZA477/EA 'Mig Eater' with an early incarnation of its shark mouth mission markings.** Mick Lee

pylons, and if needed a single weapon on the centerline. Also fitted were two 2,225ltr fuel tanks and a pair of AIM-9 Sidewinder AAMs, together with a pair of Philips BOZ-102 chaff and flare launchers on the outer wing pylons. The aircraft also sported a small conical antenna on the spine behind the cockpit for us with their newly installed GPS or SATCOM system. For their desert operations the Tornados wore a camouflage scheme more in keeping with their operating environment than their traditional European colours. The AMI paint catalogue AER-MM-P100 included a Matt Sand Yellow 29, which was then darkened to suit (the nearest reference being FS.33594). The paint was then oversprayed across the basic colours, with the undersurfaces remaining in their semigloss natural metal state. The national insignia in their standard six positions were reduced in size to 300mm diameter and were also oversprayed with a thin paint wash. Most of the stencil detail was

ZD744/BD Buddha, sporting a low-vis pale pink and pale blue shark mouth. Mick Lee

73

Desert Storm Tornados

Dhahran		
ZA370/A		
ZA371/C		
ZA372/E	Sally T	
ZA373/H		
ZA400/T		
ZA397/O		
ZA376	Mrs Miggins (uncoded)	
ZD745/BM	Black Magic (previously Melchie)	
ZD895/BF		
ZA374/CN	Miss Behavin; additional 'N' added to code to make 'CNN'	
ZA403/CO	Bomb load exploded on release, destroying the aircraft; crew ejected	
ZA457/CE	Bob	
ZA847/CH	Where do you want it?	
ZA490/GG	GiGi	
ZA461/DK		
ZA707/BK		
ZD715/DB	Luscious Lizzie	
ZD740/DA	Dhahran Annie (previously Black Adder)	
ZD843/DH	Damaged by ZA403's bombs, 23 January 1991	

Tabuk		
ZD719/AD	Check Six (ALARM)	
ZD739/AC	Armoured Charmer (TIALD)	
ZD746/AB	(ALARM) Belle (ALARM)	
ZD747/AL	Anna Louise (ALARM)	
ZD748/AK	Anola Kay (ALARM)	
ZD810/AA	(ALARM)	
ZD845/AF	Angel Face (ALARM)	
ZD850/CL	Cherry Lips	
ZD851/AJ	Amanda Jane (ALARM)	
ZD893/AG	Crashed after take-off, 20 January 1991	
ZD744/BD	Buddha	
ZD848/BC	Bacardi and Coke (TIALD)	
ZD892/H	Helen; crashed 20 January 1991	
ZA452/GK	Gulf Killer	
ZA446/EF	(TIALD)	
ZA447/EA	MiG Eater	
ZA460/FD	Fire Dancer	
ZA465/FK	Foxy Killer	
ZA466/FH	Crashed on landing, 18 October 1990	
ZA467/FF	Shot down over Ar Rutbah radar station, 22 January 1991	
ZA473/FM	Foxy Mama	
ZA393/CQ	Sir Gallahad (TIALD)	
ZD850/CL	(ALARM)	
ZA396/GE	Shot down over Tallil air base, 20 January 1991	
ZA452/GK	Gulf Killer	
ZA406/DN	(TIALD)	
ZD844/DE	Donna Ewin (TIALD)	

Muharraq		
ZA396/GE	Hit by Roland SAM over Tallil, 20 Janaury 1991; crew ejected	
ZD890/O	Hello Kuwait-G'dbye Iraq	
ZD718/BH	Crashed on low-level training mission, 13 Janaury 1991	
ZD791/BG	John Peters and Adrian ('John') Nichol's aircraft, shot down over Shaibah air base, 17 January 1991	
ZD809/BA	Awesome Annie	
ZA392/FN	Shot down over Shaibah air base after JP233 attack 18 January 1991; crew killed	
ZA455/EJ	Triffid Airways	
ZA471/ER	Emma; roman numeral II added in between E and R tail code	
ZA459/EL		
ZA475/FC	Triffid Airways	
ZD717/CD	Hello Kuwait-G'dbye Iraq; shot down over Al Taqaddum air base after attack on 14 February 1991; navigator killed	
ZD792/CF	Nursie	
ZD744/BD	Damaged by birdstrike, 18 January 1991	
ZA399/GA	Zimmer Woman Hello Kuwait … G'dbye Iraq	
ZA456/M	Mel Hello Kuwait … G'dbye Iraq	
ZA463/Q	Flying High – Garfield	
ZA469/I		
ZA472/EE		
ZA475/P	Triffid Airways	
ZA492/FE		
ZD892/H	Helen	
ZA790/D	Debbie	

removed, except for the rescue markings, and individual codes were painted in white on the tail fins and nosewheel doors. The leading edges received a coat of anti-abrasive black paint to reduce the wear caused by the desert sand, and the red intake edges were narrowed, with the interiors being painted black (first 12in) and then dark sea grey (5ft). Due to the harsh conditions none of the aircraft remained in pristine condition for more than a few days, and all showed signs of extreme wear on their return home, with some displaying a distinct 'pinkish' hue. By the end of hostilities the aircraft had flown 226 sorties in thirty-two missions and dropped 565 1,000lb Mk83 bombs. Due to political sensitivities, the aircraft did not receive anything in the shape of artwork during the war.

Saudi Storm Birds

Although little has been published concerning Saudi Tornado operations in the Gulf War, they played an important role in the bombing campaign. No.7 Squadron of the RSAF was already operational on the Tornado IDS in August 1990, whilst its sister unit was still forming. The RSAF IDS aircraft, practically identical in equipment fit to the RAF's GR.1s, undertook the same counter-air and interdiction missions as their UK counterparts. Their first mission, flown against Iraqi airfields on the first night of the war, was reportedly an anti-runway attack against H-3 airfield by four Tornados (probably armed with JP233) on 17 January, and they lost a single aircraft on the 19th in a non-combat related mission. No. 7 Sqn shouldered the brunt of the RSAF combat operations in the war, flying some 665 combat sorties, of which 590 were interdiction and 75 were offensive counter-air.

Post-War Policing

Operation Southern Watch

Following the Gulf War, Saddam Hussein began to turn his attentions against his own people, the Kurds in the north and the Marsh Arabs in the south, who both began to suffer at the hands of the Iraqi forces. The United Nations agreed that the Iraqi action was contrary to the spirit and the terms agreed at the end of the Gulf War, as well as violating many humanitarian policies. This brought into play resolutions enforcing a 'Safe Havens' policy to protect the Kurds and enable them live in peace. Part of the Safe Haven policy was the imposition – by a Coalition comprising of the US, the UK and France of a 'no-fly' zone – extending over the whole of Iraq north of the 36th Parallel, the UK contribution being titled Operation *Warden*. Later, the Coalition also imposed a 'no-fly' zone to cover the area extending over the whole of Iraq south of the 32nd Parallel to provide protection to the Marsh Arabs. The major difference between southern and northern zones was that no Coalition ground forces were involved in the southern zone, and no safe-havens were established: it was a policy purely of 'do not operate in this area – or else'.

To enforce this policy a Coalition air force was assembled. Below the 36th Parallel Operation *Southern Watch* came into being, the major element of this air arm being provided by the United States, in the shape of the USAF's 4404th Composite Wing (provisional), along with a naval task force. The Allied contribution was provided by France and Britain, in addition to certain other types of missions being flown by Arab air forces over their own airspace. The RAF contribution received a great deal of media attention when it was first announced in the August of 1992 that a Tornado force would be deploying from RAF Marham. Named Operation *Jural* the primary task was to be that of reconnaissance. The initial deployment comprised three Tornado GR.1As from No.2(AC) Squadron and three GR.1s from No.617 Sqn, crews being from the respective units, although in due course the GR.1As were replaced one for one by GR.1s. When the Tornado detachment arrived in Dhahran there was no certainty as to what to expect, or what type of missions would be required. While the 'Pink Panther' aircraft adapted themselves to the heat of the desert, the detachment personnel constructed a shanty town by a mixture of formal and informal building.

A typical mission package would consist of fighter, strike, reconnaissance and defence suppression aircraft, the aircraft types involved including the following: F-16, F-15, F-14 and Mirage 2000 fighters for CAP; F-15E, A-6 Intruder and Tornado strike aircraft; Tornado GR.1As for reconnaissance; and F-4G, EF-111 and EA-6B Prowler defence suppression aircraft. The size of the 'package' was decided by the tasking agency but the employment of the package, within the constraints of the task, was the job of the air commander. Additional support was provided by a variety of AAR resources plus E-3 AWACS and E-2 Hawkeyes. The 'mix and match' of these assets was very variable, with packages running from fewer than ten aircraft up to forty plus.

The primary aim of the RAF mission was reconnaissance, and the detachment included a RIC inhabited by skilled PIs whose task it was to examine the returned images and decide what elements of interest could be found. All sorties were flown at medium level, although RAF crews maintained their low-level proficiency by flying some sorties in Kuwait. The distances involved in operating over Iraq from the main Coalition bases means that AAR was an essential part of any task; the Tornado force tended to work with its own VC-10 tankers, but if these were not available then the USAF KC-10s provided an excellent alternative. With a fixed time to cross the border incorporated in the mission task, any pre-task tanking becomes the first critical point: all aircraft must take on board the required amount of fuel in the planned time and any delays would create a ripple in the plan. It is all too easy for a tanker to appear with one of its hoses not working, thus halving availability as the aircraft have to take it in turns on the remaining hose.

Due to the continuing intransigence of the Iraqi leadership, at the time of writing the *Southern Watch* continues, though not from its original base of Dhahran. Following the American re-appraisal of security around the base, it was decided that the continued safety of the aircraft and personnel could no longer be guaranteed, and thus during late 1996 the Coalition air forces relocated to Al Kharj – or 'Al's Garage', as it is known in RAF parlance – which is politely reported to be something of a 'slum'!

Crews from Nos14 and 17 Squadrons took over the *Jural* detachment in December 1992, and crews from Honington, Marham and Brüggen replaced them in March 1993. No.9 Squadron maintained the detachment from June-

A pair of Saudi Tornados, practically identical in equipment fit to the RAF's GR.1 undertook the same counter air and interdiction missions as its UK counterparts. BAe

August 1993, passing the role to No. II (AC) Squadron that December, and the reconnaissance team stayed until March 1994. The Brüggen-based units have maintained the detachment since then. The RAF maintains a six-aircraft presence at Al Kharj on a rotational deployment, all being of the IDS variety, with at least two TIALD pods being used along with Vinten GP.1 reconnaissance pods.

The Tornado force also took over the Warden detachment at Incerlik, taking over from Harriers in 1995. A pool of

twelve GR.1s at Brüggen were at the time of writing being given Operation *Jural* codes tailcodes in the 'Jx' range. The crews man three GR.1As and three GR.1Bs to police the northern no-fly zone.

Operation *Bolton*

During 1998, Tornado GR.1s from RAF Brüggen and Lossiemouth and GR.1As from Honington were based at Ali Al Salem air base, some 56km from Kuwait

City, in response to the heightened state of tension in the area caused by Iraq's decision not to allow the UN Weapons Inspectors access to their sites. Under the shadow of bomb-damaged HASs – a reminder of the previous Gulf conflict – aircraft from Nos 9 and 12 Squadrons, TIALD-equipped aircraft from Nos14 and 617, and reconnaissance jets from No.2 were despatched as part of Operation *Bolton*, a deployment which allowed the urgently dispatched HMS Illustrious, with her Fleet Air Arm Sea Harriers and RAF

Harrier GR.7s, to return to the UK. Instead of applying 'nose art' as had been the custom during Operation *Granby*, a more culinary theme was adopted by some GR.1Bs with individual aircraft being named after gourmet dishes such as 'Lobster Bisque' and 'Royal Game'. The Tornados later began operating alongside their compatriots at Al Kharj in Saudi Arabia, and the RAF's presence in the Middle East has now all come under the Operation *Bolton*, which has superseded *Jural*. Aircraft also began to to sport white

tail chevrons, on to which was superimposed a small Union Flag as a theatre-specific Operation *Bolton* marking. The aircraft wear a mixture of the new two-tone grey and traditional grey/green camouflage, with some sporting the latest incarnation of their squadron markings in reduced form on their noses. Operation *Bolton* also saw the operational debut of the RAF's Paveway III LGBs, which were carried but not used in anger.

Operation *Bolton* Aircraft

GR.1s ZA393/BE (14 Squadron) and ZD843/CJ (17 Squadron), GR.1A ZA405/Y (2 Squadron), using callsigns 'Viper 1-3'.

GR.1B ZA400/AJ-A (617 Squadron), GR.1A ZA398/S (2 Squadron) and GR.1 ZD747/AL (9 Squadron), using callsigns 'Snake 1-3'

GR.1B ZA457/AJ-B (617 Squadron), ZA490/FJ (12 Squadron), using callsigns 'Python 1-2'.

GR.1B ZA490/FJ was reported to have diverted to Crete due to unservicability and was replaced by ZA450/FB.

ZD843/CJ 'Viper 2' of 17 Squadron, fitted with a TIALD pod and camouflaged Hindenburger wing tanks, is readied for an Operation Bolton **from Ali Al Salem air base in Kuwait.**

CHAPTER FOUR

Electronic Tornados

Tornado ECR

To fulfil the Luftwaffe's electronic warfare requirements, a specialist derivative of the IDS was developed, known as the ECR – Electronic Combat and Reconnaissance – but generally called in Germany the EKA (*Elektronische Kampfführung und Aufklärung*). The primary role of the ECR was to replace the RF-4E Phantoms and RF-104G Starfighters, and it is interesting to note that from production Batch 5 onwards all German Tornados were made compatible with the AGM-88A HARM anti-radar missile. The project was approved by the German Parliament in May 1986, and that June Panavia was authorized to build thirty-seven of the aircraft for delivery between 1990 and 1992, from the seventh production batch. The Tornado ECR contains many advanced features such as the Mil Std 1553 datbus and the 128k computing power of the Tornado ADV. The main differences from the standard IDS are: the Emitter Locator System (ELS); the Infra-Red Imaging System (IIS); a Forward Looking Infra-Red (FLIR) sensor; an ODIN operational data link; up to four HARM missiles; the inclusion of external fairings for the sensors; and the lack of the usual twin cannon armament.

The ELS, developed by Texas instruments and integrated into the Tornado by DASA, is a precise direction-finding system, able to locate, classify and display hostile radars, and allowing the crew to either avoid or surpress the emitter site; it began its flight tests in 1989. The ELS is capable of identifying a large number of hostile emitters in a dense signal environment; the databus distributes the data to both the pilot's and the WSO's tactical displays, and can be used to cue and

46+26, one of JBG-32's Tornado ECRs, shown here in the latest Luftwaffe camouflage scheme. Of note are the HARM missiles and the underfuselage reconnaissance fairing. Panavia

Low-angle view showing the undernose forward-facing steerable Carl-Zeiss FLIR, mounted in a 'teardrop' turret under the nose. Author

release the HARM missiles. The ELS also contributes to the reconnaissance mission, enabling the identification of both mobile targets and targets of opportunity. It has its system antennae located in the forward edge of the fixed part of the wing, and uses a surface acoustic wave channelizer to determine the frequency, arrival time and pulse of the signal. Six 1750 digital processors are used to determine the signal type using powerful passive ranging techniques. A specially designed radome enhances the performance and protects the antennae and down converters located in each wing rib, with the channelizer positioned in the space vacated by the cannon. The local oscillator is located behind the WSO in the 'spine' equipment bay. The display on the WSO's TV Tabs or the pilots CEDAM shows the aircraft's position and track, and the precise ELS field of view. Threat radars are shown in relation to the aircraft by the circular symbols which indicate the lethal range of the threat and its position.

The ELS is augmented by a Honeywell/Sondertechnic panoramic horizon-to-horizon internal IIS which provides high resolution thermal coverage of the area overflown by the ECR, and the IIS is connected via the databus to the main computer which furnishes it

with flight navigation and control data overlaid with tactical symbology. The IIS's 'eye' is located under the fuselage, having the same basic shape as the reconnaissance sensor to be found on the RAF's Tornado GR.1A, and its installation was facilitated by the removal of the twin 27mm cannons. Examination of the displayed image by the crew makes for valuable in-flight evaluation minutes after acquisition and is available to ground forces via the ODIN link. Dry silver film storage of the thermal map allows review and evaluation of the recorded image, which enables the WSO to zoom, freeze or search the displayed image, whilst the video continues to store data. The rather complex system consists of an AN/AAD-5 IR scanner receiver, a power distribution unit, a film processor, dry silver film, film developer and control panel. The image is composed on a line-by-line basis, which to the unaided eye resembles a conventional black and white image. The Italian ECR variant (see page 82) employs a different recording medium: the Recorder Film Processor Unit is replaced by a Tape Recorder Formatter Unit, and this data is recorded on video rather than film, and therefore the recording storage capability is increased.

The ODIN enables the crew to hand over

target and threat data in digital format to other aircraft and ground stations. Any data received is detected by ODIN and is fed to the aircraft's transceivers. ODIN enables the WSO to complete a prepared format for the transfer of information, which are extracts from the standard NATO Recce Report and CAT-06 in-flight report. Target and defence information can be drawn from the ELS and IIS, and target weather information can also be included in the ODIN format. All receivers of an ODIN transmission are alerted to the in-coming message by a blinking warning light on their TV Tab.

The IIS is also augmented by a forward-facing steerable Carl-Zeiss FLIR, mounted in a 'teardrop' turret under the nose, and rotatable through 180°. Situated to the starboard side of the underfuselage, it produces an infra-red image which can be displayed on the pilot's HUD or CEDAM and on the WSO's TV Tabs. Since this is a passive sensor, the approaching aircraft is difficult to detect if the TFR is not operational. The first two prototype ECRs, 98+03 and 45+75, lacked the FLIR turret but carried the IIS fairing with ELS, and instrumentation pods on their centre-lines. The definitive ECR featured all of the Batch 6 Tornado improvements with the 128k main computer, Mil Std 1553D databus, Mil Std 1760 weapons interfaces and the more powerful RB.199 Mk105 engines. HARM firings were undertaken in the USA at the China Lake test facility in the early 1990s, 45+29 and 98+02 being amongst the aircraft involved.

The first production ECR made its maiden flight in October 1989, and the official first handover took place on 3 May 1990. Squadron deliveries began to JBG 38 at Jever on 21 May, and eighteen were on strength in April 1991. The final seventeen aircraft went to JBG 32 at Lechfeld from June 1991 to January 1992. Thirty of the ECRs arrived without their ELS equipment, and therefore operated at a reduced level, relying on the RHAWS and HARM seekers to aquire and pinpoint targets, and the first fully retro-fitted ELS aircraft arrived on 8 February 1993. The five ELS-equipped aircraft

were used for trials. The aircraft initially formed single squadrons within both JBG 32 and JBG 38, and were later consolidated within JBG 32, which became the sole ECR unit from October 1994.

Germany's ECRs were the two protoypes and the last thirty-five German IDS airframes, and wore the serials 46+23 to 46+57. None was dual-controlled, and were plane sets 817, 818, 821, 823, 827, 830, 833, 837, 839, 842, 844, 847, 848, 851, 854, 856, 858, 860, 864, 866, 869, 871, 873, 876, 879, 881, 884, 887, 890, 894, 896, 898, 900, 903 and 906.

Operational ECR

To add support to the NATO-led Operations *Deny Flight* and *Deliberate Force* over Bosnia, between August

1995 and November 1996 a detachment of eight German Tornado ECRs was based at Piacenza in Italy under the umbrella of *Einsatzgeschwader* 1, which was established to co-ordinate German Tornado operations over Bosnia. In keeping with the 1990s vogue for low-visibility, the aircraft all sported an overall light grey camouflage scheme which, it is understood, has now been applied across the entire ECR fleet. For their Balkan operations the ECRs carried their usual compliment of BOZ and Cerebus pods, as well a as pair of AIM-9 Sidewinder AAMs and their normal complement of two HARM missiles.

On 31 August 1995, a flight of five ECRs flew the unit's first operational sortie; this also marked Germany's first participation in a combat zone since the end of the Second World War, and thus an important, although restricted, foreign

A Tornado being prepared for a *Deny Flight* **sortie over Bosnia, as evidenced by the full load of flares in the BOZ pod.** Panavia

Close-up of 322 Staffel's 'Dragon' giving credence to the unit's 'Flying Monsters' legend, as seen at the 1998 RIAT. Gary Parsons f4 Aviation

policy change by the Bonn Government. As part of the legacy of the Nazi regime and World War Two, the German Parliament was reluctant to send troops or aircraft into any conflict zone, and as recently as the Gulf War preferred to send money rather than materiel. The decision to move into the Balkans was a difficult one, and seen as more 'symbolic' than 'operational'. The aircraft did not have any opportunities to fire their missiles in anger, but they did take part in the strikes against Bosnian Serb positions in September 1995, flying as anti-radar cover as part of a larger package. Retaining their original fin badge markings of AKG-51, the aircraft also adopted the EG1 badge of a stylized number 1 on the engine intakes.

Operational experience quickly demonstrated that the ECR could not practically operate both SEAD and reconnaissance roles simultaneously, and the IIS would better serve as part of a pod-mounted system. However removal of the IIS would adversely affect the SEAD role, and so the ECR's future is at something of an impasse.

ECR Units

Jagdbombergerschwader 38

JBG 38 was the first Luftwaffe Tornado unit to form and is described in detail on page 00. Initially it had only a single Staffel, but it gained a second in 1989 with 382 Staffel, this being the first unit to equip with eighteen Tornado ECRs at the Jever base in January 1990. 382 Staffel's life as an ECR unit was, however, short-lived, and it transferred its aircraft to JBG 32 in October 1994, receiving standard IDS versions in return.

Jagdbombergerschwader 32

Flying its last Starfighter mission in April 1984, JBG 32 began to receive its first aircraft at its Lechfeld base on 27 August that year. JBG 32 has always had a close association with ECM and EW, and indeed housed a third Staffel, 323, dedicated to the ECM training role with the Hansa jet. JBG 32 became the Luftwaffe's second ECR operator in June 1991, receiving the last seventeen Tornado ECRs produced. It was originally thought that the ECR would replace 323 Staffel's Hansa jets, but instead they were delivered to 321 Staffel, whose standard IDS aircraft were distributed amongst other operators. JBG 32 became the 'official' operators of the ECR on 1 July 1994 when its second Staffel, 322, re-equipped with the ECRs formerly operated by JBG 31's 382 Staffel. 321 Staffel's insignia is that of a roaring Panther, whilst 322 uses a fearsome dragon, and carries the legend 'The Flying Monsters', a point well illustrated on the aircraft that the unit sent to the 1998 RIAT at RAF Fairford.

American Interest

In the late 1989 a German Tornado ECR was sent to the USA to give Pentagon officials the opportunity to study the aircraft at close hand, hoping to convince them of the Tornado's ability. This stemmed from an agreement announced on 16 December 1988, whereby Rockwell began promoting the Tornado ECR as a possible follow-on aircraft to replace the USAF's F-4G 'Wild Weasel' Phantoms. A number of designs had previously been mooted by Panavia to gauge the interest of the American market, having a re-designed tail fin akin to that of the EA-6 Prowler and using existing systems from that aircraft. However, the Americans' in-built resistance to anything that does not bear Uncle Sam's trademark, and a serious lack of funds at the time, gave the ECR little chance. In any event, when the F-4G was finally withdrawn, the USAF turned to the US Navy, using their Prowlers to provide EW support.

Italian Tornado 'ITECR'

In light of a perceived SAM threat to their aircraft, the AMI decided to obtain a SEAD capability, and following their experiences during the Gulf War a contract was issued to provide a limited number of Italian Tornado IDS aircraft with a HARM capability. Integration testing was completed in October 1991 and as a result twenty Tornados were modified to carry HARM at the AMI's Central maintenance Depot at Camerai and at Alenia's aircraft plant at Turin, for subsequent delivery to the 550 Stormo. The first pair of 'interim' ITECRs was handed over to 50o Stormo's 155o Gruppo in February 1992.

Although this 'interim' HARM capability was useful, it was clear that a more capable SEAD system was required, with enhanced detection abilities. Despite some protracted financial wrangling Italy finallydecided to acquire sixteen 'full-specification' ECRs, these being convert-ed from existing IDS airframes rather than being built new, and therefore retaining their original engines. The aircraft also have greater emphasis on 'home grown' electronics, a revised ARWE – 'Advanced Radar Warning Equipment' – RHAWS produced by Elettronica. The Italian aircraft will carry the IIS, but they will record its imagery direct to video rather than the dry silver film used in the German ECR. Therefore the aircraft carries a Tape Formatter Unit instead of a Film Processor. Like the German ECR, the Italian ITECR has the FLIR turret under the nose and the IIS fairing under the fuselage, and also lacks the two cannon.

The first of the ITECRs, MM7079, converted by Alenia at Turin, undertook its maiden flight in July 1992, and was subsequently handed over to the AMI just as the Luftwaffe was receiving the last of its new-build ECRs. During late 1995 the Italian 'interim' ECR's worked hand in hand with their German counterparts

The 'Flying Monsters' ECR in the air. Gary Parsons f4 Aviation

A Tornado IDS of the Aeronautica Militaire Italiano. Author

when the two types were co-located at Piacenza to take part in operations over Bosnia. The two types operated in concert with the German ECRs making up for the Italian aircraft's lack of an Emitter Location System. The first 'full specification' ECR aircraft first flew on 20 July 1992 and was delivered in February 1998. Crews from 155° Gruppo of the 50°

Stormo undertook the first ITECR conversion courses in early 1997 at Torino-Caselle. 155° Gruppo are the recognized SEAD specialists within the AMI, and also undertake a secondary reconnaissance committment, using the Aeritalia/MBE underfuselage reconnaissance pod.

RAF 'Wild Weasel' – Sounding the 'ALARM'

The need for an indigenous anti-radar missile had been recognized by the RAF for many years, highlighted perhaps by its experiences with the American-supplied Shrikes used by Vulcan bombers against Argentine radars during the Falklands War of 1982. BAe was given a contact in 1988 to supply its very promising ALARM missile, an innovative design for an 'intelligent' anti-radar missile. Problems were experienced with the ALARMS's ROF Nuthatch rocket, but these were solved with the German Bayard motor, and the missile completed trial firings at China Lake in the USA with No.32 JTU during 1990.

With the start of the Desert Shield operations in Saudi Arabia, ALARM was pressed into service. The original plan had called for No.9 Squadron to be the dedicated ALARM operators, and at the time of the growing Gulf crisis only one crew from the unit had attended a course at BAe on the use of the new weapon. However, modifications the unit's aircraft were well underway, including a Mil Std 1553B digtal databus enabling the aircraft

---

Texas Instruments AGM-88A HARM

The Texas Instruments AGM-88A High Speed Anti-Radar Missile, or HARM, is able to identify and home in on radar transmitter antennae, and is highly resistant to ECM employed by hostile radars. Largely autonomous, HARM carries a wide band fixed-array antenna in the nose, backed by an on-board digital computer. Three modes of operation are available: Target of Opportunity Mode – Range Known (HARM will aquire the target in flight); Target of Opportunity Mode – Range Unknown (HARM serves as an electronic warfare receiver); and Self Protection Mode (HARM provides a quick reaction when a threat is aquired, the parameters are relayed to the missile and the pilot fires and jinks away).

Specifications for AGM-88A:

Wingspan:	3ft 71/4in (1.1m)
Length:	13ft 91/4in (4.2m)
Diameter:	93/4in (0.25m)
Launch weight:	798lb (362kg)
Max. speed:	1,417mph (2,280km/h)
Minimum range:	4 miles (6km)
Maximum range:	50 miles (80km)
Propulsion:	Single-stage dual thrust solid propellant rocket motor
Guidance:	Passive broad-band radar
Warhead:	Proximity- and laser height sensing-fuzed high explosive fragmentation, 146lb (66kg)

Texas Instruments AGM-88 HARM missiles fitted to a Luftwaffe Tornado ECR, part of
***Einsatzgeschwader* 1, as denoted by the '1' badge on the engine intake.** Panavia

In desert garb, one of No.9 Squadron's aircraft fitted with two BAe ALARM anti-radar
missiles. Iraqi radar operators soon gained a healthy respect for the new missile. BAe

ZD850/CL 'Cherry Lips', with two ALARM mission symbols. RAF

ZD748/AK, gun-toting 'Anola Kay' with eight ALARM mission symbols. Author

ZD851/AJ 'Amanda Jane' with nine ALARM mission symbols. Author

to 'talk' to the missile. A further twist in the tale came in mid-October 1990 when it was decided that it should be No.20 Squadron that used ALARM in the Gulf instead; its familiarization with the system took the form of a briefing from a No.9 Squadron crew and a week of becoming proficient with the computer system used to programme the missiles. After a week of flying SAPs, No.20 Squadron despatched eight crews to Tabuk in November, all having to practise IFR, which they had not done prior to their involvement in the conflict.

To say that ALARM was untried is something of an understatement, as only one live firing had been undertaken, along with at least five motor tests: under the leadership of Wg Cdr Bob McAlpine, the sixteen-man team had the task of 'writing the book' on ALARM. Initially the missile could only be carried singly on the inner wing pylons, displacing the 495gal fuel tanks, but by January of 1991 the underfuslage stations had been modified to carry up to three missiles, whilst the tanks returned to their wing stations. All but one of the nine ALARM aircraft were provided by No.9 Squadron, four of their number also having NVG-compatible lighting.

During the months before combat began, ELINT aircraft were mapping Iraqi radar frequencies and, armed with this information, the crews were able to work out the best method of operation. Missions were planned in close co-operation with the strike forces, so that the ALARM missiles were 'loitering' overhead as the air attack began. Having been fed with the relevant information by computer tape beforehand, along with the aircraft's intended height, speed and location at the moment of launch, the missile would be instructed to follow a pre-programmed pattern, looking for a particular radar signal, perhaps that of the SA-6, and if that was not evident, then to search for siganls from another system, such as the SA-2. Because of the weapon's digital database, the missile can be instantly updated if the parameters need changing, so the navigator can then input different sets of instructions right up to the moment of release.

'The ALARM was sounded' at 2310 local on 16 January when two GR.1s crewed by Flt Lts Roche and Bellamy in ZD810, and Flt Lts Williams and Goddard in ZD850 set off to support Tornados

ZD746/AB 'Alarm Belle' with six anti-radar mission markings. Author

final ALARM sortie was flown on the afternoon of 13 February when ZD748 and ZD851 supported a TIALD mission against Al Taqaddum. A similar mission involving ZD746 and ZD851 against Habbanniyah on the 26th was aborted due to bad weather. In total, twenty-four ALARM missions were flown during which 121 rounds were fired. The 'lead ALARMist' was ZD746 with twelve successful and two aborted missions to its credit. Both ZD851 and ZD746 both flew eleven successful and two aborted missions each. The ALARM aircraft sported a very neat line in 'nose art' and 'sharkmouths' which added a fearsome – and humorous – dimension to the aircraft.

which had left an hour earlier, bound for Al Asad airfield to lay down JP233s. The duo successfully launched their missiles some five launch! It was also a little uncomfortable for the ALARM crews who sometimes found themselves desigated as 'hostile targets' by AWACS aircraft as they were approaching at low-level,

and had to give a burst from their IFF transponders. From 25 January, the ALARM aircraft worked at medium level along with the rest of the strike packages, thus removing the low-level problems.

By early February, despite the best efforts of BAe at Lostock, stocks of ALARM were almost exhausted. The

ALARM Aircraft:
ZD719/AD 'Check Six'
ZD746/AB 'Alarm Belle'
ZD747/AL 'Anna Louise'
ZD748/AK 'Anola Kay'
ZD810/AA
ZD845/AF 'Angel Face'
ZD851/AJ 'Amanda Jane'
ZD850/CL'CherryLips'

The BAe ALARM Missile

ALARM is an acronym for Air Launched Anti-Radiation Missile, a 'smart' munition which does not need assistance from complex and expensive specialist sensors on board the launch aircraft. All that is required of the pilot is to initiate launch from safely outside the effective cover of the air defence systems the aircraft will be attacking. ALARM is a passive system, hunting the skies and selecting its target in response to instructions and data programmed into the missile before launch. What makes ALARM so unique is its 'loiter' capability:

the missile flies in a upward trajec-tory and then deploys a parachute, allowing it to 'search' for hostile emmissions. Once a radar threat is detected within its parameters the parachute is ejected, the rocket motor fires and the missile homes in on its target – ALARM is not a point-and-shoot weapon like HARM or Shrike.

Five modes of operation are available: the already mentioned Loiter Mode; Direct Mode, which is designed to give the least time between launch and kill; Dual Mode, which

provides the flexibility of direct attack whilst maintaining the loiter option; Corridor/Air Surpression Mode, which gives a large area of coverage; and Universal Mode, similar in all respects to the Corridor/Air Suppression Mode except that it is optimized for medium- to high-level launch. ALARM contains a passive radar seeker, a forward-looking rangefinder which triggers the warhead for optimum lethality, a missile contol computer, a navigation pack with 'strap down' INS, and a blast fragmentation warhead with outstanding armour piercing abilities.

ALARM Statistics:

Wingspan:	0.73m
Length:	4.1m
Diameter:	0.23m
Launch weight:	200kg
Max. speed:	2280km/h
Maximum range:	20km
Propulsion:	Two-stage solid propellant rocket motors
Guidance:	Pre-programmed passive radar seeker
Warhead:	Laser proximity fuzed direct action high-explosive

An ALARM missile, caught at the point of launch. ALARM is a passive system, hunting the skies and selecting its target in response to instructions and data programmed into the missile before launch. BAe

ALARMs were also used to escort American F-15E Strike Eagles, and so effective was the new munition that the Iraqi radar emissions fell so low that from January 26 only two missiles were needed to be carried per aircraft – which was just as well as there was no stockpile of ALARMs to draw on! BAe

CHAPTER FIVE

Maritime Strike

RAF Tornado GR.1B – Overwater Attacker

Being traditionally a maritime nation, the United Kingdom had always gone to great efforts to protect itself against possible assault from the sea. From the 1970s the airborne maritime strike role was performed by the old, but still highly effective Blackburn (BAe) Buccaneer, armed initially with BAe/Matra Martel and later BAe Sea Eagle anti-ship missiles. By the early 1990s the retirement of the Buccaneer was long overdue: although the 'Brick' served an essential purpose, its weapons had become 'smarter' than the aircraft itself, the airframes had become tired, and they continued to carry avion-

ics that were lacking, even after the FIN 1063 INS upgrade.

Giving the Tornado a maritime role was made possible by the reduction in the strength of No.2 Group, formerly RAF Germany, following the reduction in east/west tensions as the Cold War came to an end. Nos15, 16 and 20 Squadrons lost their front-line roles, leaving a pool of airframes available for other uses. The Buccaneer's final bow therefore took place at RAF Lossiemouth on 27 March 1994, its role as the teeth of No.18 (Maritime) Group being taken by a new version of the RAF's main strike aircraft, the Tornado GR.1B. Of the two Buccaneer units at RAF Lossiemouth, Nos12 and 208 squadrons, only No.12 retained its identity during transition to the Tornado,

with No.208 being replaced by the 'Dambusters' of No.617 Squadron. A former Fleet Air Arm base, Lossiemouth is also home to No.16(R) Squadron, the Jaguar OCU.

It had been hoped at one stage that the RAF might have bought the Sea Eagle-armed 'Tornado International' to meet its overwater needs, but this paper project, based on a modified ADV airframe, did not attract any interest. Therefore, to provide a full maritime attack capability, the Tornado GR.1B was developed. It can be armed with up to four Sea Eagle sea-skimming anti-ship missiles, can strike over 400 miles from base and can launch its weapons from a stand-off range of over seventy miles.

The GR.1B airframes are in effect

A Tornado GR.1B from No.617 Squadron the 'Dambusters' based at RAF Lossiemouth displays its Sea Eagle sea-skimming anti-ship missiles. BAe

standard IDS variants, adapted for the maritime role, yet retaining all of the GR.1's avionics and weapons fits, including the FIN 1010 INS, TFR, Doppler and laser rangefinder; when not carrying the Sea Eagle missiles it is impossible to tell them apart from the standard GR.1. Modifications were made to allow the operation of the Sea Eagle, the GR.1B's primary weapon, with new computer software being added and modified underfuselage shoulder pylons fitted to carry the missile. The 'Tornado In Service Maintenance Team' (TISMT) at Boscombe Down found some spare capacity in the aircraft's main computer that allowed for firing and update command lines to be wired via 'Pan Data Links' into the inboard wing and shoulder stations. Inside the rear cockpit an ex-Buccaneer Missile Control Panel has been fitted to manage the Sea Eagles, and the navigator's SMS panel has had the Sea Eagle firing parameters added to it. The aircraft was also the first to adopt the in-vogue 'Low Infra-Red' two-tone grey

camouflage scheme, tailor-made for maritime operations.

The GR.1Bs were delivered in two batches from RAF St Athan, where the modifications were undertaken. The Batch 1 aircraft could only 'point and shoot' the Sea Eagle and so were restricted to line-of-sight attacks only. The Batch 2 aircraft are now able to download target information into the missile's own computer and the round can be fire from a reported distance of some 110km, over the radar horizon, in 'fire-and-forget' mode, thus increasing the aircraft's survivability. Some twenty-six former RAF Germany Batch 3 Tornadoes were converted into GR.1Bs, and the first 'Proof of Installation' (or Pinst in RAF jargon) aircraft, ZA409 and ZA411, were re-worked at BAe Warton; being twin-stickers, they were sometimes incorrectly referred to as GR.1B(T)s. The first 'true' GR.1B, ZA407 made its first flight on 18 September 1993.

The first step in the Tornado's development of a maritime role was to re-equip

the two RAF Marham-based strike attack squadrons, Nos27 and 617, with recently upgraded ex-Laarbruch GR.1s, which now carried the more powerful RB.199 Mk103 engines: these aircraft would become the GR.1Bs. The original plans called for the re-numbering of No.27 Squadron, as No.12 (Designate) Squadron which, together with No.617 would move to RAF Lossiemouth in Scotland to take up the new overwater role. However, the old Buccaneer-equipped No.12 Squadron reformed with the Tornado on 1 October 1993, the day after it stood down as a Buccaneer unit, with the unit not actually making the move north until January 1994, and No.27's numberplate was then transferred to the Chinook and Puma helicopter OCU at RAF Odiham.

No.617 Squadron had previously received aircraft that had been modified for TIALD operations, but with the change of the unit's role, these aircraft were transferred to No.14 Squadron. Following the retirement of No.208 Squadron, No.617's ex-Laarbruch GR.1s

A worrying sight for any potential enemy, though the first warning of an impending Sea Eagle attack would probably actually be the missile hits themselves! Here four 'dummy' rounds are carried by a trials Tornado, complete with Saudi-painted Sky Shadow pod and BOZ-107 dispenser. BAe

The GR.1B airframes are in effect standard IDS variants, adapted for the maritime role, yet retaining all of the GR.1's avionics capabilities and weapons fits, including the FIN 1010 INS, TFR, Doppler and Laser Rangefinder. Upgrades were undertaken to allow the operation of the BAe Sea Eagle missile, the GR.1B's primary offensive weopon, with new computer software added and modified underfuselage 'shoulder' pylons fitted to carry the sea skimming munition. BAe

moved from Marham to Lossiemouth on 27 April 1994, with the GR.1As of No.13 and No. II (AC) Squadrons replacing them at the Norfolk base to form the centre for the RAF's reconnaissance force. No.208 Squadron's numberplate then re-appeared as part of No.4 FTS at RAF Valley, where No.208 (Reserve) Squadron took over from No.234 Squadron.

Each of the squadrons at Lossiemouth has twelve aircraft on strength with some fifteen crews. However, not all are available at once, as some are deployed to Operations *Warden* in Turkey and *Jural* in Saudi Arabia, as well as supporting the RAF Detachment at Goose Bay in Canada.

The GR.1B combat ready work-up for aircrews includes both overwater and overland roles, and the maritime work-up usually coincides with a Joint Maritime Course (JMC), which each unit takes part in at least three times a year. Aircrews must first be declared Attack Combat Ready, before being made Maritime Combat Ready. The maritime work-up consists of seven sorties, starting with three-ship formation sorties at 250ft, up to six-ship formations flying at a minimum of 100ft, of which one will be flown at night.

Operating the GR.1B in the overwater role is essentially no different to operating the Buccaneer. The objective is the same: to ensure the maximum amount of Sea Eagles arrive at their target at the same time. Daylight attacks were of no real problem to theBuccaneer, but when thick cloud or darkness obscured the view, the 'Bricks' found themselves in a formation closer than any the Red Arrows would be comfortable with, making the mission incredibly demanding on the crews. Not so with the Tornado: with its sophisticated navigation equipment and powerful radar, it can achieve the same results by independently navigating to a precise launch position.

A GR.1B mission is, in effect, no different to a 'traditional' bombing sortie, using AWACS or a maritime patrol aircraft such as Nimrod as the controlling agency. The maps are drawn and the CPGS inputs undertaken, the latter then being loaded into the aircraft computer. The actual mechanics and tactics of a GR.1B attack remain classified; suffice it

Sea Eagle missiles fitted onto special adaptor pylons and carried aboard ZA457/AJ-J of No.617 Squadron. BAe

to say that the aim is to attack the highest-value enemy naval asset, be it a carrier or a conventional ship, and to do that the aim is to have as many missiles in the air as possible, to saturate the ship's defences. A typical plan may call for six GR.1Bs operating at low level in widely spaced pairs, each trailing the one in front, and if required making contact with an airborne tanker. The AWACS or MPA would then update the flight with the latest Surface Picture or SURPIC, and the relevant data would then be programmed by the navigator into the Sea Eagle's own computer, in an operation known as Vector Assisted Attack or VASTAC. In the absence of a SURPIC provider, one Tornado would climb and aquire the target on its own radar before dropping down again, and the information gathered would be fed into the missiles' systems. TSMT also provides a neat 'fix' for the

possibility of a 'pop-up' target acquisition by one of the aircraft. The system now contains an algorithm that allow the navigator to enter the height of the target ship's mast and the current height of the aircraft, and this then produces a calculation as to how high the Tornado must climb in order to 'aquire' its prey. The Tornado's advanced navigation system also allows for a precise launch time for the missiles, so as the formation speeds in they would spread onto different attack headings, and be able to launch their missiles at precisely the right moment so that each arrives on target +/–5 seconds apart. The missile is updated from the aircraft's own systems and can be off-boresighted for a high or low attack, allowing the missile to discriminate between targets. The major headache for the GR.1Bs is that the enemy may put a picket ship in front of the fleet's highest value asset, and these ships very

unsportingly do not remain stationary!

The maritime units are not limited to over-water operations, and retain their interdiction, OCA, BAI and precision bombing operations, and crews are regularly deployed to Saudi Arabia to take their part in patrolling the 'No-Fly' zones, as well as continuing their low flying

GR.1B Aircraft		
ZA374	ZA375	ZA399
ZA407	ZA409	ZA411
ZA446	ZA447	ZA450
ZA452	ZA453	ZA455
ZA456	ZA457	ZA459
ZA460	ZA460	ZA461
ZA465	ZA469	ZA471
ZA473	ZA474	ZA475
ZA490	ZA491	ZA492

The latest 'low observable' incarnation of the No.617 Squadron 'flashes'. Author

Buccaneer. They continued with their 'Buccs' until 1993, when they became operators of the GR.1B Tornado. The squadron adopted a two-letter code commencing with FA – F being for 'Fox', hence the Fox's head on their tail fin.

No.617 Squadron

Après moi le deluge – 'After me the flood'

No.617 Squadron, the world-famous 'Dambusters', was formed as a heavy bomber unit at Scampton in 1943, equipped with modified Lancaster BIII Special aircraft, with the specific task of breaching the Moehne, Eder and Sorpe dams using the now-legendary 'bouncing bombs' designed by Barnes Wallis. The squadron was also tasked with delivering special weapons such as the 'Tallboy' and 'Grand Slam' bombs.

After the war the unit flew Canberras until disbanding in 1955, to return in 1958 as part of the 'V Force' with the Vulcan. Disbanding again in 1981, No.617 Squadron re-formed in 1983 on the Tornado GR.1 as a strike squadron at RAF Marham in Norfolk. Maritime strike was added to their roles during 1994, with the colloquially and affectionately coined 'Six Foot Seven' Squadron remaining as one of the RAF's high profile units.

Sea Eagle

As the Sea Eagle is a 'fire and forget' missile, once it has been programmed by the Tornado crew with the position and distance to the target, they have no further part to play in its final run-in. Powered by a Microturbo TRI-60 turbojet engine with some 787lb st available, Sea Eagle has a range in excess of traditional solid fuel missiles, and carries a high-explosive, armour-piercing warhead. Once launched, it flies by reference to its own computer, making a 'pop-up' move at a pre-determined point to aquire its target with its own radar before dropping to wavetop level again to maintain the element of surprise. Able to be programmed to attack from any selected bearing, it is able to discriminate between several potential targets, and once locked on is very difficult to deceive, having a range of sophisticated ECM programmes available to it.

practices at Goose Bay in Canada and participating in exercises such as 'Red Flag' in the USA.

RAF Maritime Strike Squadrons

No.12 Squadron
'Leads the field'

Formed on 14 February 1915, No.12 Squadron were the sole recipients of the Fairey Fox biplane. Heavier equipment followed down the years with the Wellington, Lancaster and Lincoln, and the unit became an early operator of the Canberra, eventually equipping with the Vulcan, which it flew until 1967, before re-forming in 1969 on the Blackburn

Germany's Marineflieger – Baltic Defenders

Like the Lufwaffe, the German Marineflieger (naval air arm) bought Tornados to replace its ageing Starfighters. It operated 110 F-104Gs for strike, attack and anti-shipping duties, along with twenty-five RF-104s for reconnaissance. The importance of the Marineflieger's role in watching over the strategically important Baltic Sea led to the Tornado order for the Marineflieger being set at 112 aircraft, including a pair of twin-stickers; this allowed the Marineflieger to equip its two primary units, Marinefliegergeschwader 1 and 2 (MFG 1 and MFG 2), with forty-eight aircraft each, plus a few in reserve. With the delays in the service delivery of the maritime Tornado, the Marineflieger were forced to soldier on with the Starfighter, whilst the Luftwaffe bought a number of F-4F Phantoms to bridge the gap. It was therefore important

No.12 Squadron nose flash. Author

that the Marineflieger should be the first the receive the Tornado, and MFG 1 had the honour of being the first unit to form on the new Panavia aircraft. Training and conversion was rapid, in spite of the fact that, the Starfighter being a single-seater, the Marineflieger did not have any backseaters! Sixteen aircraft came from Batch 2, thirty-two from Batch 3, forty-eight from Batch 5 and twenty from Batch 6, with the lions share of Batch 5 aircraft going to MFG 2.

The Marineflieger Starfighters were equipped with the elderly AS.30 anti-ship missile, and there was a desperate need for a more modern missile for the new Tornados. The replacement came in the shape of the DASA AS-34 Kormoran, which offered a moderate range and very straightforward installation to the aircraft. A total of 174 Kormoran I missiles were delivered from 1989, with the heavier, digitized Kormoran II replacing them in service during 1995. The Marineflieger aircraft are also fitted to carry the AGM-88 HARM missile, making them a highly effective and specialized force.

Around ninety-six Tornadoes were also plumbed to carry the Sergeant Fletcher 28-200 'Buddy-Buddy' re-fuelling pod, of which seventy-six are reported to have been delivered. In time of war, the Marineflieger aircraft would also have been tasked with opposing hostile coastal landings, and therefore were equipped with the Hunting BL755 CBU and Mk103 bombs, in addition to their usual Mauser cannon, AIM-9 Sidewinder AAMs and Cerebus II and BOZ-100 self protection pods.

MFG 1 flew its final Starfighter mission on 29 October 1981 and the first Tornado delivery was made to Schleswig-Jagel on 2 July 1982, with the unit's aircrew undergoing their basic training at the TTTE at RAF Cottesmore. The unit was referred to as the Naval Tornado Conversion Unit until formal commissioning on 2 July 1982. The Marineflieger Tornados were externally identical to the Luftwaffe's IDS, except for their over-water camouflage scheme of Basalt Grey RAL7012 upper surfaces and Pale Grey RAL7035 lower surfaces. MFG 1 was

declared operational with its two Staffels on 1 January 1984, and its Tornados quickly proved to be an effective replacement for the Starfighter, with its two-man crew, powerful radar and all-weather abilities. With the ending of the Cold War, however, pressures mounted to reduce the number of aircraft in the German inventory, and as a result MFG 1 was de-activated on 1 January 1994, handing over its aircraft to AKG 51, which also moved into its Schlewig-Jagel base.

MFG 2 was the last of the German front-line Tornado units to form, on 11 September 1986, with forty-eight HARM-capable Batch 5 aircraft. The unit's first Staffel majored on tactical reconnaissance, while the second was assigned to using both HARM and Kormoran missiles in the anti-shipping role. The system practised was for the HARM-equipped aircraft to surpress the ship's surveillance radars, whilst the Kormoran-carrying aircraft launched their anti-ship missiles. The first Batch 5 aircraft was 43+85, delivered in a three-tone wraparound disruptive camouflage scheme which was later rejected in favour of a Dark Grey and Dark Green scheme.

When the aforementioned post-Cold War cuts took place, MFG 2 became the only Marineflieger Tornado unit; although it performed the same anti-shipping role as MFG 1, it was far more versatile with its additional roles of reconnaissance and HARM-shooting. The disbandment increased the size of MFG 2's force to some sixty aircraft. No.1 Staffel aircraft are now equipped with the MBB/Aeritalia reconnaissance pod on their centerline stations.

AMI – Anti-Surface Warfare

The Italian Air Force also operates Kormoran-equipped Tornado IDS in the anti-shipping role. The 36o Stormo's 156o Gruppo converted to the Tornado during 1984, and becasme operational at Gioia del Colle that August. Within the Gruppo are 381a, 382a, 383a and 384a Squadrigile, and their main tasking is that of maritime strike and interdiction using the Kormoran AShM. 156o Gruppo Tornados undertook low-level flypasts over Serbian shipping during Operation *Sharp Guard* above the Adriatic in 19XX, supporting NATO's blockade of Serb

An MFG-1 Tornado IDS armed with twin Kormoran anti-shipping missiles, the Marineflieger's primary air-to-surface munition. BAe

shipping; 36o Stormo aircraft also took part in combat sorties over Bosnia as part of Operation *Joint Endeavour*, carrying pairs of GBU-16 LGBs in conjunction with CDLP-carrying Tornado designator aircraft.

Tornado J

The Tornado J was proposed as a solution to a Japanese requirement for a new maritime strike aircraft to replace the Mitsubishi F-1s. The proposal succumbed to the fact that the basic Tornado lacked the range required by the Japanese forces. The Tornado J was to have been a joint development between Panavia and Mitsubishi, and was to have been built around the longer ADV airframe, but incorporating many of the features included in the IDS and ECR.

No.617 Squadron badge. Author

ABOVE: **A pair of naval Tornados display the 'old' and the 'new' camouflage schemes. The first of the Navy's Batch 5 aircraft was delivered in a three-tone wraparound disruptive camouflage scheme, but this was rejected in favour of a Dark Grey and Dark Green scheme.** Panavia

LEFT: **46+18 displays the Marineflieger anchor emblem.** Author

A Desert Sand-coloured Tornado GR.1 from No.617 Squadron. Note the unusual tail coding, adopted to commemorate the Lancaster bombers of their illustrious predecessors, the 'Dambusters'. Author

A superb study of the Tornado GR.1B in its LIR grey camouflage scheme, armed with two BAe Sea Eagle missiles. This example belongs to No.12 Squadron, which shares the RAF's over-water role with No.617 Squadron. Rick Brewell

Developed as a long-range interceptor for the RAF, the Tornado F.3 was required to mount lengthy CAPs to protect UK airspace. BAe

Tanking Tornados. An F.3 takes on fuel from one of the RAF's Hercules tankers – since retired – whilst a German Tornado ECR can be seen plugged into a USAFE KC-135. Author

Tri-national Tornados. A formation from the TTTE at RAF Cottesmore where, for the moment, all of the IDS basic training takes place. RAF Cottesmore

For the RAF *Desert Storm* was the 'Tornados' War'. Armed with BL755 CBUs, a GR.1 awaits its mission, whilst groundcrew haul more equipment around the shelter.
RAF

A Tornado GR.1 formation, as seen from the back seat. Author

An impressively sleek all-grey GR.1 from the TTTE, used for the 1996 air show season. RAF Cottesmore

An Italian Tornado IDS. Author

One almost feels tucked under the wing, in this close-in view of a GR.1 during a pre-Gulf War familiarization sortie over the desert. RAF

Prior to a Red Flag sortie at Nellis AFB in Nevada, a GR.1 gets the once-over from a ground crewman. RAF Tornados have a fine tradition of excellence at these gatherings. RAF

ABOVE: A formation of 'Bats' from No.9 Squadron take their turn 'plugging in' to an
Armée de l'Air tanker during a joint exercise. RAF

The only export customer for the IDS was the Royal Saudi Air Force, who bought twenty-
four aircraft as part of the Al Yamamah I and II deals. BAe

ABOVE: An excellent view of a fully-armed F.3, showing off its four semi-recessed Skyflash AAMs and the wing-mounted AIM-9 Sidewinders. RAF

Right: One of a small number of Royal Saudi Air Force Tornados used for reconnaissance, broadly similar to the RAF's Tornado GR.1A. BAe

**Prototype P.03/XX947, the first Tornado with dual controls. First flying on 5 August 1975, it was
used for stalling and spinning trials. It was also the first Tornado to be delivered in camouflage,
and the first with a nose radome rather than a representatively-shaped fairing.** BAe

Above: A trio from 'Treble One', protectors of the UK's northern
sector. BAe

ABOVE: An Arctic-camouflaged Tornado GR.1A. RAF

RIGHT: Another maritime
Tornado, this time from the
German Navy's MFG 2. Panavia

CHAPTER SIX

Tornado Reconnaissance

In the post-Cold War era, the Royal Air Force recognized the rising importance of accurate reconnaissance. Given the fact that the world's political map is in a constant state of flux and the uncertainty of where the next threat may come from, reconnaissance has assumed an ever-greater importance. Although the original three partner countries of the Panavia team had tried to reach an agreement for a common dedicated reconnaissance aircraft, it became clear that due to the requirements of the individual users, this would prove to be impossible. Therefore the UK decided to develop its own reconnaissance version to replace its Phantoms, Jaguars and some Canberras in the role.

Tornado GR1A

As a result, now spearheading the RAF's tactical reconnaissance force is the unique Tornado GR.1A, which serves with two squadrons based at RAF Marham in Norfolk, the home of the RAF's reconnaissance force. Nos II (AC) and 13 Squadrons and their high-tech GR.1As currently share their operating location with the elderly and 'traditionally' equipped, yet amazingly useful, Canberra PR.9, but these aircraft will move to RAF Waddington on the return to the UK of the Germany-based strike units. In addition to the primary reconnaissance role, both units have a secondary attack role, being split 80/20 between reconnaissance and bombing. In addition to normal reconnaissance operations, both squadrons regularly support commitments in Turkey, Saudi Arabia and more recently Kuwait, and each unit deploys for at least three months each year.

The lack of internal space in the Tornado gave rise to initial studies to fit the aircraft with an external pod, but the drag this would impose was deemed to be

One of the GR.1A's SLIR windows and the open aperture for the Vinten Type 4000 IRLS (Infra-Red Line Scan), part of the Tornado Infra-Red Reconnaissance System. BAe

unacceptable, and to fit a 'photo-nose' like that on the RF-4 Phantom would have meant removing the radar. It was therefore decided to concentrate efforts on the development of a small electro-optical package that would record images directly onto video tape. This new system would be based on the IR technology mastered by BAe, W.Vinten and CDC Systems, using TICMS (Thermal Imaging Common Module System) and SPRITE (Signal Processing In The Element) with cooling provided by Stirling Cycle Cryogenics. As a reconnaissance system, the GR.1A remains a world-leader. When it entered service in 1989 it was the

world's first filmless reconnaissance aircraft, thanks to its revolutionary infra-red/video system.

Fourteen GR.1As were initially converted from standard models by BAe. The modifications involved removing the two 27mm cannons and installing the sensors, recording equipment and the cockpit controls that integrated the reconnaissance system into the backseater's station. A further sixteen were built as GR.1As from new (two from Batch 5 and fourteen from Batch 7), the reconnaissance system integration being performed this time by the RAF's No.431 MU at RAF Brüggen. A single 'PINST' aircraft, ZA402, was delivered

A 'hard copy' from the TIRRS system showing a rail-over-river bridge.
via No.II (AC) Squadron

to BAe Warton for development work in June 1984, and made its maiden flight as a fledgling GR.1A on 11 July 1985. Trials of the intended sensor package were undertaken in autumn 1985, and this was followed by twelve aircraft from Batch 4 being converted. It is also worth noting that only two new-build aircraft received by the RAF from Batch 5, ZD996 and ZE116, were GR.1As, the rest of the batch being diverted to the Saudi order as GR.1s. The aircraft were initially provided only with the structure to make them GR.1As, complete with the underfuselage fairing, but not the tinted side windows. ZA402 remained with BAe, the other aircraft being issued to the Brüggen and Laarbruch wings commencing in April 1997, whilst others spent a brief time at the TTTE.

The most obvious advantage of the Tornado's IR system is its complete disregard for ambient light. IR systems are just as effective at night as they are in daylight, and are much less affected by weather conditions. An IR picture can reveal far more than a 'light' picture can, providing the interpreter is fully versed in the relatively new skill of IR imagery exploitation. There are, of course, disadvantages to the system. In its primary use at low level, it puts the carrier at a tactical disadvantage in some scenarios, and its resolution is nowhere near as sharp as a wet-film process. However, the ability to view imagery without the need for film processing outweighs the reduction in the quality over a picture-based system. Although less impaired by weather conditions than

light cameras, IR systems do suffer some loss of quality in heavy moisture conditions and at certain times of day. Despite these drawbacks, the overwhelming advantage of the Tornado's IR/video system is the speed with which gathered imagery can be processed into usable intelligence, which can be a huge tactical advantage.

At the heart of the aircraft's abilities is the 'TIRRS' (Tornado Infra-Red Reconnaissance System), which consists of three sensors, recording equipment and cockpit controls. The primary sensor is the Vinten Type 4000 IRLS (Infra-Red Line Scan), mounted in a blister on the underside of the fuselage. This is a panoramic sensor with horizon-to-horizon coverage, operating in the 8- to 14-

micron waveband. Its 'window' is a slit aperture in the underside, which has an air baffle and a protective cover when not in use. Complimenting the IRLS are two SLIR (Side Looking Infra-Red) sensors which look sideways from either side of the forward fuselage. Each sensor has a dull brick-coloured 'window', which is in effect a glass sandwich with thorium fluoride inside to aid image enhancement. The SLIRs have a field of view from the horizon down to 10-degree depression, and are used to fill in the image close to the horizon in better detail than is possible with IRLS. A recent modification to SLIR now allows the sensors to be further depressed, giving a coverage of +4 degrees to –14 degrees from the horizon, though this extra depression can only be selected on the ground prior to take-off. The SLIRs are also roll-stabilized, so that they remain looking at the horizon when the aircraft banks.

Imagery is produced by an EO (electro-optical) backplate which is made up of thousands of CCDs (Charge-Coupled Devices). Lenses focus the heat energy onto the EO plate, and each CCD is then energized to a greater or lesser degree according to the amount of energy striking it. This creates a digital electric signal, which is handled by a Computing Devices Ltd recording system and transferred to analogue video tape in real time. These tapes are essentially the same as standard E-180 household VHS tapes, but run at three times the speed for better definition. Each holds sixty minutes of imagery, and this imagery can also be viewed on one of the navigator's 625-line TV tab screens in the rear cockpit.

The video tapes and recorders are numbered from 1–6, and each has a specific function: No.1 is the primary recording tape for the IRLS; No.2 the primary for the left-hand SLIR; and No.3 the primary for the right-hand SLIR. No.4 is the back-up tape for the first three, though the first ten minutes can also be in-flight editing; No.5 is the back-up for the left SLIR; and No. 6 has a similar job for the starboard SLIR and also has ten minutes of editing time available.

In addition to the TIRRS, the GR.1A can carry a Vicon 18 Series 601 podded sensor system in situations where low-level operations are precluded, rendering the TIRRS virtually useless. Manufactured by Vinten Ltd, the GP.1

pod is a medium-altitude, wet-film, day-time system. It contains as its primary sensor a 690 LOROP camera, shooting on to film. The main 450mm lens mounted longitudinally within a 45-degree mirror at the front reflecting through 90 degrees into the camera. The main sensor window is mounted in the pod's nose cone, which allows the camera to rotate at any angle, including vertically down. In the rear of the pod is a smaller panoramic camera which provides accurate orientation of the LOROP pod's image; it has a 3in lens and uses 70mm film.

A groundcrewman inserts the video cassettes into the aircraft's recorders. The video tapes and recorders are numbered from 1–6, and each has a specific function. Author

Photographic Interpretation

For faster analysis of the imagery, the navigator uses the system to produce an edited mission tape. This task is usually undertaken whilst the aircraft is on its return journey, so the edited tape is available immediately on return to base. This tape is used to mark events which are then recorded across to the back-up tapes, and is collected by the PIs back on the base. The PIs use their specialist ground systems to interrogate and analyze the tapes in their specially equipped RICs. The initial ground interpretation equipment was installed at Laarbruch and Honington, intended for work in-situ, and each containing several IAWs (Imagery Analysis Workstations), but with the ending of the Cold War, and the need to take the RICs anywhere in the world

came the introduction of portable EIAW (Enhanced Imagery Analysis Workstation), which is of modular construction, and a number of these units entered service in 1997. The EIAW takes two hours to strike down and around three hours to set-up. Under NATO rules the PIs must have their initial report ready within forty-five minutes, and a more detailed study available within hours. This account is then briefed over secure line to the controlling agency and the 'hard-copy' is whisked away to arrive at GHQ 'almost immediately'. The PIs combine both verbal and written comments from the crews with the actual video imagery to produce these findings, and on training sorties the results are posted on the crew-room notice board – a sobering thought for an careless team!

GR.1A Details and Mission

Located in the rear cockpit of the GR.1A is the 'control centre' for the reconnaissance system, operated by the navigator, who could be better described by the Americanism of 'Wizzo', or Weapons Systems Officer. The backseater's office is centred around the radar and navigation systems, with its two TV tabulator displays and the circular radar/moving-map display. The TV tabs have a number of 'soft key' function pads, and these keys change in their notation depending upon which 'page' is being displayed on the TV tab. The two TV tabs are the link between the navigator and the main computer, and these have three basic formats. 'Plan' format displays the overall mission, with the various waypoints being shown as letters 'A', 'B', 'C', and so on. Fixed points are indicated by a number '1', '2', '3', and targets by letters 'X', 'Y', 'Z'. The aircraft's current position is displayed as a small circle which is overlaid with a latitude and longitude. The 'Nav' format shows the aircraft's position at centre screen, surrounded by a circle through which is placed a vertical line representing the current track. Information such as the next waypoint can also be seen on this display. The third format is 'Fix/attack', which represents a bird's-eye view of the aircraft's position relative to the planned target, which enables the navigator to compare his radar picture with this simplified image, allowing him better to

assess the situation at a glance. There is a fourth format, 'Recce', which displays the sensor's view on the backseater's left-hand TV tab. At front left is the reconnaissance control panel, unique to the GR.lA, and this generates a number of 'windows' on the TV tab, and controls the VCRs and sensors.

The rear left-hand side of the cockpit contains the air filter for the AR5 respirator system, and also contains the switches for the lighting and the Secondary Attitude Reference System, the SARS, which forms part of the INS. Also situated in this section is the cockpit voice recorder, which is also used to load the route information into the main computer via the cassette tape. In front of the navigator and to his right-hand side are the chaff/flare controls and the RHWR, and along the bottom line of the centre console is the navigation mode selector, steering selector and height sensor selector. Directly above these can be

found the CMPRD and above that an altimeter, air speed indicator and angle-of-attack indicator. Below these and to the left are an artificial horizon and weapons control panel No.1, the pilot having panel No.2 in the front seat.

Planning and execution of any GR.1A reconnaissance mission is no different to the preparation that goes into a GR.1 'attack' mission, and No.II (AC) Squadron were more than happy to explain to the author the virtues of their ultra-capable machine. Flt Lt Rick Haley explained:

I think one of the most important points is the real-time capablity of the Tornado. The navigator can actually look at the pictures in the rear cockpit as he flies over the target, possibly even doing a de-brief on the flight back to base. Added to the bad weather capability, it's quite an improvement over the Jaguar, which we flew previously.

Before the arrival of the Tornado reconnaissance kit, we had been confined to flying just

A No.II (AC) Squadron Tornado GR.1A outside its HAS at RAF Laarbruch, before the unit moved to Marham. Author

'Visreps' – visual reconnaissance sorties – whereas now we have a video film-confirmed Visrep, which is of much greater value to the forces on the ground.

We get good images which we can blow up in size and use for whatever purposes are necessary. We have two SLIRs and IRLS for the vertical view, so for example, if we wanted to look at a radio mast we would stand off to one side and use the SLIR, and if it was perhaps the positioning of some enemy vehicles, we would use the IRLS and go straight over the top. So in effect we have full horizon-to-horizon coverage. The Tornado GR.IA has an impressive night reconnaissance capability too. Thanks to an excellent Terrain Following Radar, Ground Mapping Radar and reliable navigational system accuracy, it is theoretically possible for the Tornado to fly automatically (after take-off), locate the target, record the appropriate reconnaissance details and return to base completely 'hands-off'. Back in the days of the Jaguar, there was no TFR, no GMR and only a limited night capability. The single-seat concept also meant that the pilot had to fly the aircraft, navigate accurately and monitor all of the on-board systems. With the two-man Tornado, the pilot can keep his concentration on flying the aircraft, avoiding the ground, and keeping a better lookout for marauding fighters and missiles.

The navigator divides his time between a number of tasks. Lookout is vitally important, monitoring the RHWR and maintaining a visual search for aircraft. Operation of the Sky Shadow ECM pod and the Swedish-designed BOZ-107 chaff-flare dispenser, together with continual monitering of the fuel state and navigation kit (occasional update inputs) may be necessary. He must also advise the pilot of turn directions, target data, speed changes, terrain information and possible threats.

Normal fuel load is quoted in various publications as being 8,600kg, giving a typical flight time of around an hour and forty-five minutes or two hours, depending on the weather and required landing fuel.

Occasionally we fly high-low-high sorties to the UK, not as often as the strike squadrons, as there's only a limited number of suitable reconnaissance targets in the UK and there are many more targets of training value over here in Germany. There's lots more kit to see, lots more of interest. However, if the weather dictates that the UK is a good choice we'll go over there. Sometimes we land in the UK too, re-fuel, and fly another low-level sortie before making a high-level transit back to Laarbruch. Some of our pilots are tanker-qualified too, so we have the option of aerial refuelling.

Take-off speed is about 155kt with our usual fit of external fuel tanks. You can expect to leave the runway somewhere beteeen 170–180kt. The actual speed would obviously depend on temperature and aircraft configuration. Cruise speed is 420kt, which is really a speed limit imposed by the German low flying system. We would accelerate on the IP-to-target runs, to give us better simulation of a realistic speed, as obviously we would like to go through high-threat areas a little faster, to give us a little more energy to combat any fighters, and to give the guys firing missiles a harder time. 420kt is a good speed for us to fly our route, as it gives us a convenient seven-miles-a-minute that the navigator can mark on his maps, and 480kt obviously gives eight-miles-per-minute, which is a good speed for our target run. Landing speed is going to be about 160kt, and we're limited by our Alpha – angle-of-attack – on landing, because of the danger of scraping the fin on the external fuel tanks under the fuselage. It's basically ten units of AOA on approach, increasing to twelve units, increasing to fourteen, possibly even going up to between sixteen and eighteen units on the runway for aerodynamic braking, before using the thrust reversers. So we fly a fairly flat approach and use the buckets – the thrust reversers – on touchdown. Speed is variable upon weight, and if we had a problem with hydraulics, maybe the wings could be stuck back at 45 or 67 degrees, in which case the landing speed would increase greatly, up to 220–230kt.

Operational flying height is in reality just 100ft, and the kit has been shown to work well at that height. Maintaining that height in a two-man jet is really quite easy and, providing the navigator has full confidence in the pilot, he can have his eyes peering out of the cockpit almost all of the time on lookout. With a two-man crew, navigation is really a very minor part of the job, and with the guy up front flying the aircraft, the chap at the back can be looking for a threat coming. I think that perhaps it takes longer for the navigator to get used to flying at 100ft, trusting the pilot, than it does for the pilot to get used to actually flying the aircraft at that height. In the UK the Tornado crews are permitted to fly (outside of restricted areas) down to a minimum height of 250ft, with a small number of designated areas where the aircraft can descend to just 100ft (naturally such flying is conducted over sparsely populated countryside, and these areas may soon be withdrawn). In Germany however, a combination of flying accidents, airspace congestion and political will has dictated a more restricted environment, with a base limit of 1000ft in force. In the Netherlands the restrictions are equally tight, with a minimum height of 1000ft being applied to military training. Naturally, when a realistic operational height is just 100ft, these peacetime restrictions prevent the Tornado crews from maintaining a regular degree of practice, at the more realistic heights, more often, which is why the RAF has elected to spend more time training its crews at Goose Bay in Canada where the restrictions are almost nil.

A typical training sortie starts in the planning room, part of No.II (AC) Squadron's bomb-proof Pilot Briefing Facility, the nerve centre where day-to-day operations are planned and controlled, and where the aircrew would shelter between sorties, during exercises or wartime conditions. Normal training missions usually include five targets, and although occasional bombing attack missions are flown as pairs or four-ships (the squadron also has a bombing capability), reconnaissance sorties are flown by single aircraft. The pilot and navigator will plot the locations of the pre-determined targets (chosen from a library of suitable locations by another member of the squadron) on 1:50,000 scale Ordnance Survey maps. Consideration is given to lighting conditions (the sun's position can be important in visually locating a target), local terrain and possible threats. Daily Notams (Notices to Airmen) are also taken into account and, with all avoidance areas, towns, restricted areas and other features noted appropriately, the navigator will draw up a suitable route, linking the targets. Weather conditions and endurance (fuel state) is also accounted for when determining the route, which is drawn up on a 'half-mil' [1:50,000] map. Once the route is established, the navigator takes his map to the CPGS and places it on a magnetic table. By feeding-in the location of Laarbruch and the aircraft's HAS plus other known reference features, the electronic sensor system built into the CPGS will automatically record the latitude and longitude of each target, by simply 'walking' an electronic cursor around the route, inserting targets as appropriate. This information is then fed into a cassette tape, which is later down-loaded into the aircraft's computer.

Good planning is essential and we have to look carefully at our positioning, in order to get the best view of the target. With bridges you usually have to fly about a hundred yards offset and fly along the line of the bridge to get the perfect picture which the photographic interpreter needs. In most cases an offset position is desirable, as it gives the crew a chance to visually examine the target, and if the recce

Inside its HAS a newly delivered GR.1A belonging to No.13 Squadron is prepared for flight. Note the absence of the SLIR windows, as the aircraft still awaits its full 'recce-fit'. Author

system should fail you at least have a visual backup. If you go straight over the top of the target it would be difficult for the crew to give a visual report as the downward view is obviously very limited from the cockpit. Targets are categorized from a choice of seventeen, ranging from airfields to industrial facilities. The task will identify the target category and it is the crew's mission to successfully obtain the best imagery and visual report possible on the target. A record of the planned route will be recorded and if the flight extends outside of West German airspace a full flight plan is filed. After a few final checks and authorization notes, the crew are ready to 'walk', collecting their lifejackets, G-pants, gloves and helmets en route.

Once inside the HAS, the Tornado will already be fed with external power supply, and the on-board INS will be aligning with the HAS co-ordinates. A check of the '700' servicing record, and the pilot signs for his aircraft, before conducting a walk-round external check. The navigator climbs aboard and straps in, getting the INS and the recce equipment

going, while the pilot checks the exterior of the aircraft for fuel or oil leaks, removing safety locking pins and so on. The pilot then straps in and starts the auxiliary power unit, which is used to fire up the main engines. The starboard engine is started first and the computer then conducts a BITE check on the aircraft systems, flying control surfaces, inlet controls and so on. As No.II (AC) Squadron's aircraft regularly fly with externally mounted stores, a careful check of the computerized stores management system is made, so that the external fuel tanks and ECM pods can be quickly jettisoned if a problem develops during take-off. Once the computer is satisfied that everything is functioning correctly, the aircraft is ready to roll: the crew will continually talk to each other during start-up, cross-checking each stage of the sequence. The navigator will put a casette into the cockpit voice recorder, load the route into the main computer, check the details have gone in properly, do a map-follow, making sure turning point and target details are in correctly, the recce kit is started up, INS is already aligned and the secondary attitude and

heading reference system, another gyro platform, is started up. Doppler is switched on, also the laser, in case we do any targetting with it, plus a few other items. Both engines are running, hydraulics are checked, fuel and electrics, and we're ready to go.

The ground crew will ensure that all external panels are closed and all the safety pins removed, confirm correct and positive movement of the flying controls and, following a flash of the nosewheel landing light, the aircraft is marshalled out of the HAS onto the taxiway. In Laarbruch's first-generation HASs there is only minimal wingtip clearance for the Tornado's wingtips, and emerging from the HAS is a tricky business. The ejection seat safety pins are removed – they get left in before we emerge as we don't want to accidentally eject into the HAS roof – and a series of pre-take-off checks are performed whilst heading for the runway:

Navigator: Pilot
Wing sweep: 25 degrees
Airbrakes: In and locked
Flaps: Mid position

Trims: Set for take-off

Cross-drive clutch:Auto lightout

Emergency Jettison: Emergency Jettison selected (front cockpit); Wing external tank selected (rear cockpit).

Flight Controls: Full and free movement

Hydraulics: Left on, right automatic; both with correct pressure

Emergency power system:Auto Position

Fuel:Check contents both cockpits; Check fin is feeding

Ignition: Normal selected

Oxygen: Check breathing, contents, flow; Check 100 per cent flow

Intake anti-icing: Auto

External lights: All functioning

Command eject systems: Both seats selected

Canopy: Closed and locked, caption light out

Safety pins: Removed and stowed

Take-off emergency brief: Abort for AC/DC red caption, burner-blow-out, or engine failure; select thrust reverse over-ride; if airborne, both engines in combat power, ensuring landing gear is retracting; if handling becomes difficult, call navigator to jettison external stores; if it is still impractical to stay with the aircraft, call 'Eject,

Eject' and the navigator will take both crew out.

The crew talk to the airfield control tower to confirm that they are taxying, and obtain wind speed and direction details, altimeter pressure settings, and the runway direction in use. After reaching the holding point, just short of the runway threshold, the crew call up the tower and request permission to line up on the runway and take off. Once on the runway some final checks are performed:

Navigator: Pilot

Air system master: Emergency ram air selected

Rapid Take-off panel: Gang bar up, all switches selected

Harnesses: Tight and locked, visors down

IFF:Normal peacetime squawk selected; others selected as required

Landing lights: On

Weapons control panel: Last check, no faults

Master arm selection switch: Live

The pilot ensures that the thrust reversers indication lights are out and that low-response nosewheel steering is selected. The engines are run-up against the brakes, a check of the instruments, more power-up to maximum dry power, check that the afterburners are functioning,

and the brakes are released. Rolling down the runway looking for 100kt airspeed, the navigator checks the speed to ensure that front and back cockpit readouts are the same. At 155kt the control column is moved backwards and the nose starts to rise, and the Tornado is airborne. Once into the air the landing gear is selected up, and at 225kt the flaps are retracted. At 250kt the reheat is cancelled, the master arm switch is set to standby, and the air conditioning is switched on (for take-off the system is off, to give slightly greater engine thrust). At 350kt the wings are swept back to 45 degrees. The navigator continually talks to the control tower, on their approach frequency, advising them of the Tornado's departure, as the pilot brings the terrain-following radar into life. Once TFR is selected, the Tornado is effectively flying automatically, while the navigator continually checks the system for performance and accuracy.

No.II (AC) Squadron almost always fly to the first planned target using automatic TFR, simulating IFC (Instrument Flying Conditions):

In addition to the TIRRS, the GR.1A can carry a Vicon 18 Series 601 podded sensor. Gary Parsons f4 Aviation

A No.II (AC) Squadron GR.1A replendent in the latest LIR grey colour scheme at low level. Formed during World War One, No.II (Army Co-operation) Squadron has a long tradition in the reconnaissance role. Rick Brewell

This way the pilot can leave the aircraft to fly itself to the first target, and check that everything is working okay, monitoring and checking from cockpit-to-cockpit and keeping a good lookout.

After locating the first target the Tornado is flown hands-on with TFR de-selected:

For the next target we might aim for an offset position so that the pilot can see the object we're aiming for. The navigator will hit the freeze button on the reconnaissance display as we go past the target, and as we come off the target the navigator will say what he sees on his TV screen and the pilot will say what he sees, coming-up with a fairly accurate Vis-rep, a visual report. With bridges and such we have to fly at about a hundred yards offset and fly a line to get that perfect image that the PI needs. It also gives the crew the chance to visually examine the target, backing up with the 'Mk1

eyeball', should the recce kit fail. Targets are categorized from a choice of seventeen, ranging from airfields to industrial facilities, and in addition to normal flying training recce crews are also heavily involved in developing their recognition skill in terms of enemy armour.

Typically then for recce'ing a bridge – and in order to obtain the best position – the aircraft would be 'stepped down' to a lower altitude in order for the crew to get a better look and allow the sensors the best chance of obtaining a good image. Although the recce system can be pre-programmed to start at a set point in the mission, the GR.1A backseaters like to switch on the kit well in advance of the target. Accelerating to around 480kt, the navigator will confirm that all the systems are functioning and the aircraft will fly an offset pattern along the outside of the bridge, using the SLIR to record imagery as they fly along and also using the IRLS to 'look inside' the spans as the pilot applies bank.

'On track', is the comment from the back.

'Kits running ... good mark ... speed OK', and in the distance as the pilot sights the target he begins to describe what he sees as the aircraft sweep's past:

'Confirm taking down the left-hand side', announces the pilot.

'Banking ... now!'

As soon as the navigator sees the bank begin come on it is heads out. The general rule of thumb is that the pilot describes the top sections and the navigator looks at what is below. The navigator hits the 'freeze' button on the recce display as they go past, so that they have a picture of the bridge to refer to as they come off the target.

'Beam and deck ... four spans ... steel construction ... concrete base', comments the navigator.

Its composition is duly noted, as are any defences or activity around it, and any alternate crossings within 200m. The imagery is captured on tape, and described in both written and verbal format by the crew. It may be that the navigator will be required to transmit an 'If-Rep' (In-Flight Report) back to their controlling agency, using a coded format, in which case a quick review of the tape is in order as the aircraft speeds to its next location. If there's some confusion, the navigator can select 'replay', have another look and undertake some discussion with the pilot. So a great deal of the real interpretation is now done in the air. Then we would try to produce an in-flight report. The content of the report will be the target, time over target, type of target, status of the target, activity at the target, defences in the area and some coded formats we use. We would normally do this kind of report for one of the five targets on our training sortie.

The Tornado GR.1A carries six VCRs, three primary and three 'nav' VCRs. The latter three are used as back-up machines and also to allow the navigator to re-run recorded data while the primaries are still recording. One of the nav VCRs will also be used to create a final edit tape, containing all the useful recorded information from the sortie. This tape will be given to the photographic interpreters together with the visual reports, after landing. Another of the planned targets may be located without the use of the Tornado's high-tech systems. Assuming that the equipment has broken down, the crew will use their maps and 'traditional' navigation techniques to locate the target. After successfully completing the reconnaissance aims of the sortie, additional tasks can include a visit to a bombing range to drop practice bombs. Coming back to Laarbruch, the pre-recovery checks are performed. The wing sweep position is checked, the instruments are confirmed as being properly erected (head-up and head-down displays), and the radio altimeter is re-set to zero; the radalt can be a bit of an annoyance, as while we're flying around we have it set to safety height which in Germany is 1000ft, so if we touch or go below that height, we get an audio warning. We do take great care about height as it's a very sensitive matter in Germany. When we're coming back into Laarbruch however, we reset it to zero to stop it annoying us as we approach the runway. The RHWR is switched off, as it would be another noisy distraction during landing. In bad weather the intake anti-icing and cockpit de-mist systems are selected on, and the navigator will call up the approach frequency and advise the controller that the Tornado is roughly twenty miles from base.

The approach controller will advise the crew on weather conditions, dictating a visual or radar-guided approach to the runway. For a normal good-weather visual recovery the aircraft returns at 400kt, at 1000ft, with a 25-degree wing sweep (fully forward, normal cruising position being the mid-sweep 45-degree setting). At about three miles from Laarbruch the pilot will call 'initials' to the tower, and providing the call is confirmed by the tower, the next call is on the left-hand break over the airfield, requesting permission to land or 'roll' (touchdown and take-off). We will pitch into the break roughly in line with the runway threshold. Turning downwind we check that the wings are fully forward, airbrakes are in and locked, check fuel state which dictates our landing speed, flaps at mid position, and that the Spin Prevention and Incidence Limiting System is off. The SPILS is an automatic safety device, but in this critical part of the flight it is de-selected, in case we need to pull that little bit more angle-of-attack if we have some sort of problem. We don't want to have that in our

No.II (AC) Squadron's 'Wake Knot' marking. Author

A brace of No.II (AC) reconnaissance jets bank over as they prepare for landing back at Laarbruch. Author

way. Make sure the arrestor hook light is out, as it could be a little embarrassing if we arrived with the hook down and caught the arrestor barrier.

Navigator: 'Check the harnesses are tight and locked, select gear down and look for three greens indicated, and check brake pressures.'

After touchdown, the navigator checks that the lift-dump spoilers are all deployed, the nosewheel is slowly lowered, and the thrust reversers are activated. At 50kt the reverse has to set to idle, in order to avoid reingesting the hot exhaust gases into the engine. Turning off the runway the pre-shut-down checks are performed, these being essentially a reverse reading of the pre-take-off checks: we will have called the squadron operations room while we were airborne to tell them that we were inbound, and once off the runway we call them again to tell them our servicablity state, so that they can have the apppropriate equipment waiting for us back at the shelter. If we haven't been able to issue an in-flight report whilst

actually in the air, we could do that while we're taxying back to the HAS. Radar and the majority of on-board systems are switched off, before being marshalled back into position, facing forward in front of the HAS doors.

The ground crew will hook-up an RT cable to the aircraft so that any problems can be discussed, while the VCR tapes are unloaded and taken to the photographic interpreters, the Tornado's engines still running. Once cleared to shut-down, the engine power is cut, the arrestor hook is lowered and attached to the HAS winch cable, and the Tornado is slowly pulled back into its protective shelter. Once inside, the chocks are placed under the wheels, brake pressure is released, safety pins are all checked as being in the safe positions, and the crew climbs out. We fill in the 700 form and because the reconnaissance kit is relatively new, we fill out forms to describe how well the equipment performed, as at this stage we're still very interested in how it performs on a day-to-day basis. After discussing any problems we might have had with the aircraft with the

approriate tradesman, we then go to the Aircrew Reconnaissance Facility to begin what is really the most important part of the mission.

Inside the ARF we discuss our visual reports with the photographic interpreters and, depending on the sortie, this can take maybe forty-five minutes or more. We'll write out our reports, and at present we often have an aircraft out over the target with a normal hand-held camera to take normal photographs before the infra-red equipment arrives. The PIs will then take the photographic imagery and the infra-red imagery, and take our visual reports and mark them, and the next morning they will be up on the wall at the weather brief, so it's a sobering thought. Your report will be up there right next to a photograph. Obviously our visual reports are very important, helping the PIs to interpret the infra-red imagery they have before them. We also make a verbal report onto the cockpit voice recorder tape, and this is also given to the PIs so they can use this to help interpret the combined information.

The report has to be off-station to the appropriate HQ no later than forty-five minutes from tape down-load. Speed is of the essence. Time is a vitally important factor in No.2 Squadron's operations, and life at Laarbruch is no nine-to-five routine: the job is a difficult and dangerous one and the crews, hard-working professionals. The aircraft is a superb reconnaissance platform – a very capable machine indeed.

RAF Tornado Reonnaissance Units

No.II (AC) Squadron 'Hereward'

Formed during the World War One, No.II (Army Co-operation) Squadron has a long tradition in the reconnaissance role. More recent times have seen the unit based in Germany flying the F-4 Phantom and the Jaguar, both carrying podded reconnaissance equipment. The unit's first Tornado GR.1As began to arrive in 1989, albeit without the neccessary reconnaissance kit installed. The unit moved to its current home at RAF Marham from RAF Laarbruch during December 1991. The unit is allocated the HA–HZ code sequence, but have never worn them, choosing instead to carry code letters that spell out 'SHINY TWO ER AC U', with the squadron's twin-stickers being coded II and IV.

The unit originally carried the traditional grey/green overland camouflage scheme, punctuated by the odd ARTF finish of white covering the grey for Arctic operations in Norway. Currently, the aircraft wear the latest LIR Medium Sea Grey scheme. The 'Wake Knot' can be found on a white circle on a black rectangle flanked by white triangles on the nose, repeated on the fin tip.

No.13 Squadron

Adjuvamus Tuendo – 'We assist by watching'

This was the last of the Tornado squadrons formed in the RAF, and equipped with new-build Batch 7 aircraft. No.13 Squadron officially re-formed on 1 January 1990, and was declared operational in the January of 1991 at RAF Honington; it moved to RAF Marham on 1 February 1994. Its aircraft carry the code

Seen here in its 'high-vis' state, No.13 Squadron's nose markings in glorious green, yellow and blue. Author

range KA–KZ, although the unit only carry a single letter on their tail fins.

Grey and Green tactical has now given way to LIR Grey, and the flamboyant markings of green and blue shot through with a yellow lightning flash are very welcome. The tail fin is adorned with a shield carrying a Lynx's head flanked by a yellow and blue band across the RWR. Like its sister unit, No.13 Squadron have had occasion to paint their aircraft in arctic garb for cold weather operations.

Tornado GR.4A

The MLU for the Tornado (described on page 00) will also result in the current GR.1As becoming GR.4As. In the near future the GR.4As will receive the RAP-TOR/EO LOROP pods, in addition to the undernose FLIR and cockpit modifications. The second aircraft to undergo the MLU upgrade, ZA371, was delivered to BAe on 3 June 1996, eventually returning to service with No.13 Squadron at Honington in mid-1998.

Gulf War - 'The Scud Busters'

Following the invasion of Kuwait, Nos II and 13 Squadrons, at Laarbruch and Honington respectively, were informed that the need had arisen for them to deploy their nearly-new specialized reconnaissance equipment to the Gulf. Ground technicians were given time to fine-tune the aircrafts' sensitive equipment and bring the GR.1As up to Granby modification state to meet the demands of combat conditions. Wg Cdr Al Threadgould, the OC of No.II (AC) and the RAF Recce Detachment Commander Squadron takes up the story:

We arrived at Dahrhan a mere two days before hostilities broke out. The deployment was delayed for many reasons until the last moment, and so we arrived with three aircraft on the 14th, three more on the 15th as the war began in the early hours of the 17th! So for most of us our first taste of recce flying in the region was an operational sortie into Iraq, with no desert training at all. This is a testament to the high level of training proficiency we maintained in our European operations.

The 'Recce Det' left for the Gulf during the hours of darkness on 13 January,

Now in LIR grey, No.13 Squadron's aircraft have lost their colourful RWR tail markings, but retained their Lynx emblem. Gary Parsons f4 Aviation

with Wg Cdr Threadgould leading the Laarbruch contingent, and Wg Cdr Glenn Torpy the Honington contingent. A Hercules transport ferried out all the neccessary ground and support crews as well as an Air Portable Reconnaissance Interpretation Centre and its associated PIs and specialist technicians.

The six GR.1As were all drawn from No.II (AC) Squadron, with that squadron providing six crews and No.13 Squadron four. The aircraft carried the 'pink panther' scheme, and little else in the way of markings. In-theatre the aircraft received a pair of 495gal 'Hindenburger' wing tanks; they also carried two 330gal tanks on their underfuselage shoulder pylons. For self defence the Sky Shadow and BOZ-107 pods were carried on the outer wing stations, and as all of their missions were to be nocturnal, the aircraft dispensed with the usual AIM-9 AAMs; as one pilot later commented:

Lets face it, someone in an Iraqi fighter would have to be pretty brave to try to engage us at max dry power, flying at 200ft or below in the pitch black of a desert night!

Wg Cdr Threadgould continues:

The tasks we undertook fell into four basic areas, in no order of importance: 'route searches', 'BDA assessment', 'FBA searches' for the US Army's forward planners, as well as the 'anti-Scud' missions. Our first sorties in fact saw us on 'Scud-Hunts', and these assignments above all others attracted the most media interest. We were given the positions where the Scud missiles were likely to be, and we would then fly a search pattern along the latitude/longitude lines, seeking out targets. In fact on our first night out, after my aircraft developed a fuel feed problem causing an abort, Sqn Ldr (now Wg Cdr and the current 'Boss' of No.II (AC) Squadron) Dick Garwood and Sqn Ldr Jon Hill, flying ZA400 in the company of Flt Lt Brian Robinson and Flt Lt Gordon Walker of No.13 Squadron in ZA371, found a Scud missile on its launcher, and their images really put recce on the map. Sadly there were insufficient strike assets available in the area to 'take-down' the site, and the Scud went unmolested.

The missions we undertook for the US forces were specifically tailored for the 82nd Airborne Division, designed for when they made their important push through the tri-border area at the beginning of the ground war. We provided them with superb imagery on video of the terrain and obstacles in their path. We were told that their helo pilots sat watching our tapes with their leg maps unfurled marking areas of interest to them! Indeed the commanders of the 82nd Airborne agreed, 'The GR.1A was awesome!' Some of the ultimate missions we undertook were the 'route searches', tracking the Iraqi Army as they retreated from Kuwait, and these were amongst the most interestingof our trips, as the Iraqi's still had plenty of firepower. The final sorties picked out targets leading into the now infamous carnage near Basra that closed out the war.

Sgt Kev Knight, one of No.II (AC) Squadron's PIs, explained:

In general the ground support kit performed very well. Once we had our four workstations set up and running it all went OK, although it was pretty hot inside the Portakabins that we had to work inside. Once the recce missions were down and we got hold of the mission video tapes, we split them into the various sensors and produced our initial report inside the 45-minute time slot. Important targets were passed to Command HQ, and we would then go back over the tapes again for another four hours until the next mission came in – and the process would begin all over again. Sometimes, however, it was a long and tiring shift.

Sgt Steve Cox, an Avionics Technician with No.II (AC) Squadron, recalls:

The number of sorties we flew far exceeded our expectations, but the aircraft held up beautifully. In peacetime you can often fly the aircraft with one or two components not serviceable with little effect on the overall sortie; however, in a combat situation everything had to be perfect and 100 per cent. The biggest worry right from day one was sand ingestion into the engines and the sensitive recce equipment, but as it turned out all the systems functioned normally despite the low flying over the desert.

Wg Cdr Threadgould continues:

Overall the GR.1A worked extremely well, considering the newness of its systems. The TFR autopilot was superb, and I was happy to let it fly the aircraft more than I thought I would be, considering we were hitting 200ft at 550kt at night. The recce kit also performed well, and indeed surpassed our expectations. It produced some outstanding results across the board and gathered an enormous amount of information. We were happy to go in a low level when everyone else was going medium to high, and we were able to get in and out of an area most times before we were seen. During our 82nd Airborne sorties we did not bring back many 'target pictures', which was exactly what the Americans wanted to see, so when their push forward came they were able to go through the lines of least resistance.

One of the busiest crews of the Recce Det were No.II (AC)'s Flt Lt Rick Haley and Flt Lt Angus Hogg. Together they flew seventeen missions, and clocked up the longest Tornado IDS sortie of the war with a 4½-hour mission. Rick Haley describes a typical trip:

We would arrive for work at 3pm or 9pm in two groups, generally working 12-hour shifts. As the Lead Crew for the shift we would divide up the night's tasks and Intel would then brief us on our mission and our objectives. The navs would then get together and plan out the trips, and then we would study the targets, co-ordinate tankers if neccessary, and plan out the entire flight in terms of fuel, headings and allocation of targets. Each aircraft would have a call-sign, such as 'Fiesta One Four', 'Fiesta One Three' and so on. We planned a normal two-ship mission with a third aircraft being fully prepared as a back-up. The route was carefully planned in terms of avoiding enemy defences and other Allied activity in the region, and the premium position to get the best view of the target. We would then feed the mission plan into the CPGS and produce a cassette tape to feed into the aircraft's systems. Then it was an escape and evasion brief, out-brief, pick up our NBC kit and 'walk' an hour before take off. To say 'walk' is a slight exaggeration, as Dhahran Air Base is massive, and our aircraft were some five miles from the crew room! We toted our NBC kit and gas masks out to the aircraft in our transport, and when we got to the jets all three would already be fired up, their nav systems aligned and ready for us to 'crew-in'. As we were the evening's Lead Crew we would lead the flight on the long haul to the main runway. Take-off was in echelon, with a ten-second spacing. Once airborne we would switch to Dhahran approach frequency and contact AWACS and, if we needed to, one of the RAF's tankers, which was usually a No.101 Squadron VC-10. Once we were happy with the systems we clipped on our NVGs and called the 'spare' aircraft to turn for home. In the rear Angus ensured the nav and recce kit was OK and we make a quick check in with our number two aircraft, with Flt Lt Sam McLeod and Flt Lt Dave Knight aboard. Once all was in the groove we began our descent run. I'd engage the TFR at 2000ft and then step it down to 200ft as we crossed the border, whilst Angus was setting up the recce sensors and video recorders. Keeping a close watch on the RHWR scope for SAMs and radar-laid AAA indications, we sped across the desert, staying well separated, but in close contact for safety

One of No.13 Squadron's Tornado GR.4As, seen at the 1998 RIAT at RAF Fairford. Note the updated and reduced squadron markings and the FLIR fairing. Gary Parsons f4 Aviation

The so-called 'White Witch'. ZG729/M of No.13 Squadron, in an arctic scheme, emerges from its HAS. This particular jet was not 'quite dry' when the pilot hit the afterburners for take-off, and blobs of white paint later adorned your author! Author

reasons. A SAM-8 indication came up on the RHWR but at our speed we outran it and the indication died away. Angus used the IRLS whilst I used my NVGs to look at the first target run, which was an artery road, and keep it directly under the aircraft. I must admit that I found it amazing that the Iraqis were actually driving around with their headlights on, and they still had their towns fully lit, which was a great help to us. We also had a few moments when AAA came very close to the aircraft, and lit up the inside as it sped over our canopy, trying to track our noise. After around fifty minutes inside Iraq with our tasks completed, we turned and picked up our egress heading, keeping a keen eye on the map for any SAM sites. A quick check with Sam and Dave and AWACS, and we adopted a standard recovery route into Dhahran. During this phase Angus was reviewing the mission tapes, marking any important items to pass on to the PIs after we land. The landing was routine, and once the aircraft had been shut down and the PIs and intelligence guys have been briefed, it was off to the aircrew feeder for some steak and chips

and a climb into bed – just as the morning sun comes up over the desert.

Tornado LRV - Luftwaffe Reconnaissance Version

The ending of the Cold War gave the German Luftwaffe a surplus of Tornado IDS aircraft, and allowing the accelerated retirement of their specialized RF-4E reconnaissance Phantoms. Their replacements were to be specially-equipped Tornados, and Panavia was asked to submit options for six reconnaissance conversions of varying degrees of sophistication. Due to budgetary constraints a 'modest' conversion programme consisting of an external Aeritalia/MBB reconnaissance pod was installed for some forty ex-Marineflieger aircraft, mostly from MFG 1, was announced in 1994. These aircraft would then equip AKG 51 'Immelmann' which would take over the insignia and

traditions of AKG 52; at least nine of the ex-MFG-1 aircraft had HARM capabilities. The unit later gained a number of ex-Luftwaffe IDS aircraft and transferred the former Marineflieger aircraft to other units.

The 'modest' recce capability really was very modest, and the aircraft initially had only nine reconnaissance pods between them, although it was reported that some

An aggressive-looking MBB/Aeritalia reconnaissance pod fitted beneath a Luftwaffe LRV Tornado. Gary Parsons f4 Aviation

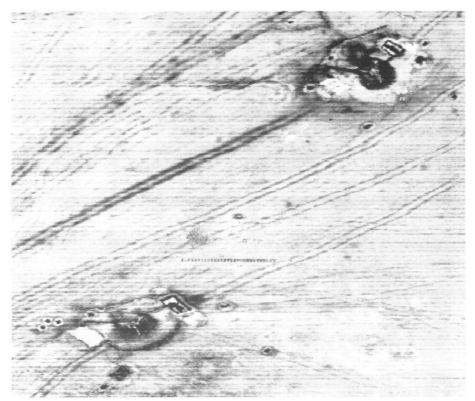

Iraqi emplacements, shown up by their thermal significance and anomalies discovered by the Tornados when the surface sand was disturbed. RAF

Wg Cdr Al Threadgould aboard one of No.2(AC) Squadron's reconnaissance jets prepares for another mission into Iraq. via Mike Tomlinson

GR.1A 'Scud Buster' Aircraft	
ZA370/A	25 Mission Symbols
ZA371/C	28 Mission Symbols
ZA372/E	14 mission symbols
ZA373/H	22 Mission Symbols
ZA397/O	
ZA400/T	
Mission Symbols in the shape of 'Palm Trees'	

thirty more were quickly obtained. The pod contained a pair of Zeiss optical wet film cameras and a Texas Instruments RS-170 IRLS. For the future, the reconnaissance role will be enhanced by a new pod which will carry two optical cameras, an IRLS, a data storage system and a BITE capability. This will give the navigator more control over the pod's functions and will also allow for the real-time gathering of data supported by a new air-to-ground data link. Although titled here as the 'LRV', these reconnaissance-equipped aircraft retain the IDS designation within the Luftwaffe.

Aufklärungsgeschwader 51 'Immelmann'

The original AKG 51 ceased operations from its Bremgarten base in March 1992, and following the retirement of its RF-4E Phantoms in late 1993, AKG 52 moved to Schleswig-Jagel, where it changed its designation to AKG 51, whilst retaining its own panther's head badge in place of AKG 51's owl insignia, and 511 Squadron's diving eagle . The unit then re-formed on the Tornado on 21 September 1993, taking

over the aircraft of MFG 1. Six AKG 51 aircraft formed the backbone of the German participation in Operation Deny Flight with Einsatzgeschwader 1 at Pincenza in Italy in August 1995. The aircraft originally wore standard Luftwaffe three-tone camouflage, but this has given way to a new light grey medium altitude finish.

Italian Reconnaissance

The Aeronautica Militare Italiano's 50° Stormo's 155° Gruppo are not only the AMI's recognized SEAD specialists, but also undertake a secondary reconnaissance committment using the Aeritalia/MBE underfuselage reconnaissance pod. Their

Al Threadgould and Tim Robinson prepare for a dusk into night mission. via Mike Tomlinson

High over the desert, having just taken on fuel, one of the 'Scud Busters' banks away and prepares to make a high-speed low level dash into Iraq. RAF

aircraft wear standard AMI camouflage with stylized blue fin flashes and unit badge on the aircraft's tail-fins.

Al Yamamah Recce - Saudi GR.1A

No.66 Squadron RSAF was the second Saudi Tornado squadron to form at Dhahran and was in the process of becoming established as the Gulf War broke out. No.66 Squadron were the recipients of the Al Yammamah I aircraft, which included four TIRRS-equipped reconnaissance machines, and operate a 'mix' of aircraft including standard IDS and twin-stick trainers. The unit is destined to move to Tabuk in the near future. The Saudi machines carry the most colourful of the current batch of Tornado camouflage schemes.

TIALD - Airborne Designation

'TIALD represents the very cutting edge of 'smart' electro-optical systems', explained Group Captain Bill Hedges, Commander of the RAF Detatchment Tabuk during a press briefing following the arrival of this latest laser designation system in the Gulf War. Unlike earlier generations of laser designators such as Pave Tack and Pave Spike, TIALD locks its laser automatically to its target even though the parent aircraft may be

manoevring to avoid SAMs or enemy aircraft.

The GEC-Ferranti-designed TIALD system is primarily a day/night/adverse weather laser designator pod which can pinpoint targets for PGMs, whose renowned accuracy is in fact wholly dependant on the laser 'spot' being skilfully directed onto the target. As the PGM does not recognize the target, only the laser spot, it is vital that the targeting pod is pointed with precision, and remains locked on to the target until it is struck. To accommodate this the TIALD pod has a TV wavelength at 0.7–1.0 microns, a 1.06 micron laser and a themal imager at 8–12 microns, which allows the system to have a compact size, with optics that ensure the sensors are boresighted precisely with the aiming mark, affording unmatched precision, which allows TIALD to pick off targets well beyond normal visual range. Once fixed, the cross-hairs are automatically kept in place by a computerized system which compares each scan, looking for the shape and colour contrast of the selected target.

TIALD's large sightline or 'Field Of View Regard' allows maximum scope for manoeuvre on approach, which is coupled with an auto tracking facility that enables the aircraft to adopt evasive tactics if under fire during the terminal phase of its attack. During target acquisition, the pod is set to 'Field Of View' mode, either 'Narrow' for target identification and designation, or 'Wide' for acquisition. The 'Narrow' field is further enhanced by an electronic zoom facility. Once the target has been overlaid by the cross hairs, the system can be switched to 'Autotrack' which maintains the target aspect without the pilot needing to make any further

GR.1A Crews

No.II(AC) Squadron	No.13 Squadron
Wg Cdr Al Threadgould	Wg Cdr Glenn Torpy
Flt Lt Tim Robinson	Sqn Ldr Tom Perrem
Sqn Ldr Dick Garwood	Flt Lt Brian Robinson
Sqn Ldr Jon Hill	Flt Lt Gordon Walker
Flt Lt Angus Hogg	Sqn Ldr Al Gallagher
Flt Lt Rick Haley	Flt Lt Mike Stanway
Fg Off Jerry Spencer	Flt Lt Andy Tucker
Flt Lt Harry Seddon	Flt Lt Roger Bennett
Flt Lt Sam McLeod	
Flt Lt Dave Knight	

All smiles as Wg Cdr Threadgould brings home the No. II (AC) portion of the Recce Detatchment to RAF Laarbruch. Author

inputs. To enable maximum coverage in differing weather conditions, TIALD carries both thermal imaging and TV sensors, both of which operate simultaneously, either image being displayed at the flick of a switch onto the navigator's cockpit MFD; this allows the selection of the best performer either prior to, or during, an attack. The image from both of these sensors can be recorded simultaneously and continuously, thus making it a useful reconnaissance tool as well.

In January 1988 the first GEC-Ferranti 'A' model TIALD pod, was delivered to the RAE at Farnborough, and was quickly integrated onto the 'Nightbird' trials Buccaneer, XV344, for a 35-month intensive flying programme, with most flights being undertaken by the RAE's Flt Lts John McRae and Barry Hardy-Gillings. During Phase 5 of the programme set, between 24 May and 10 December 1990, the laser and software integration was completed; a further forty-seven flights took place, including for the first time laser firing and guiding of LGBs. Those selected for this phase and the subsequent LGB trials were Flt Lts Frank Chapman and Steve Thomas aboard the test Buccaneer, and Flt Lt Steve Pethick and Sqn Ldr Bob Fisher in the LGB-equipped Tornado, a GR.1A from No.13 Squadron. TIALD was ordered in June 1988 to meet ASR 1015, which called for a day and

night laser designation system to equip a 'pathfinder' squadron of Tornados. This unit was to be No.9 Squadron at Brüggen, but when urgent development became necessary to meet the crisis in the Gulf, and No.9 Squadron was already committed to the bombing role, it was No.13 Squadron at Honington, still waiting for the bulk of their reconnaissance aircraft, that took up the gauntlet.

Desert Designation - TIALD in Action

As part of the British build-up to the war

in the Gulf it was proposed by the MoD that consideration should be given to a TIALD Accelerated Programme or TAP, the intention being to give the RAF bomber force any possible advantage it could. Initial investigations revealed that GEC could not meet the timescale to undertake software changes to integrate TIALD onto the Tornado, and EASAMS of Camberley were approached, who confirmed they could re-write the Operational Flight Programme (OFP) to accommodate TIALD within the six-week deadline. The OFP programme

A Saudi GR.1A from No.665 Squadron RSAF. BAe

One of the No II (AC) squadron aircraft held in reserve, seen here crossing the English Channel coast. Author

ZA372/E 'Sally T', the only GR.1A to receive attention from the Gulf 'artists', was named after Wg Cdr Threadgould's wife. *Author*

moved to Boscombe Down, where after just twenty-seven days the first operational TIALD was removed from its Buccaneer host and delivered to the A&AEE, where it was rapidly integrated onto Tornado, three days after the start of Desert Storm. The RAE test pilots completed three shakedown trips and found no problems, and the pod was given unrestricted flight clearance. At Honington the Tornado Engineering and Investigation Team modified four Tornado GR.1s, taken from the Brüggen wing, to take TIALD, these changes involving additional wiring in the port under-fuselage pylon, the addition of a power supply as well as the Phase 1 Gulf adjustments.

TAP work continued apace with the four aircraft modified for TIALD and four crews from No.13 Squadron at Honington. During this period further software modifications optimized the pod for video recording, and the team undertook day and night sorties in Central Europe and the UK, despite being ham-

pered by a serious patch of bad weather. Spearheaded by No.13 Squadron's Sqn Ldr Greg Monaghan, the TIALD Team carried out vigorous trials from Boscombe Down under the codename Operation *Albert*. On 30 January the first Tornado-led laser firing was carried out, and on 2 February the TIALD pod fitted to a Tornado designated an LGB for the first time, resulting in a direct hit on a target at Garvey Island in the North of Scotland, On 6 February, a mere fifty days after the programme started, the four TAP Tornados were en route to the Gulf, following a decision that the final TIALD trials would be better run in the clear skies over the desert. A back-up team of engineers from GEC-Ferranti complete with the one fully operational pod used in the trials work, and a second pod hastily prepared from the working spares used to back up the first unit, left the day after in a Hercules transport. A third pod was undergoing urgent work during the conflict, but was not completed by the time of the ceasefire.

With the arrival of the two pods and four TAP Tornados (later joined by a fifth) at Tabuk, there was just time to unpack the equipment, paint the pods in desert sand (one arrived in black and one white), before local area familiarization flights were underway, ending with a successful LGB attack by Sqn Ldr Greg Monaghan and Flt Lt Jerry Cass on the Badr range south of Tabuk. Whilst at Tabuk the No.13 Squadron crews were augmented by another two crews from No.617 Squadron and a further two crews, one each from No.II (AC) Squadron at Laarbruch and No.14 Squadron at Brüggen. After delivering attrition replacement aircraft, the Boss of No.617 Squadron, Wg Cdr Bob Iveson (well known for having been shot down in Harrier GR.3 ZX988 during the Falklands war of 1982) assumed command of the TIALD team at Tabuk.

On 10 February, TIALD went into action for the first time, against hardened shelters on the sprawling H3 airfield complex in south-west Iraq. The two pods, carried aboard ZD848/BC flown by Wg Cdr Iveson and Flt Lt Chris Purkiss, accompanied by Flt Lts Gareth Walker and Adrian Frost in ZD739/AC, were to designate bombs for a four-ship attack. Iveson's laser malfunctioned just after the first two-ship cell released their weapons, but the LGBs were picked up by Walker and Frost's TIALD pod, and the latter pair became the first crew credited with a TIALD kill. From then on, Tabuk-based Tornados only used LGBs, and complemented the Bahrain-based Buccaneers with their AN/AVQ-23E Pave Spike daylight-only pods. As part of the pre-flight preparation, target co-ordinates were fed into the TMC, and inbound to the target the navigator would boresight the radar to that position. Around twenty miles out he would select 'slave-mode', directing the TIALD pod to look in the same direction as the radar. At fifteen miles, narrow field would be selected, magnifying the image to enlarge the target. He would then refine the TIALD point with his hand controller, placing the aiming mark directly over the target. Auto-Track would then be selected and the system took over.

Typically, the laser was engaged for thirty seconds before impact of the LGB, following the 'weapons release' call by the bombers, and impact was generally met by the announcement of 'splash' from the TIALD operator. Typically again, the TIALD GR.1s carried two long-range 'Big Jug' Hindenburger wing tanks, BOZ-107 and Sky Shadow pods on the wings, with the TIALD being attached to the port underfuselage shoulder pylon. Tactics generally dictated an approach at 20,000ft in cells of two or three aircraft, with a second trio some way behind, awaiting their turn following the first attack. After the first 'hit' the navigator would use his joy-stick to position the laser on to the next target, verifying its position with his x2 and x4 zoom facility. Because the TIALD-equipped aircraft were lightly loaded compared to the bombers they were supporting, they needed no in-flight refuelling, allowing them to leave thirty minutes later to meet up with their comrades after their tanker 'prod'. The TIALD aircraft supplemented their fuel with an additional 330gal tank on the

starboard shoulder position, which was jettisoned before the pod was operated. The bombers carried standard RAF Mk13 or later versions of the classic 1,000lb bomb, fitted with a Texas Instruments CPU-123B guidance unit; because of the extra length and guidance fins, only three of these weapons could be carried on the underfuselage stations.

For each mission a spare aircraft was prepared in case of a snag, and to support the high number of Tornado TIALD missions, four more aircrew were added to the team, and fourteen GR.1s were allocated to drop LGBs. Typical of the Tornado's war was the attack on 19 February by Gerry Monaghan and his navigator, Flt Lt Harry Hargraves, who scored 'the biggest bang in Iraq' during an attack on Unbaydah bin Al Jarrah, flying aboard ZD848. Their Tornado cell hit an ammunition store and the ensuing fireball and smoke rose to 15,000ft. As the ground offensive drew nearer, the TIALD crews were switched to disabling the airfields near the Kuwait border.

One of AKG 52's LRV Tornados seen here making a stopover at Aviano AFB in Italy, and being prepared for a *Deny Flight* **sortie as part of Einsatzgeschwader 1. Of note is the ALQ-101 ECM pod in place of the usual Cerebus.** Author

An AMI reconnaissance-equippped Tornado from the 50° Stormo's 155° Gruppo. Author

TIALD Team: (l–r) Flt Lt Frank Chapman, Flt Lt Steve Perthick, Sqn Ldr Bob Fisher and Flt Lt Colin Thomas. GEC

A suitably cool-looking Italian reconnaissance aircrew. Author

TIALD War Diary

10th February

The first series of offensive strikes using TIALD involved four sorties against hardened aircraft shelters in the huge H3 air base in western Iraq. Several shelters were totally destroyed.

11th February

Two sorties were carried out against the Hachama rail bridge, near Samawah, south of Baghdad. Six laser-guided bombs caused severe damage to the structure. Later that day a further two successful sorties were made against hardened aircraft shelters at H3.

12th February

The first strike was carried out against fuel storage tanks and pilot briefing facilities at Ruwayshid air base in western Iraq, where seven laser-guided bombs struck targets. This was followed by a sortie against hardened aircraft shelters in H3, with another six direct hits. On this third day of TIALD operations the Royal Air Force disclosed the existence of the new weapon system. Air Commodore Ian Macfadyen broke the news at a press conference in Riyadh, which flashed round the world on CNN.

13th February

The emphasis was now firmly on hardened aircraft shelters with two strikes at Al Asad followed by a further two sorties against Al Taqaddum air base near Baghdad.

14th February

All three sorties were made against shelters in H2 air base, with bombs clearly penetrating the reinforced concrete, blowing off the doors from the inside.

15th February

Six sorties were made, against shelters in H2 and Mudaysis air bases in central Iraq. Runways were also struck for the first time at Mudaysis.

16th February

Further shelters were destroyed at H3 and at Jalibah South East air base near the Kuwait border.

17th February

Two sorties were carried out against hardened aircraft shelters in H3 base, followed by strikes against two bridges, the Al Samawah rail bridge south of Baghdad and the Ar Ramadi Highway bridge to the west of Baghdad. Six bombs struck the former and three the latter, causing major structural damage.

18th February

A further six sorties took place against the Ar Ramadi bridge, resulting in twelve direct hits, and fuel storage tanks at Tallil in southern Iraq.

19th February

Fuel and ammunition storage at Ubaydah bin al Jarrah Air Base south of Baghdad were the targets, and considerable destruction was caused. Although the first ammunition store destroyed appeared to be empty, the second resulted in the biggest explosion of the war. The fuel stores also resulted in enormous explosions. After the strikes TIALD aircraft carried out bomb damage assessment against bridges over the River Tigris, confirming eight destroyed within two minutes.

20th February

With the date of the land war fast approaching, Central Command in Riyadh changed the emphasis to disabling airfields near the Kuwait border. The TIALD Task Force was charged with cutting runways to deny facilities to the enemy flying aircraft reinforcements with chemical weapons down from northern Iraq. This phase commenced with runway attacks at Shaibah Air Base in the south, adjacent to the Iranian border. Due to the excellent serviceability of TIALD and consequent high usage rate, the fifth TAP Tornado, which had been kept at Boscombe Down as a spare, was flown to Tabuk.

21st February

This was the most intensive operating day of the war, with eight sorties flown against runways at Shaibah. Twenty-four laser-guided bombs gouged holes in the operating surfaces, thus disabling the whole complex.

22nd February
Runways were put out of action at Ubaydah bin Al Jarrali with seventeen laser-guided bombs blasting craters.

23rd February

A final attack against runways took place with strikes against Mudaysis, Ghalaysan and Wadi Al Khirr air bases, all in southern Iraq. Twenty-eight laser-guided bombs struck the targets. TIALD designated four targets on each pass.

24th February
In the early hours of the morning the land offensive began. To deny supplies to the Iraqi defences, the TIALD Task Force was switched to attacking fuel and ammunition storage, and completed six sorties against Jalibah South-East and Tallil air bases down near the Kuwait border.

25th February

Fuel storage facilities at Al Asad were attacked and, to prevent Iraq bringing reinforcements from the north, sorties were flown against the As Samawah
26th February

Iraq started to withdraw from Kuwait.

27th February

Strikes resumed with attacks against hardened aircraft shelters and fuel dumps in Al Asad air base, west of Baghdad, with a total of sixteen bombs hitting targets. That evening a further two night sorties took place against large helicopter hangers at Al Habbaniyah air base near Baghdad This proved to be the last RAF air strike of the war .

TIALD was equally useful for reconnaissance and battle damage assessment, as the thermal imager was very effective in pinpointing actual damage, as opposed to fake damage painted on to buildings and runways by enterprising Iraqi troops. For crews used to single pass attacks at 200ft, the use of the pod was a revelation; the aircraft's video recording system was always active during a sortie, and although the 200-line TV tabs in the aircraft hampered cockpit assessments, back on the ground and played at 625 lines, the clarity was impressive.

The two pods, named 'Sandra' and 'Tracy' (of Viz magazine's 'Fat Slags' fame) flew aboard five GR.1s, and of the ten navigators who used them on operational missions only three had had previous TIALD experience, the other seven requiring only one training flight –

TIALD aboard a Tornado at Boscombe Down for the first time. GEC

A hanger at Habbaniyah containing helicopters attacked on 27 February. GEC

Ammunition storage at Ubanydah seen here on 19 January. The hit on the dump was the biggest 'bang' of the war. GEC

TIALD was that simple to operate. Flt Lts Kevin Noble and Jerry Cass received the GEC award for 'Top TIALD Aircrew', and ZD739/AC, nicknamed – with a heavy American influence – 'Armoured Charmer', being the aircraft which flew the most TIALD missions, notching up thirty-six 'splashes'. The two TIALD pods accounted for 229 direct hits in eighteen days, the aircraft flying some seventy-two successful missions and twenty-three aborts.

Gp Capt Hedges concluded:

TIALD was one of the great success stories of the war. It gave us the ability to bomb accurately by both day and night, and the video recording facility enabled us to assess our own results immediately. It was a triumph of co-operation between the RAF and the GEC-Ferranti engineers.

Southern Watch TIALD

After the withdrawl of the Coalition forces from the Gulf, Saddam Hussein turned his attentions to the Kurds in the North of the country and the Marsh Arabs in the south. The UN decided that the forced repression of these peoples was against the spirit of the terms that ended the Gulf War and passed resolutions enforcing a 'Safe Havens' policy to protect both groups. The latter were keen to acquire a degree of regional autonomy for their lands, centred on the great rivers Tigris and Euphrates and extending down to the city of Basra; the Iraqi leadership chose a policy of extermination. To police these 'Safe Havens' a Coalition air force was again assembled. In the north a no-fly zone was established with aircraft based at Incerlik in Turkey under Operation *Provide Comfort*, and in the south Operation *Southern Watch* came into force with a no-fly zone being established below the 32nd Parallel.

The UK's participation in Southern Watch was known as Operation *Jural*, and in August 1992, the RAF announced the involvement of RAF Marham's Tornado force. As the task was primarily reconnaissance the initial deployment consisted of three GR.1As from No.2(AC) Squadron and three GR.1s from No.617 Squadron. In due course the GR.1As were replaced by GR.1s. A RIC was also established. During December 1992 the six Tornados from Marham were replaced by a further six TIALD-equipped GR.1s from No.31 Squadron at RAF Brüggen.

Since the Gulf War many more of the RAF's Tornados had been wired for TIALD, and the squadron dedicated to its operation is now No.14, based at Brüggen. With TIALD now available, its carrier aircraft have been deployed back to the Gulf during times of added tension, such as Iraq's continued brinksmanship surrounding UN Weapons Inspectors' examining Iraq's weopons of mass destruction. The latest 'effort' in mid-1998 led to eight TIALD-equipped Tornados from No.14 Squadron being based at Al Kharj in Kuwait.

Italian CLDP

The 36° Stormo's 156° Gruppo has been involved in bombing missions over Bosnia where the aircraft have tended to carry a pair of GBU-16 Paveway II LGBs. This has led to the AMI acquiring its own autonomous laser designation facility, with 156° Tornados now also being assigned to carrying an externally mounted Thompson-CSF CLDP (Combined Laser Designator Pod) for designing targets.

TIALD-modified aircraft

ZD739/AC	'Armoured Charmer' Full-colour artwork with thirty-six 'splash' mission symbols.
ZA393/CQ	'Sir Gallahad' Name only stencilled on the port side of the radome, 7 'splash' symbols.
ZA406/DA	No artwork, ten 'splash' symbols.
ZD848/BC	'Bacardi and Coke' Artwork unfinished before the ceasefire, nineteen 'splash' symbols.
ZD844/DE	'Donna Ewin' Full-colour artwork, twenty 'splashes' and a No.17 Squadron 'mailed fist' emblem.

All aircraft carried a 'TIALD 91' legend on their noses.

TIALD Aircrew

No.II (AC) Squadron:	Flt Lts Wayne Haigh and 'Moose' Poole. Seven missions.
No.13 Squadron:	Sqn Ldr Stu Morton, Flt Lts Kev Noble, Jerry Cass, Bill Bohill and Jim Ross. Forty-five missions.
No.14 Squadron:	Flt Lts Tim Marsh and Ken Smith. Seven missions.
No.16 Squadron:	Wg Cdr Bob Iveson, Flt Lts Chris Purkiss, Gareth Walker Adrian Frost and Harry Hargreaves. Sixteen missions.
No.617 Squadron:	Sqn Ldrs Greg Monaghan and Brian Cole. Twenty missions.

'Sandra', one of the two TIALD pods rushed into service during the Gulf War. Stuart Black

Artwork applied to ZD844/DE 'Donna Ewin', complete with TIALD 'spash' markings. Steve Morris

A production TIALD pod beneath the fuselage of a No.14 Squadron Tornado. Gary Parsons f4 Aviation

Top TIALD scorer ZD739/AC 'Armoured Charmer'. Author

CHAPTER SEVEN

Tornado Air Defence Variant

Two of the original six roles envisaged for the Tornado programme were air superiority and interception/air defence. Although the three nations involved in the Tornado project each had their own agenda for air defence, it was Britain's obligations that were of the greatest importance. The RAF is tasked with

maintaining the integrity of the United Kingdom's Air Defence Region, or 'UK ADR'. This is an area significantly larger than the whole of NATO's Central Region, as it extends from Iceland to the English Channel and from the Atlantic approaches to the Baltic. Therefore, unlike her allies, Britain had little need

to detect and oppose small, agile fighters at short ranges; instead, the primary threat came from large formations of long-range Soviet aircraft such as the giant Tu-22M bombers, carrying cruise missiles down through the Greenland/Iceland/UK gap from their home bases in the North Cape or Kola

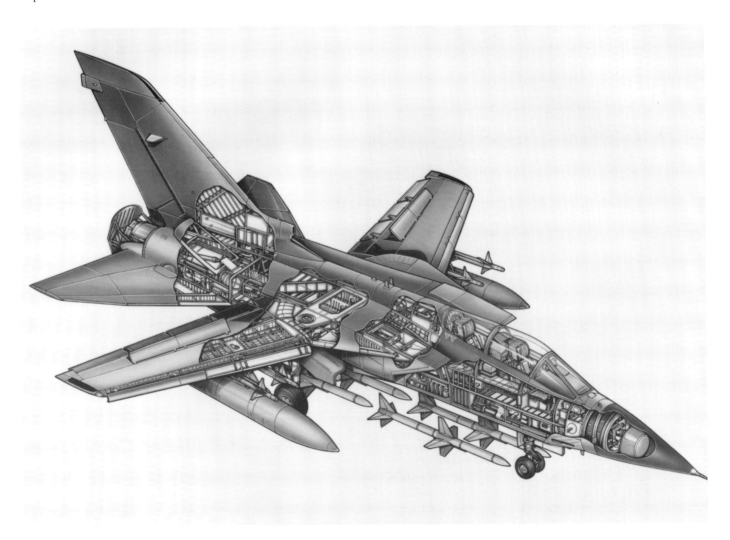

Tornado F.3 Cutaway Diagram. BAe

Peninsula. To cope with this threat the RAF needed a long-range, long-endurance – loitering on CAP between 300–400 miles from base – BVR missile-equipped interceptor, able to patrol the huge UK ADR, capable of detecting and engaging a number of targets in all weathers, from a stand-off range using a powerful radar and reacting to information provided by AWACS or ground radars.

With the growing threat from Warsaw Pact air power in the late 1960s and 1970s, the RAF's Lightning interceptors and their 'interim' replacement – the Phantom – were not thought able to cope sufficiently with the advancements of Soviet designs and were judged to need urgent (in governmental terms) replacement. When the original MRCA was still in the planning stages, the RAF's Operational Requirements Branch considered the possibility of producing an indigenous variant of the MRCA to replace the Lightning and Phantom. What emerged from their studies was the Tornado ADV, launched as a proposal in 1969 under AST 395, described as a derivative of the Panavia 200, having an advanced radar and BVR air-to-air capabilities. Although Panavia had announced the development of a 'Radpac', designed to give the basic IDS an improved air-to-air facility with AIM-7 Sparrow AAMs, the basic Tornado became increasingly orientated toward air-to-surface roles, and finally lost its pretensions to be a fighter in 1970.

The RAF's OR Branch, though enthusiastic about the ADV, were directed to look at other air defence options to see if any were more cost-effective. The Grumman F-14 Tomcat was examined, but found to be to prohibitively expensive if bought with the AIM-54 Phoenix missile and AWG-9 radar, around which it

had been designed and without which it offered little improvement over the already in-service Phantom. The single seat F-16, undoubtedly a superb dogfighter, was unsuitable for the RAF's stated mission. The F-15, an excellent fighter in the Central European theatre, was also studied in both its single and two-seat forms, but was ruled out due to its limited radar and ECCM capacity; this remained the case when, in the face of a shortfall of available RAF air defence aircraft in the mid-1980s after the Falklands War, the US Government offered the RAF four squadrons on a lease basis, citing their concerns over the lack of air defence assets to protect their UK-based aircraft. The French Mirage 2000 was also considered at one stage.

After these aircraft were rejected, the Government announced that 165 of the RAF's 385 Tornados would be of the new ADV derivative. The full-scale development of the ADV was launched on 4 March 1976 and authorized on the 5th, and an Instruction to Proceed with the manufacture of two prototypes was received by BAe Warton on 11 March 1977. Despite its different role, the Tornado ADV would have around 80 per cent commonality with the IDS version.

Central to its role, the Tornado ADV would be armed with four medium-range missiles, these being the British adaptation of the American AIM-7 Sparrow, the BAe Skyflash. Mounting these weapons on wing pylons was considered, but abandoned because of the drag it would cause. The ideal location turned out to be on the aircraft's broad underfuselage, though this was not big enough to accommodate the missiles without interfering with undercarriage operation. The solution was simple – to stretch the fuselage. By inserting a 1ft 9in plug immediately behind the cockpit

(the minimum permitted without changing the aircraft's CoG) the Skyflashes just fitted, placed in a staggered formation to aid launch and non-interference with the undercarriage bays. The added bonus of the fuselage stretch was an extra fuel tank (Tank 0) holding 200gal of fuel.

Further modifications came to accommodate the new airborne intercept (AI) radar and its associated equipment. This came in the shape of an elongated and more pointed radome that gave less drag and added 2ft 8in to the forward fuselage, thus making the ADV some 4ft 5 1/2in longer than the IDS. Other modifications were less noticeable. The inboard fixed glove vanes were re-shaped to have a sharper sweep than those of the IDS in order to compensate for the slight increase in the forward CoG and the Kruger flaps were deleted. The port cannon was deleted as it was felt that a single gun was sufficient, given the ADV's proposed engagement zone. The internal space was then reorganized to accept an integral IFR probe, and the additional ADV avionics were so built as to further reduce drag, which would have been very pronounced had the IDS 'bolt-on' style had been adopted.

Systems

The ADV, as could be expected, has very different avionics and instruments to the IDS. The ADV was given double the original IDS's computing power, stepping up from the 64k of the IDS to 128k; also introduced was a Marconi TACAN, Cossor ILS and IFF (later included in the IDS) and a revised communications suite. The latter consists of a GEC-Plessy VHF/UHF, Rohde and Schwarz HF/SSB, and SIT emergency UHF with a Comms Control Unit by Ultra and an Epsylon CVR. The ADV lacks the IDS's TFR, LRMTS, Secondary HARS and Decca 72 Doppler. After some concern was voiced, the ADV was fitted with a D-band IFF, which incorporated a radar mode allowing a pulse to interrogate an IFF transponder, not just a dedicated interrogator. In the cockpits the ADV lacks the moving map and TFR E-scope, and instead the pilot had a HDD CRT to view intercepts or anything being viewed on the backseater's CRTs. The navigator has two centrally-mounted CRTs, together with a displayed data video recorder and a GEC Marconi

---

Specification – Tornado ADV

Weights:	Empty 31,857lb (14,450kg); maximum take-off: 61,700lb (28,000kg)
Dimensions:	
Wingspan:	Swept 28ft 2in (8.6m); forward : 45ft 7in (13.9m); length:61ft (18.6m); height 19ft 8in (6m)
Performance:	Maximum speed Mach 2.2
Fuel capacity:	Maximum internal 1,920gal (7.270ltr); maximum external: 1,981gal (7,500ltr)

Foxhunter Radar

The most critical change to the basic Tornado concept for the ADV was the provision of a dedicated 'fighter radar'. The set chosen for the ADV was the newly developed GEC-Marconi AI-24 Foxhunter set, a FMICW (Frequency Modulated Interrupted Continuous Wave) system operating in the 3cm I-Band. Marconi-Elloitt, with Ferranti as its major sub-contractor, received a contract to develop the new radar in 1976, building on their vast experience of existing radar sets. One of the primary requirements in its design was the radar's ability to operate against hostile ECM jamming. The new radar consisted of eight liquid-cooled LRUs around a central transmitter, while the front-end was mostly analogue with a coherent travelling wave transmitter tube which gave high power over a wide variety of bandwidths. The twist-cassegrain antenna was light and simple, and gave a greater consistency and lower side-lobes than the latest planar arrays used by the current US fighters. The set also incorporated a J-band illuminator for the Skyflash missiles, with high PRFs being used for long range detection and low PRFs for targets that gave little Doppler shift. Able to detect targets in excess of 100nm, it is not limited by target altitude – even in the most demanding case of 'look-down' against low-flying targets: Foxhunter possesses a multiple synthetic symbology Track-While-Scan capability, where the target returns are displayed to the crew. A built-in processor suppresses ground clutter and a built-in Cossor IFF-3500 interrogator which has its dipole aerials mounted on the main reflector to aid friend or foe identification. The navigator/WSO designates the target to be tracked, whilst the TWS of multiple targets calculates the ground speed, track and height of other targets and the radar continues to search for others. The new radar brought with it a new cooling system and the inclusion of a pop-out ram-air turbine to power the emergency systems in the event of a double flame-out.

Serious technical problems beset the development of the Foxhunter radar, which had been flying aboard an MoD(PE) Canberra since 1975, added to which its introduction was delayed mainly due to the RAF continually changing their minds on what it should be capable of doing. Shortcomings were cited in the un-acceptably large sidelobes which increased the detectability and vulnerability of the aircraft, and there was a severe problem with the TWS capabilities. The third of the ADV prototypes was due to be the radar development aircraft, but initially had to fly with lead ballast in its nose, in place of the radar set. It was reported that most of the original F.2s were delivered without radar, which lead to a somewhat bitter joke that the aircraft were fitted with a 'Blue Circle' radar, the name deriving from a British cement company whose name name echoed the colour-based names for weapons and avionics during the 1950s and '60s. It was later admitted that the aircraft carried steel bars for ballast and not cement!

Finally, on 17 June 1981 ZA283 became the first ADV fitted with a B-series radar, and for some time remained the only aircraft so equipped. The first twenty pre-production sets were delivered to BAe Warton in July 1983, but not fitted on the production line until 1985. By now the 'Foxhunter' was four years late, and 50 per cent over its original budget. It is generally accepted that all of the F.2s flew with the pre-production radar sets, which allowed at least some realistic air intercept training to be undertaken. Unlike the IDS aircraft, which were given to units under their batch numbers, the ADVs were assigned under their block number. For the F.3, although this designation covered its overall, the single and most crucial difference between the aircraft blocks was their radar fit. The first of the radar units to be delivered to the RAF were still well below the original specification, and were known as 'Type W'. Seventy 'Type W' sets were produced for the first sixty-two aircraft – eighteen for the original F.2s and forty-four for the first F.3s – and these were subsequently upgrade to 'Type Z' Standard in a programme which began in 1988. The following eighty aircraft all received the 'Type Z' radar which had increased TWS and range, and broadly met the RAF's specification. All of the 'Type Z' sets began life as 'Type W' and were subsequently brought up to the 'Stage 1' Standard. An interim standard 'Stage 1+' (described on page 00) was hurriedly rushed into service for aircraft taking part in the Gulf War, where the Foxhunter set was upgraded to 'AA' Standard, better cooling, and greater ECCM.

FH 31A artificial horizon. Twin-stick trainer versions lose one of the CRTs, the remaining one being moved to the centre of the instructor's rear instrument panel.

Unlike the Tornado F.2, the Tornado F.3 is equipped with an automatic manoeuvring device system (AMDS) to reduce the pilot's workload, particularly in combat, giving the optimum sweep settings and combat flap and slat settings for the particular performance and flight weapon load. An automatic wing sweep system is also employed on the F.3, with the wing sweep angles offering 25 degrees for low speed and 67 degrees for high speed, with intermediate settings of 45 and 58 degrees. The AWS thus provides the pilot with the best settings for the aircraft's flight envelope and gives the pilot one less thing to worry about during combat.

Although the Foxhunter radar is the aircraft's primary sensor, it is not the only method of gathering information. The aircraft's RHWS detects, analyzes and displays hostile emissions received by the external antennae, which can be found on the rear of the tail fin and in the wing-nibs. The cockpit displays a 'user friendly' read-out giving target type and direction. Priority threats such as SAMs and air-intercept radars override all other selections, giving both audio and visual warnings. The aircraft also carries a fire-control system and a comprehensive Missile Management System (MMS), which controls the firing of the AAMs and gun, and the jettisoning of the external fuel tanks. The pilot is able to take control of the fire-control system by pressing the 'air override' button on his control stick, and can select the appropriate weapon without taking his hands off the control stick. Initial selection of the air-override will

SPILS

The Spin Prevention Incidence Limiting System (SPILS) is an integral part of the flight control system. This prevents loss on control whilst at high angles of attack by limiting the maximum attainable AOA and moderating the pilot's control inputs, which would normally result in a spin entry. When engaged, SPILS provides the pilot with 'carefree handling', allowing the aircraft to be manoeuvred to its limits in close combat. SPILS has its own computer and control panel on the left console in the front seat of the aircraft.

automatically select the radar in air combat mode, arm all the missiles and gun, and select 'dog-fight' mode for Skyflash as the primary weapon.

The AIM-9 Sidewinder short-range heat-seeking missiles have their own selection within the Fire Control System, which provides steering cues in the HUD, whilst the gun selection pushes the system into radar or stadiametric ranging with additional inputs from the flight control system's rate gyros and the Main Computer.

Skyflash and Sidewinder were due to be replaced eventually by the Hughes AIM-120 AMRAAM (Advanced Medium Range Air-to-Air Missile) and the BAe/Bodenswerk ASRAAM (Advanced Short Range Air-to-Air Missile), respectively, but this decision was cancelled in 1982 on economic grounds. However, in March 1996 the British Government announced a reversal of that decision in a programme that will encompass radar improvements to allow the aircraft to engage simultaneous targets using both AMRAAM and ASRAAM missiles; an upgrade contract, reportedly worth £125 million, was awarded to BAe. This contract will greatly enhance the aircraft. The flexibility of Tornado allows it to be upgraded throughout its life to maintain its operational effectiveness into the 21st century.

ADV Prototypes

Three Tornado ADV prototypes were produced, officially designated Tornado F.2s, differing little from the production F.2s. All three aircraft were fitted with a comprehensive system of air-to-ground telemetry which allowed for real-time analysis of the aircrafts' progress during their rigorous flight test schedule. The flying time was extended by the use of IFR and the aircrafts' progress through the flight regime was swift and relatively painless. Of the three prototypes the first, ZA254/AT-001, was rolled out at BAe Warton on 9 August 1979 amidst much ceremony. Resplendent in a white, black and Light Aircraft Grey colour scheme, the aircraft undertook its 1hr 32min maiden flight on 27 October, with test pilot Dave Eagles at the helm and Roy Kennard in the back seat. The aircraft reached Mach 1.25 during this flight, Mach 1.6 on its second flight and Mach 1.75 on its third, ably demonstrating more rapid acceleration than the IDS, although its straight line speed was pegged to the same 915 mph limit.

ZA254 began flying representative CAP sorties and in 1982 undertook 375 flights from its base at Warton, with a 2hr 2min loiter on station, achieving this with only two small 330gal wing tanks, as used

ZE200/DB lets fly with a Sidewinder. BAe

Prototype F.2 AT-03/ZA283. Note the 'cut-in' section below the rudder, denoting the installation of the Mk103 engines. BAe

---

BAe Skyflash Missiles

Skyflash launch. BAe

The Foxhunter radar was designed to be compatible with BAe's Skyflash missile, which was a derivative of the American AIM-7E-2 Sparrow, combining the Sparrow's proven airframe, rocket motor and warhead, but including a Marconi radar seeker and an EMI proximity fuse. New guidance controls were developed by BAe, together with a new autopilot, actuators and power supplies. Developed in 1969, Skyflash I was ordered in 1978, entering service with the RAF's Phantom units that year, later entering service with the Tornado ADV. It was hoped that the Skyflash II, which offered

mid-course correction and an active terminal guidance phase, would be the Tornado's primary weapon; despite its promise it was abandoned before it could enter production.

It was originally planned that Skyflash would be carried on the wing pylons, but the induced drag was unacceptable, so instead the fuselage was slightly stretched whilst staggered low-drag recesses were applied to the rear lower fuselage pair of missiles and semi-submerged recesses applied to the front pair. Separation of the AAMs from their recesses is achieved by the use of a pair of revolutionary

Frazer Nash twin-ram cartridge-powered ejector/launchers, which force the missile down and away from the aircraft's underside, applying a four ton force. Before launch, Skyflash is tuned into the correct frequency through its reference aerial. The Foxhunter set illuminates the target area, and when a target is identified the missile is ready for launch. After ejection the boost motor ignites and the seeker begins its search for its target. The Foxhunter continues to illuminate the target and the reflected signals are received by the missile's seeker.

Skyflash can destroy subsonic and supersonic aircraft from all aspects and can 'snap-down' or 'snap-up' to engage targets at high or low level, with the snap-up capability reported to allow the ADV to intercept targets flying at over 60,000ft. It is also able to discriminate between close formation targets, and is effective against those trying to evade its lock. The Tornado ADV is the first fighter able to launch is missiles throughout its entire flight envelope.

Skyflash Specifications

Length:	9ft 6in (2.9 m)
Diameter:	6.2in (165mm)
Wingspan:	17.7in (45 cm)
Launch weight:	214lb (97kg)
Speed:	2,295kt
Range:	27nm (50km)
Warhead:	22lb (10kg)
Guidance:	Semi-Active Radar Homing

The first ADV prototype, ZA254, lights her afterburners. Three such prototypes were produced. BAe

on the IDS. The aircraft did not use IFR and flew overhead Warton for fifteen minutes on its return before touching down with 5 per cent of its fuel reserves remaining. ZA254 later accomplished live Skyflash firings, despite not being fitted with a radar or a complete avionics fit. AT-001, AT-002 and AT-003 were also notable for having a seemingly IDS-style RWR fairing on their tails. In fact the 'front-end' housed a video camera for recording the flight trials. ZA254 was put into storage at BAe Warton at the end of its test career, and is currently planned to become the gate guardian at RAF Coningsby.

The second prototype, ZA267/AT-02, was fitted with dual controls and a representative main computer and rear cockpit displays, but no radar. Its first flight was on 18 July 1980 and it was subsequently

used for armament trials. Although it made its first appearance in its 'primer' coat, it was soon painted up the same as AT-01. AT-02 was notable for its prominent 'calibration' marks, and proved the concept of the Frazer Nash launchers, a new innovation for the ADV. Gun trials were also neccessary, as the ADV's fuselage is longer than that of the IDS and so gun gas ingestion characteristics were different. In the early test firings, shell cases were coated the optical device used for monitoring the engine turbine blades temperature, and subsequently the gun had to be re-cleared for operational use. ZA267 was also used for high-altitude zoom-climb trials, revealing that the aircraft could exceed 70,000ft, and was finally fitted with a B Model radar in 1983. AT-02 also received the first of the more powerful RB.199 Mk104 engines, des-

tined to replace the IDS-style Mk103 in the production F.3s. ZA267 is still operating with the MoD(PE) at Boscombe Down as part of the Fixed Wing Test Squadron (see page 00).

ZA283/AT-03 flew for the first time on 18 November 1980 and was intended for radar trials, although it initially flew with lead ballast in the nose. This aircraft was painted in the 'air defence grey' as used on the RAF's F-4 Phantoms, (semi-matt Barley Grey BS4800.18B.21 and Light Aircraft Grey BS381C-627) and finally looked like an operational aircraft. The radar was finally flown as part of the aircraft on 17 June 1981. Happily the development radar sets were very reliable and BAe was able to recover lost time by flying long-duration Foxhunter trials. To facilitate this work Tornado and Lightning aircraft were operated as targets, accompanied by a Buccaneer fitted with a 'buddy-buddy' IFR pack. AT-003 began flying with a Model B Foxhunter set in March 1983.

Tornado F.2

The first production batch of eighteen ADVs for the RAF were of what has been described as an 'interim' standard, without auto wing sweep, able to carry two underwing Sidewinders and powered by the IDS-type RB.199 Mk103 engines. The aircraft was also fitted with only a single FIN 1010 INS, even though it was recognized the aircraft needed two, and, as described earlier, had no radar. The first six F.2 aircraft were fitted with dual controls, and two of the remaining twelve were also twin-stickers, generally referred unofficially to as F.2(A)s. The first production aircraft was in fact ZD899, but it was ZD900 which made the first flight, during March 1984. The production aircraft differed from the prototypes in having no forward-looking RWR fairing on the tail. As has been described earlier, the delays associated with the Foxhunter radar saw the aircraft flying with the 'Blue Circle' set until mid-1984. Sixteen of the eighteen F.2s were based at RAF Coningsby, where No.229 OCU was officially formed on 1 May 1985 to undertake the training of instructor crews, and then of ab initio and conversion pilots to the F.3. To confuse matters, No.229 OCU 'unofficially' formed on 1 November 1984 as a cadre of senior staff. The unit's first pair of ADVs arrived on 5 November: ZA901/AA piloted by Dave Eagles and crewed by AVM Ken Hayr (AOC of No.11 Group), and ZA903/AB carrying Jerry Lee, Chief Test Pilot of BAe Warton, and Wg Cdr 'Rick' Peacock-Edwards, with the last F.2 to be received being ZD491/AU. Initial training on the ADV fell to BAe, which began with a four-week Service Instructor Aircrew Training Course at Warton, followed by twenty flying hours per person. From 10 May 1985 the responsibility of training aircrew reverted to the OCU. With the arrival of the PP radar sets on the F.2, the aircraft was able to undertake a limited combat capability, and so was declared to NATO as an emergency air defence unit in May 1985. In December 1986 this declaration was increased when the unit took up the 'shadow' designation of No.65 Squadron, a milestone achieved with eighteen instructor crews. Thus the unit found itself in the unusual position of being given a reserve role before any front-line units were formed! On 21 October 1985 the ADVs participated in their first air defence exercise when No.229 OCU's F.2s were involved in the three-day Priory 85/2 event. Saturday 14 June was also a red letter day for the unit, as nine of their number were selected to overfly Buckingham Palace on the occasion of the Queen's official birthday, whilst at Coningsby the public got its first view of the F.3 when ZE154 – still on charge at BAe – was specially flown in from Boscombe Down.

The first of the F.3s began arriving at RAF Coningsby on 28 July 1986 with ZE159; giving the F.2s the somewhat unusual honour of not having trained a single student! F.3 training officially began on 1 December 1986 for pilots of No.29 Squadron, who were mostly ex-Phantom crews. The sixteen F.2s were subsequently placed in storage at RAF St Athan, with a little over 250 flying hours per airframe, but with relatively high fatigue indices, with the last F.2 leaving No.229 OCU in January 1988. Of their number, ZD899 remained at Warton for trials work; ZD900 continued to be used by the DTEO at Boscombe Down; ZD935 went to the ETPS, also at Boscombe Down; ZD902 went to the DRA at Farnborough, where it later became the TIARA test aircraft; ZD939 became an instructional airframe for the Saudi Support Team at Warton; ZD937 was used as a BDR trainer; and ZD935 ended its life as a ground instructional airframe at RAF Coningsby in 1993.

In close, an F.2 from No. No.229 OCU. Stuart Black

126

Hopes were high that the F.2s might be brought up to F.2A standard, almost identical to the F.3 but retaining the RB.199 Mk103 engines. However, the ending of the Cold War put paid to such plans and they remained in storage. Export plans fell on stony ground and eventually it was decided to scrap the twelve aircraft for spares recovery. But as is described on page 134, before this could be done the aircraft were reprieved as 'donors' for allegedly contractor-damaged F.3s. The F.2A designation has since been unofficially applied to the TIARA test aircraft, ZD902.

Tornado F.3

The second batch of fifty-two aircraft, to be designated F.3, were ordered in August 1982, and a third batch ordered in January 1984. After the 'interim' F.2, the F.3 brought with it a plethora of improvements. The most obvious was the introduction of the more powerful RB.199 Mk104 engine. This new powerplant introduced a 14in extension to the afterburner section and used a DECU 500 digital engine control system developed by Rolls-Royce and Lucas Aerospace. This was the world's first full authority digital engine control, or 'FADEC'. This modification gave an extra 10 per cent thrust and reduced afterburner fuel consumption by 4 per cent. The new engine also gave rise to an increase in the size of the trailing edge fin below the rudder which now extended aft, unlike than the 'scalloped' shape found on the F.2s. The F.3s were also fitted with a second FIN 1010 three-axis digital INS, allowing the two units to

monitor each other's performance. Also added was a 128k Litef Spirit III main computer and advancing stages of radar development up to the definitive Stage 1+ sets described elsewhere. Extra offensive punch was added with the provision for a further two AIM-9 Sidewinders on stub pylons attached to the inner wing pylons, and self defence was also addressed – though not satisfactorily until the aircraft was called upon to go to war! The Tornado F.3's offensive and defensive war fit is described on page 121. Carrying the full markings of No.65 Squadron for the first time, two Tornado F.3s, accompanied by four GR.1s from No.617 Squadron, flew non-stop over 4,500 miles in a 10 1/4-hour mission, refuelled by TriStar and VC-10, to take part in Exercise Swift Sword in Oman.

No.65 Squadron became No.56 Reserve) Squadron in 1992 following the Government's re-structure of the UK's defences and the retirement of the Phantom. Another result of the retirement of the Phantom from RAF service was the re-equipment of No.1453 Flight in the Falkland Islands. As part of the UK's continuing 'air policing' role, protecting the sovereign airspace around the disputed islands, four Tornado F.3s – which required no special modifications for their work south of the equator – left RAF Coningsby between the 6–8 July 1992. Led by Wg Cdr Al Lockwood, the journey was split into two legs; Coningsby to Ascension Island and Ascension Island to RAF Mount Pleasant in the Falklands. The No.1453 Flight's F.3s have a role to play for some time to come, and aircrew from all the F.3 squadrons undertake five-week tours on the islands.

At its peak the RAF had seven front-line and one reserve unit with the Tornado F.3, but with the falling of the Iron Curtain and the ending of the Cold War one of their number, No.23 Squadron, was disbanded in February 1994, and as a result of a further Strategic Defence Review by the Labour Government in 1998 a further reduction in squadron strength seems likely.

On 21 August 1988 four F.3s from No.29(F) Squadron left their home base at RAF Coningsby for a 'round the world' deployment named Exercise *Golden Eagle*, flying out to the Far East, Australia and the USA. The aircraft also visited Oman, Malaysia, Singapore and New Zealand, taking part in the Lima Bertsatu 88 air defence exercise along the way. Following this they aircraft deployed to Korat AFB for two weeks of DACT with the Royal Thai Air Force. On their return to Coningsby they had completed the longest-ever peacetime deployment of UK air defence aircraft. The F.3's first invitation to the USAF's Red Flag exercises took place in October 1992, at Nellis AFB in Nevada. Six aircraft from the Leeming wing crossed the Atlantic to join eight GR.1s. All of the F.3s despatched for the six week-long exercise were of the 'Stage 1+' type. The first pilot to log 1000 hours on the F.3 was Sqn Ldr Paul Burnside of No.11 Squadron, who reached the milestone on 29 April 1989.

Tornado F.3 – Stage II

The planned introduction of a new single-board computer processor will bring all of the RAF's surviving F.3s radar systems up to the proposed Stage II(AB) standard, allowing for automatic target acquisition and tracking, and discrimination of head-on targets through the analysis of their first- and second-stage compressor discs. Due to have been delivered in 1991, the Stage II modification kits have suffered the inevitable delays, as have items such as the automatic wing sweep and a fleet-wide JTIDS fit.

JTIDS

At the time of writing, a limited number of Tornado F.3s are operating with a secure, spread-spectrum ECM-resistant data link called JTIDS: Joint Tactical Information Distribution System. This provides access to target data gathered by AWACS, ground defence radars or other similarly equipped interceptors. This data can then be shared between aircraft to avoid target duplication, share the fighters' information with the controlling authority and allocate targets to individual aircraft. Tornado F.3s have successfully developed fighter tactics operating with E-3 Sentry AWACS from No.8 Squadron in exercises and over Bosnia. JTIDS-equipped F.3s work in concert with the AWACS aircraft, the latter downloading battlefield information to the Tornados' computers.

JTIDS operates on a jam-resistant waveform pattern that allows differing types of information to be shared securely between the networked participants – perhaps it could be described as 'the secret Internet'. The potential for JTIDS is therefore enormous. Currently it includes major HQs, ships and other combat support aircraft, but in the future JTIDS could even be available to field HQs, combat vehicles and even troops.

Tornado ADV Units

No.229 OCU/No.65 Squadron/No.56(Reserve) Squadron

Born out of No.226 OCU at Stradishall on 15 December 1950, this unit was established at RAF Leuchars with the Meteor, Vampire

Tornado F.3 front cockpit. BAe

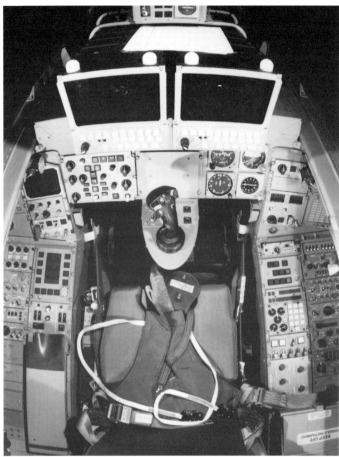

Tornado F.3 rear cockpit. BAe

A pair of Tornado F.3s escorting IDS variants over the desert. Author

and target-towing Beaufighters and Martinets. The unit moved to RAF Chivenor in 1951 with the Sabre and Hunter, plus a plethora of other aircraft such as the Oxford, Chipmunk, Mosquito and Tiger Moth. In 1969 the unit assumed the semi-operational task of air defence over Gibraltar. The unit disbanded on 2 September 1969, its aircraft being transferred to No.1 TWU at RAF Brawdy. Re-born at Coningsby, it was 'unofficially' re-formed on 1 November 1984. The 'shadow' designation of No.65 Squadron was adopted by the OCU on assuming its operational role. Similarly, later No.229 OCU was disbanded, only to re-appear as No.56(Reserve) Squadron, former operators of the Lightning and Phantom in the air defence role.

The unit's markings are a red and yellow flash on the nose with roundel, and a sword, point uppermost with a heraldic torch in saltier. Codes AA–AL are worn by the dual control aircraft and AM–AZ by the 'single stickers'. No.65 Squadron markings are a lion passant before fifteen swords in a pile upon a white disc flanked by white bars containing red chevrons; No.56(R) Squadron markings are red and white chequers on the nose, with a golden Pheonix rising from a red flames motif on the tail fins.

No. 5 Squadron

Frangas non Flectas – 'Thou mayest break but shall not bend me'

A reconnaissance unit during World War One, No.5 Squadron flew the BE2, BE8 and Bristol Fighter. During World War Two they operated Mohawks and later Tempests, disbanding in 1947. After a brief return for target-towing duties, No.5 was reformed at Wunstorf, flying Vampires and Javelins, before re-equipping with the Lightning at Binbrook in 1965. The squadron retired its Lightnings and re-formed as a Tornado unit on 1 May 1988 at RAF Coningsby. The unit's markings are sometimes a red tail stripe with two gold swords in the shape of a 'V' on a green maple leaf within a white disc, and recently a low-visibility maple leaf without stripe. A red arrowhead is worn on the forward fuselage. On the occasion of the RAF's 80th Anniversary, ZG791/CD wore special stylized squadron markings featuring an overlarge maple leaf with a yellow '5' and the logo 1918–1998 painted on its fin.

No.11 Squadron

Ociores acrioresqe aquilis – 'Swifter and keener than eagles'

Formed in 1915 as a fighter unit, No.11 Squadron was transferred to India and Burma, flying Hurricanes and Blenheims during World War Two. In 1948 the unit moved to Germany, eventually taking on charge the Meteor and Javelin. Having received Lightning interceptors in 1967, the unit moved to Binbrook in 1972, standing down on the Lightning in May 1988 and reforming on the Tornado at RAF Leeming in the November of that year. Its markings are a pair of black eagles on the tail fin with black and yellow fighter bars on the forward fuselage.

No.23(F) Squadron

Semper Aggressus – 'Always Attacking'

No.23 Squadron formed on 1 September

The Tornado F.3 OCU's numberplate currently resides with No.56(R) Squadron, the 'Firebirds'. BAe

1915 at Gosport and was deployed to the Western Front during World War IOne, equipped with FE2b aircraft. The squadron returned to the United Kingdom in March 1919 and was disbanded at Waddington in December that year. Reforming in the early years of World War Two, No.23 Squadron undertook shipping protection and intruder missions. Remaining in East Anglia, No.23 Squadron reformed just one year later with the Mosquito, but in September 1951, piston-engined aircraft gave way to jet-powered types with the introduction of the Vampire and later Venom night-fighters. The unit then converted to the English Electric Lightning

F.3, re-equipping with the F.6 in 1967. In October 1975, the squadron disbanded, but it reformed two months later with the McDonnell Douglas Phantom FGR.2 at RAF Coningsby. From February 1976 until March 1983, 23 Squadron enjoyed a period of relative stability at RAF Wattisham where the burden of Quick Reaction Alert duties was shared with 56 Squadron. The unit contributed to the air defence of the Falkland Islands Protection Zone in the South Atlantic from April 1983 to November 1988, moving in the process from Stanley to Mount Pleasant before that duty was taken over by No.1435 Flight. Re-equipment with Tornado F.3s took place at Leeming in November 1988 and 23 Squadron aircrew participated in the Gulf War in 1990 before the squadron disbanded in February 1994. In 1995, it was decided to respond to the expansion and increasing importance of the RAF Airborne Early Warning Force by forming a Sentry AEW.1 training unit to complement No 8 Squadron, and No.23 Squadron was accordingly selected to reform at RAF Waddington on 1 April 1996. Its markings are a red swooping eagle on the tail fin with a blue and red arrow head on the forward fuselage.

No.25(F) Squadron

Feriens Tego – 'Striking I defend'

Formed in 1915, No.25 Squadron spent World War One in France, and flew Beaufighters and Mosquitos during World War Two. Retained as a night-fighter squadron post-war, the unit flew Vampires and Javelins until disbanded in November 1962. The unit re-formed as a Bloodhound SAM squadron in October 1963 until it was chosen to be the final Tornado ADV unit at RAF Leeming.

Its markings are a falcon upon a gloved hand on the tail fin, with a white and pale blue tail flash.

No.29(F) Squadron

Impiger et Acer – 'Energetic and Keen'

It had been planned that the first ADV unit would be an entirely new squadron formed at RAF Coningsby in 1986 to replace the old Lightning. These plans were thwarted by the delays with the Foxhunter radar and the need to divert airframes to the Saudi contract. So instead of being the second ADV squadron, No.29 became the first. Formed at Gosport on 7 November 1915, it took up duties in France. World War Two saw operations with such aircraft as the Blenhiem, Beaufighter and Mosquito. Post-war such types as the Meteor NF.11, Javelin and Lightning were operated, followed by a brief disbandment before re-formation with the Phantom. Although assigned to NATO's SACEUR, No.29 Squadron deployed to the Falklands, later giving way to No.23 Squadron. On 1 December 1986 personnel assigned to No.29 Squadron began ground school

with No.229 OCU. The unit's markings are a red eagle preying on a yellow buzzard on the tail fin with red and yellow 'Triple X' crosses on the intake lips.

No.43 Squadron

Gloria Finis – 'Glory the end'

Formed in Scotland during 1916, the unit flew the Gamecock and Siskin before taking on charge the Hurricane, which it flew during the Battle of Britain. No.43 Squadron arrived at RAF Leuchars in 1950 flying the Meteor, and thence became a Hunter squadron, working in Cyprus and Aden. In September 1969 No.43 Squadron moved to the ex-Royal Navy Phantom FG.1, serving with the type until the advent of the Tornado ADV in 1989. Partnered by No.111 Squadron, they provide a key element in the northern half of the UK, and have the additional role of fleet defence. Its markings are a red, white and blue fighting cock emblem on the tail fin, with a dark blue and white chequer board on the forward fuselage repeated across the tail fin.

An F.3 of No.229 OCU. Author

No.111 Squadron

Adastanes – 'Standing By'

No.111 served during World War One in Palestine in the Near East, disbanding in 1920. It was the first RAF unit to operate as a fighter with the Hawker Hurricane, which it flew with distinction until 1947. Re-forming as part of Fighter Command in 1953, it provided the 'Black Arrows' Hunter aerobatic team, thence converting to the Lightning and then the Phantom FGR.2, and later the FG.1 at RAF Leuchars. Universally known a 'Treble One', the Squadron re-equipped with the Tornado in 1989, and partners No.43 Squadron in the northern defence region. Its markings are a black and yellow lightning flash on the forward fuselage, with a black and yellow fin stripe containing the cross of Jerusalem symbol.

No.1453 Flight

Following the Falklands War of 1982 it was decided to base fighters on the islands to provide a deterrent and policing presence. Originally was the Phantoms of No.29, then No.23 Squadrons that took on the role from RAF Stanley and later RAF Mount Pleasant. With the diminishing threat from Argentina, the need to have a squadron's-worth of aircraft on the islands was realized to be unnecessary, so the four-aircraft No.1453 Flight was born. With the retirement of the Phantom from the UK's inventory, No.1453's aircraft followed suit, to be replaced by four Tornado F.3s in July 1992 The aircraft are named after the valiant Gloster Gladiators that protected Malta during World War Two: 'Faith', 'Hope' and 'Charity'. The fourth aircraft? What else but 'Desperation'! The flight's markings are a red Maltese cross

on the tail fin and the Falkland Island coat of arms on the sides of the nose.

Tornado F.3 OEU

The F.3 Operational Evaluation Unit was actually formed on 1 April 1987, before the first front-line unit, and began life as an offshoot of the Central Trials and Tactics Organisation (CTTO) at Boscombe Down. Now part of the RAF Air Warfare Centre whose headquarters is at RAF Waddington, the F.3 OEU has its home at RAF Coningsby, co-located with the F.3 OCU and Nos 5 and 29 Squadrons. The F.3 OEU is tasked with developing tactics and proving new weaponry for use by the RAF's ADV force. The OEU most recently pioneered the use of the JTIDS data-link system, detaching to the USA to work with similarly equipped aircraft, and produced tac-

No.5 Squadron's colours. RAF

No.11 Squadron's tail emblem. Author

No.23 Squadron's tail emblem. Author

No.29 Squadron's tail emblem. Author

No.43 Squadron – the 'Fighting Cocks. Author

tics for aircraft operating over Bosnia using the TRD system. Three differing tail markings have adorned the F.3 OEU aircraft. Initially three swords in a 'Y' cutting through a blue disc were worn, this giving way to a stylized red chevron with the legend 'AWC' upon it inside a white disc, and the current version is the same flash but with the a winged sword emblem, in the same style as that applied to the SAOEU aircraft.

Empire Test Pilots School

The ETPS took on charge a single Tornado F.2(T), ZD935, in 1988, but returned it to RAF St Athan for storage in February 1990, having found little use for the aircraft in their particular role. It wore the ETPS badge on the tail fin along with a blue and white nose chevron outlined in red containing a full colour roundel.

DERA

The one-time Aeroplane and Armament Experimental Establishment or A&AEE, the unit has employed a number of Tornado F.2s for weapons testing and clearance trials, and one of its internal units, the Fast Jet Test Squadron, have also operated F.2s ZA267 and ZD900, as well as F.3 ZE155.

Marking Changes

No.111 Squadron's F.3s began to sport a revised unit insignia in mid-1998 which comprised of just the squadron's Jerusalem cross with superimposed seaxes in yellow (in turn superimposed on two red crossed swords) on the upper part of the fin. The two-letter code was retained, though much smaller and positioned on the trailing edge of the fin, and the traditional black lightning bolt was removed from the forward fuselage. Its neighbouring squadron at Leuchars, No.43, had its fighting cock

emblem repositioned on the fin and saw the demise of the black/white nose checks during the latter part of July 1997.

Further south, the two F.3 squadrons at Coningsby, had enjoyed a long-ish period of stability with their aircraft, but with upgrades to Stage Two they could see many of their current fleet being dispersed as they were modified. At Leeming, where the aircraft were of the highest modification state and part of the RAF's rapid reaction force – therefore subject to sanitization before being deployed out-of-area – it has made sense for these aircraft to operate either without individual markings or, as in the case of No.25 Squadron, with markings in a much reduced form to make it easier and quicker to remove them, should the need arise.

At Coningsby No.56(R) Sqn, the F.3 OCU, began adopting toned-down markings in mid-1997. Its co-resident, No.5 Sqn has also now begun to fall into line with the reduced size markings, with ZE729/CF, it is believed, carrying the definitive version, with a red fin band, the code letters moved to beneath the band and the middle part of the fin being taken up by another green maple leaf, retaining the yellow 'V'. The other Coningsby squadron, No.29, has responded to the changes by moving the triple XXX, or 'brewers sign', from the intake to the tip of the fin, the remainder of the markings so far staying unchanged.

Tornado ADV Bases

RAF Coningsby, Lincolnshire

Previously the RAF's main Phantom operating base, Coningsby opened in 1940 as a bomber station housing Manchesters, Lincolns, Washingtons, Canberras and Vulcans, and was chosen as an operating base for the ill-fated TSR.2. It was the first base to operate the Tornado F.3 and currently plays host to Nos56(R), 5 and 29 Squadrons.

RAF Leeming, Yorkshire

Opened in 1940 as a bomber station, Leeming switched to night-fighter training duties in 1961 with No.3 FTS forming there in 1961. The base underwent a major re-fit during 1986 to make it compatible with the new Tornado ADV. Currently it houses Nos 11 and 25 Squadrons.

A Tornado F.3 from 'Treble One' Squadron in full flow. BAe

RAF Leuchars, Fife Scotland.

Leuchars is the oldest Scottish military airfield, dating back to 1911. After World War One it was passed to the Fleet Air Arm, but later became a base for Coastal Command operations. Post-war it became a fighter base with Meteors, Vampires, Hunters, Javelins, Lightnings and Phantoms operating there over the years. It currently supports Nos 43 and 111 Squadrons with their Tornado F.3s.

'TIARA' Tornado F.2A

When the former No.229 OCU relinquished its Tornado F.2s in 1986, a brace of aircraft were snapped up by the Empire Test Pilots School at Boscombe Down and

the RAE at Farnborough took on charge ZD902. ZD902 was delivered in 1988 and was used for various equipment and avionics trials, before being flown to St Athan for conversion to 'virtual F.3' standard, but without the more powerful Mk104 engines and auto wing sweep. The aircraft's reliance on the Mk103 powerplants was seen as far from ideal, but it did receive 5 FI modifications, strengthening the panels near the wing box. On its return to Farnborough it became the intriguingly titled 'TIARA Tornado', an acronym for 'Tornado Integrated Avionics Research Aircraft', and was used for flying trials for a variety of support and research programmes to develop future aircraft concepts. Making its first flight in 'TIARA' configuration on 18 October 1995, it was delivered to its new base at

Boscombe Down where it began to examine such areas as sensor fusion, in which the project team envisaged adding differing avionics and sensors, which had been built up since 1988. This fit was based around four Mil Std 1553 databuses, one dedicated to the radar and running at 250Hz, and three running at 50Hz. Being a 'twin-sticker', ZD902 makes an ideal test platform, allowing the rear cockpit to remain 'standard' for the safety pilot, and affording the front cockpit the opportunity to be extensively modified as an experimental station, representing a forward look into the realms of a future single-seat fighter. The front-end was therefore fitted with three Smiths Industries 61/4 x 61/4in (15.9 x 15.9cm) colour MFDs below a Smiths wide-angle holographic Z-HUD, covering a 30-degree azimuth and 22-

133

degree elevation, broadly representative of the modern state-of-the art HUD design. The aircraft has a stick top from the F-18 Hornet together with a Sea Harrier HOTAS throttle as a hand controller, and is fitted with a variety of telemetric equipment, together with video recorders for the HUD, MFDs plus an 'over the shoulder' view of the cockpit; external shoulder pylon pod-mounted FLIR sensors can be carried, fitted into modified fuel tanks. One of the first items of kit flown aboard TIARA was the GEC-Marconi FIRSTSIGHT IRST (Infra-Red Search and Track) turret, interchangable with a FLIR. This is an advanced air-to-air infra-red sensor developed specifically as a tool for providing high quality digital imagery and gathering IR energy through a 150mm dome on the nose of the aircraft, just above the radome. This contains a zinc sulphide window through which IR waves are reflected down into a thermal

imaging sub-system based on a TICM Class II Miniscanner operating in the 8-12um band similar to the type employed on the Harrier GR.7, via a stabilized mirror arrangement which steadies the image in elevation and azimuth, with rotational stabilization being provided by a prism, and the IRST mirror can also be used to steer the system's line of sight . The sensor image is then digitized by the TI and then passed for processing by the unit's sub-system.The TIARA aircraft was first flown without radar, but was later fitted with the Blue Vixen radar used on the Sea Harrier, chosen for its multi-mode capabilities and its compatability with the aircraft's other sensors. TIARA will, at the time of writing, be undertaking other developmental projects such as Direct Voice Input, high-speed RHAWS, GEC's HMSS (Helmet-Mounted Sighting System), and in a definitive configuration it will also carry ASRAAM missiles.

'Airwork' Airframes Saga

During the early 1990s it became necessary to increase the Fatigue Index (FI) of the Tornado F.3 in order to preserve its life expectancy as part of a planned programme of service life extension. The work was offered out to private industry under competitive tendering, and a contract to modify an initial batch of fifteen aircraft was won by BAe. However, the follow-on contract to modify a further batch of eighteen aircraft was secured by Airwork Services, who delivered a tender for £7m, some £4m lower than the one submitted by BAe.

The first four aircraft modified by Airwork at RAF St Athan, ZE292, ZE295, ZE343 and ZE728, were returned to service, but pilots soon began reporting handling peculiarities. The aircraft were grounded and inspected by RAF technicians, who traced the problems to

On QRA alert at RAF Mount Pleasant, one of the four Falkland defenders, 'Faith', 'Hope', 'Charity' and 'Desperation'! RAF

longeron distortion within the centre section of the fuselage. The longerons had
apparently been distorted when inappropriate pneumatic guns had been used to
remove the light alloy collars covering the
fasteners which connected the panels to
the longerons. The remaining fourteen
airframes were then inspected, and twelve
were found to be severely damaged, the
other two having lighter damage. The
contract was immediately cancelled, and
all work stopped whilst repair options
were considered

It appeared that the only credible solution was to return the twelve severely
damaged airframes to Panavia in
Germany where they would receive new
centre sections. This proved to be too
costly, and in 1994 it was announced that
fourteen of the aircraft would be scrapped.
However, necessity being the mother of
invention, it was suggested that the aircraft be repaired using the centre sections
from sixteen of the eighteen surviving
Tornado F.2s, which had been placed in
storage awaiting their turn to be scrapped.
This proved to be a remarkably cost-effective solution, and BAe was awarded a
contract to undertake a trial rebuild of F.3
ZE154 using the centre section of F.2
ZD901. Both aircraft were transported
from St Athan to Warton in October
1994 with the 'marriage' proving a great
success. ZE294 was the next F.3 to benefit,

ABOVE: **No.25 Squadron
aircraft in servicing, with
panels open and showing
the unit's tail emblem**.
Dave Stock

LEFT: **Version 'two' of the
F.3 OEU tail markings**.
Author

BELOW: **Tornado F.2s
awaiting delivery at
Warton**. Bae

A low-angle presentaion of the TIARA Tornado, which is fitted with the Sea Harrier's Blue Vixen radar set. DERA via Mike Tomlinson

ZE155 in the markings of the A&AEE. DERA via Mike Tomlinson

from a donation by F.2 ZD906, and all six-teen of the most damaged airframes received new centre sections before being returned to service. The two less damaged aircraft were also repaired and subsequently returned to squadrons.

A further twist to the tale came on 28 September 1996, when ZE759 crashed into the sea off Blackpool, though there was no evidence to suggest the aircraft's loss was in any way connected to the Airwork contract. The Airwork story came to a conclusion in March 1997, when it was announced that Airwork's parent company, Bricom, would pay the MoD £5 million in compensation, though the costs of the BAe repair contract as yet remain undisclosed.

F.3 Upgrade

In order to maintain the F.3's viability until the Eurofighter reaches squadron service an upgrade programme has been established, a £125 million contract being awarded to BAe in 1997. The programme will greatly enhance the F.3, giving it the ability to carry ASRAAM and AMRAAM. Changes to the Missile Management System and main computer software will enable the F.3 to benefit from the fire-and-forget capability of AMRAAM, which will give the aircraft a much improved beyond-visual-range performance, particularly against multiple tar-

gets. The highly agile ASRAAM will greatly improve the F.3's short-range capability against violently evading targets. Design and engineering work, together with the manufacture of the modification kits, is being carried out at British Aerospace sites. Embodiment of the structural and wiring modifications will be undertaken by RAF St Athan, who will act as a subcontractor to British Aerospace.

Fighting the Tornado F.3

The Tornado crews of today face as much of a challenge as the 'Few' of World War Two. The ability to react quickly is as essential today as it was in the late summer of 1940. Crews must be prepared for war in advance of any battle and this is what peacetime training is all about. Air defence operations must be extremely flexible in order to cater for the many different types of threat that the RAF currently faces, not to mention the element of surprise which is such a fundamental characteristic of war.

Once crew members become operational on their squadron, they are technically ready to fight. They are capable of carrying out interceptions at all heights and speeds, and of engaging adversaries in air combat; they also have a good knowledge of the weapons they carry and the interplay required between the many on-board avionic systems

before those weapons can be successfully fired. Crews know their aircraft, so that it becomes an extension of themselves; they understand and contribute to the formulation of tactics to defeat the enemy. Furthermore, they are competent to fly by day and night and in all weathers; are qualified at air-to-air refuelling; and are able to work in a fast-moving environment which is electronically hostile. They are not simply pilots or navigators, but managers, leaders, tacticians, mathematicians, computer operators and fighter controllers as well, and they must 'know' the enemy!

For its stated task as a BVR destroyer the principle armament for the F.3 is the Skyflash AAM. With its advanced radar-proximity fuze, Skyflash offers a high probability of a single-shot kill against both subsonic and supersonic targets from high level down to the very lowest level. Two basic types of attack are practised: the 'bracket' and the 'single-side offset'. The 'bracket' is a pincer approach against the enemy formation, with a pair of Tornados splitting and coming at the formation at a slant angle, from both sides at once, and then turning to seek an opportunity to use their Sidewinders. Depending on weapons available and the size of the target formation, the Tornados may turn 'down threat' to engage further targets. If a target crosses its path, then the Tornado's internal 27mm Mauser cannon allows a gunfire opportunity.

Fully armed, an F.3 from the Tornado OCU with four Sidewinder and four Skyflash AAMs. BAe

One of the twenty-four ADVs supplied to the Saudi Air Force. BAe

However, the Tornado is not an air combat fighter, rather a long-range bomber-destroyer, and 'turning-and-burning' is considered 'foolhardy in the extreme'. Very simply, the crews would prefer to attack in the BVR mode, using hit-and-run tactics. The 'single-side offset' keeps the pair together on one side of the enemy formation, approaching on the slant to launch Skyflash at long range and then break away. Close-in attack is cautioned against, as it can leave the attacking fighter vulnerable to the radar-guided guns of the bombers or present a tempting target to any self-defence AAMs or forward-firing guns which aircraft such as the Su-24 'Fencer' might carry. Where fighters are involved, the tactics are basically the same, but the 'paired single-side offset' is preferred. The Tornado aircrew prefer to approach these targets fast, engage the fighters at the greatest possible range, invariably BVR, and break away.

ADV Upgrade

Work has begun in British Aerospace on upgrading the Royal Air Force's Tornado (F3) Air Defence Variant under a £125 million contract awarded last year. The programme will greatly enhance the F3, giving it the ability to carry ASRAAM (Advanced Short Range Air to Air Missile) and MRAAM (Advanced Medium Range Air to Air Missile). Changes to the Missile Management System and main computer software will enable the Tornado F3 to benefit from the fire-and-forget capability of AMRAAM which will give the aircraft a much improved Beyond-Visual-Range performance, particularly against multiple targets. The highly agile ASRAAM will greatly improve the Tornado F3's short range capability against evasive targets. Design and engineering work, together with the manufacture of the modification kits, is being carried out at British

Aerospace sites. Embodiment of the structural and wiring modifications will be undertaken by the Royal Air Force at St Athan in South Wales, acting as a subcontractor to British Aerospace.

Upgrading of the Tornado F3 with ASRAAM and AMRAAM will ensure that the aircraft remains at the forefront of the UK's air defence until its replacement, the Eurofighter, is fully operational.

Fights On!

A four ship element – Maple Flight – from No.5 Squadron based at RAF Coningsby is described here by Sqn Ldr Tony Paxton, taking us through a typical CAP practice sortie:

Following an extensive brief the crew will strap in and begin their pre-start checks. The Tornado's rear cockpit is dominated by two cathode ray tubes for the radar and other displays, but it is still one of the most roomy 'fast jets' available. The switches are set, the CRTs

Sweeping across the desert, a pair of No.5 Squadron Tornado F.3s on patrol soon after arriving in Saudi Arabia. RAF

and computers are ready and the external APU provides power to start the starboard engine which, by use of a cross-drive, is then able to start the port engine. Before this, the control surfaces on the wings – flaps, slats and spoilers – are checked with the groundcrew. The port engine is then started and the ground crew intercom line disconnected. For a modern jet fighter, with both engines running, the Tornado is relatively quiet inside the cockpit. In spite of the suiting-up and the complexity of the aircraft's systems, a scramble alert can be accomplished from being outside the aircraft to chocks off in under two minutes.

Following ATC clearance, the crews taxi out of the HAS complex, lining up behind Maple 1 and heading towards the runway. The planned pairs take-off is almost immediate following the final checks. The engines are wound up to full cold power and a quick visual check of the engine instrumentation made. Maple 1's pilot gives a 'thumbs-up' and engages afterburner at 50 per cent reheat. Maple 1 then taps his helmet and nods. At this signal, 80 per cent reheat is engaged and the brakes let off. With the ASI indicating some 135kt, the nosewheel lifts and take-off is accomplished at some 150kt. The undercarriage is immediately selected up and,

as the speed passes 215kt, the flaps are retracted, and the afterburner cancelled at 300kt. Climbing away as a pair, the first duo proceed to flight level 185 on a heading of 340 degrees turning north, and splitting into 'battle' formation with about one nautical mile separation. The F.3 flies on rails and has an impressive performance, despite its detractors, and will go supersonic in the climb and is every bit as good – or better – than many of its contemporaries. Maple 3 and 4 split away as they pass Newcastle, preparing to play the role of the 'bad guys' while the first part of Maple Flight continue to set up their CAP.

The WSOs then begin their hunt with the baseline computer-generated display of range/azimuth 'search'. The plots are displayed as short vertical lines plus a horizontal crossbar to indicate a confirmed IFF response. The target is designated by using the joystick to move a four-quadrant marker around the plot. Moving to the attack display mode the WSOs select their weapons – Skyflash AAMs – and the target is illuminated by Tornado's continuous wave signal. Further symbology is displayed on the screen and a 'dot' shows the course to steer for a collision course with the target, while a larger circle shows the allowable steering error (ASE),

the diameter of which is dependent on the missile seeker gimbal limits and range to target. Launch success zones are shown on the right of the screens with maximum and minimum launch ranges. Memory Tracking aids the re-acquisition of other targets after a launch, thus permitting a rapid sequence of attacks.

While the WSOs are handling the weapon systems, the pilots manage the attack sequence, designating and re-designating the target if necessary using an air-to-air override switch on the throttles, which can be used if close combat occurs. This throws all systems into the attack mode for instant reaction: the radar rapidly scans across the 20-degree HUD field of view, locking on to the first detected target and providing aiming cues for the Sidewinder. Compared with the AI.23 of the Tornado's predecessor, the Lightning, the AI.24 Foxhunter – even before Stage 1 and 2 improvements – represented a great leap forward for the RAF's air defenders. Adopting a one-minute 'racetrack' CAP, the 'fighters' head into 'battle' formation, flying at 2,500ft and at some 450kt. Maple 1 picks up the targets on the second turn-in and brings them in on a 'sweep right' calling 'Fox One' [a 'kill'] on the 'enemy' leader. Turning in low over the Northumbrian hills, another aircraft is spotted flashing in across their starboard quarter and they pull around onto it. Using the boresight mode on HUD and cueing a Sidewinder AAM, the pilot prepares to fire. The growl in the crews' headsets changes to a chirp and the call is 'Fox Two' [another 'kill'] on Maple 4. Someone calls 'knock it off' over the R/T and the IFF dial is reset. All four aircraft head east out over the North Sea in formation to look for a tanker top-up from a VC-10 K.2 of 101 Squadron. Maple 1 approaches the starboard drogue, connecting with the probe first time, taking on 3,000kg of fuel. After refuelling, all of the aircraft break away and head towards the lower levels. Slowing down to 350kt, with wings fully forward, Maple 1 turns east over the North Sea, as aircraft are not allowed to go supersonic while heading towards the coast. Having checked-in with Boulmer radar, the throttles are moved forward into reheat and then combat power. This setting allows a little extra thrust to be used for a limited period of time, measured in minutes. At 450kt, the wings are swept back to 45 degrees, going to full 67 degrees sweep at 550kt. At 700kt, with the Machmeter reading 1.15, the throttle is set to idle. The Tornado is still accelerating and it takes some time for the inertia to drop off and the aircraft to slow down. The 'rock-steady' of the F.3 ride is punctuated only when the aircraft is doing 750kt at low-level and the re-heat is cancelled; the decelleration is marked and sudden – like hitting a brick wall! As the speed drops, so the wings are gradually moved forward. With the refuelling now complete the formation re-set over the North Sea to practise BVR interceptions, setting up a maritime CAP against Maple 3 and Four. After two goes at being the defender, Maple 1 and Two became the target and victims of a Fox One; again the only RWR contact the enemy should receive would be the lock-on from the AI.24 radar, and their destruction would then be some nineteen seconds away. Again reverting to the hunter role and in the ensuing interception, Maple 3 passes Maple 1 before they could lock-on. The tactical situation then demanded the kill of Maple 4, which was accomplished almost simultaneously by a Fox One from Maple 1 and Fox Two from Maple 2. Maple 1 then used the Tornado's acceleration to come up behind Maple 3 to deliver another Fox One.

Recovery to Coningsby will see Maples 3 and 4 making a standard landing whilst Maples 1 and 2 overshoot. In Maple 1 the wings are set forward, speed checked, gear and flaps down. Deploying full flap for finals – 180kt with 10–15-degree AOA – final approach is made at 150kt. The pilot pre-arms the lift dump spoilers

to react when the wheels touch, and the thrust reversers are activated when all the wheels are on the tarmac. With Maple 2 also on terra firma, the aircraft taxi back to the HAS site where the port engine is shut down first and the wings are swept fully back to 67 degrees to allow the aircraft to be towed back into its protective shelter.

ADVs for Export

Oman and Jordan

So nearly the first customer for the Tornado ADV outside the three-nation European consortium was the Sultanate of Oman, which ordered eight aircraft on 14 August 1985. Due for delivery in 1987, they wore a £250m price tag which included training, support and Skyflash missiles. The plan was to use the Tornados to replace Oman's SEPECAT Jaguars in the air defence role, freeing the Jaguars to replace the ageing Hawker Hunters in the ground attack role. The delivery schedule was put back to 1988, then to 1992 before being cancelled in favour of an order for the less capable BAe Hawk 200. The 'nearly' machines were then delivered to the RAF as F.3s, wearing serials ZH552 to ZH559.

Jordan was another potential ADV export sales customer. With the shelving of their interest in the 'F-5-esque' Northrop Tigershark, Jordan asked Saudi Arabia to order an additional ten ADVs for direct transfer to the RJAF. The deal was refused by the UK, even though Jordanian pilots had evaluated the aircraft.

Al Yamamah – Tornados to Saudi Arabia

The second order for the ADV also came from the Arab world, in the shape of a massive package of BAe products sold to Saudi Arabia under the Al Yamamah (Bird of Peace) programme, described in more detail on page 60. The twenty-four F.3s included in the deal were taken from the RAF's share of Batch 6 (they were later replaced), and included six twin-stickers. The aircraft were not allocated serials in the usual strict RAF fashion. The F.3s were delivered commencing 9 February 1989 to Dhahran to re-equip No.29 Squadron; plans to equip a second unit, No.34 Squadron, were abandoned in

1993. Differing little from the RAF machines, the Saudi F.3s were in fact the first aircraft to receive the Stage One Foxhunter radar set, and wore the same grey colour scheme (albeit with Saudi markings) and carried Skyflash, Sidewinder and the larger 'Hindenburger' wing tanks. In order too expedite the service entry of the aircraft, places at the TTTE were given to Saudi crews.

A second arms package, Al Yamamah II, was agreed in 1988 and was to have included a further thirty-six ADVs. However, on contract signature the order had changed to forty-eight IDS and no ADV; it has been suggested that the Saudi Air Force was not completely satisfied with the F.3's ability to meet its air defence needs. Massive deliveries of the McDonnell Douglas F-15 Eagle have now rendered the Tornado ADVs surplus to requirements, and it has been reported that the twenty-four aircraft may be converted to a SEAD or even maritime strike configuration.

ADVs at War – Operation *Granby*

One of the first responses made by the British Government to the invasion of Kuwait by Iraq was to despatch a number of Tornado F.3 interceptors to Saudi Arabia to aid in repelling any attack on that country in the most positive manner possible.

The F.3s in question, from Nos5 and 29 Squadrons, were in fact already in the region, undertaking a regular armament practice camp at RAF Akrotiri in Cyprus, No.5 Squadron arriving there on the 7th. Twelve aircraft, six from each unit, were ordered to relocate to King Abdul Aziz Air Base at Dhahran, arriving on 11 August to take up residence at their new base, grandly called HQ, RAF Detachment Dhahran. The first RAF personnel actually arrived on the 9th, led by Gp Capt 'Rick' Peacock-Edwards, a vastly experienced Tornado man, and proceeded to set up the HQ, which consisted of eight air-conditioned Portakabins and a SAT-COM dish. The Tornado aircraft detachment was led by Wg Cdr Euan Black and was named No.5 (Composite) Squadron, so called as Wg Cdr Black was the OC of that unit. This included twenty-two aircrew, and over 200 groundcrew (the latter being more than a little proud that their

Stage 1+ Tornados

As mentioned above, the final batch of F.3s were delivered with the new 'Stage 1' radar, together with an F-18 Hornet stick-top giving improved HOTAS, bringing the weapons selection switchology as well as the radar override to the pilot's fingertips. The last eight production ADVs originally intended to fulfil the cancelled order from Oman were similarly equipped, and delivered to RAF Leuchars, and thence to RAF Leeming where the aforementioned desert modifications were undertaken. For operations in the Gulf, an interim modification was rushed through, commonly known as 'Stage 1+' (S1+), which combined a comprehensive series of modifications to the Stage 1 aircraft and was intended to enhance the aircraft's capability and survivability. By retuning the engine limiters the RB.199 engines received a 5 per cent 'combat boost' feature in maximum dry and maximum reheat modes, operated by a switch on the pilot's engine control panel. The Foxhunter radar was upgraded to AA standard, with improved cooling, software and enhanced ECCM and in-close combat capabilities.

Improvements were also made to the Hermes RHWR, allowing it to recognize all in-theatre threats, and a Have Quick secure voice radio was fitted. Unfortunately this was not sufficiently compatible with the US F-15s and F-14s, which contributed to the decision to only allow the F.3s to operate over friendly areas. AN/ALE-40(V) flare dispensers were scabbed onto the lower fuselage engine access doors, canted slightly outwards, with each unit containing fifteen flare compartments. These were replaced by Vinten Vicon 78 Series 210 units before the fighting started. For protection against guided missiles the aircraft were fitted with a Philips-Matra Phimat chaff pod, initially carried in place of the port fuel tank, but later mounted on the port outer missile rail, even though this affected the aircraft's full flap ability.

The F.3's frontal RCS was also addressed with the addition of RAM strips on the leading edges of the wings, fin, tailplane, weapons pylons and the inner faces of the engine intakes. Nickel-chrome tailplane leading edges were also fitted beneath the RAM, replacing the standard aluminium ones which were prone to 'pitting' from the exhaust of Sidewinder missile launches. During the course of the war the aircraft also received NVGs, drawing on the experience gained by the F.3 OEU and subsequently by No.29 Squadron themselves who were foremost in developing the tactics for NVG operations. With the ever-present threat of chemical weapons being used, the crews regularly practised, and sometimes operated, in full AR5 NBC respirators. The cockpit air conditioning system was upgraded and the cockpit canopy rails were also modified to prevent buckling under the desert sun, and hot weather tyres, already featured on the Saudi F.3s, were also fitted.

The AIM-9L Sidewinders were replaced by the better Raytheon AIM-9M version purchased from the US. With its WGU-4A/B seeker head the 'Mike' offered greater target discrimination in the hot climate, and carried the improved Mod 11 Mk36 rocket motor. During the course of operations the F.3s were regularly seen carrying the Tornado GR.1's subsonic 330gal drop tanks (often painted sand), giving up their 495gal supersonic 'Hindenburger' tanks to give the GR.1s a greater unrefuelled range. This had the advantage of giving the ADVs a 5g manoeuvring limit, rather than the 2.25g limit imposed by the larger tanks. A pool of some twenty-six aircraft of 'S1+' standard was therefore established.

An Italian (foreground) and a British F.3. RAF

**Groundcrew prepare one of the RAF ADVs for another CAP over
Saudi Arabian airspace.** RAF

The emblem of the 'Desert Eagles', more usually found on the cap/shoulder of RAF personnel. Paul Jackson

Tornados turned in a better serviceability rate than the USAF's F-15C Eagles). Within hours of their arrival the aircraft were mounting CAPs just to the south of the Iraq/Kuwaiti/Saudi borders, commencing a cycle that would see the F.3s patrolling this airspace twenty-four hours a day until the cessation of the conflict. Under Operation *Granby* (so called as it was the next name on the MoD's list of operational prefixes) the Tornado F.3s became the first British combat aircraft in the region, to be hastily followed by Jaguars and Tornado IDSs.

The first twelve aircraft, still carrying their high-visibility squadron markings were not ideally kitted out to deal with the hostile environment into which they had been thrust, and back in the UK a replacement batch of aircraft was being prepared. These aircraft were being brought up to a higher modification state under a programme called 'Stage 1+' which was reported by Wg Cdr David Hamilton, OC of No.11 Squadron to 'have transformed the aircraft by at least 50 per cent', which goes to prove once again that there is nothing like a war to press into service requirements that have

been shelved for budgetary or political reasons!

Media estimates at the time compared the Tornado F.3's likely performance against Iraqi fighters, but these conjectures seem to have been based on the aircraft in the UK which were operating with the early Type Z Foxhunter radar, which was widely understood not to meet the RAF's requirements. By 1989 however, deliveries of 'Block 13' aircraft fitted with the Type AA radar, now meeting the RAF's original specification, had begun. Existing F.3s then began to be filtered through RAF Coningsby where a joint BAe/RAF team undertook radar replacement and other modifications, under a package known as 'Stage 1'. These 'Stage 1' aircraft went to Nos 43 and 111 Squadrons at RAF Leuchars, but in August 1990 they were transferred to RAF Leeming for further upgrading for use in the Gulf.

By 29 August the first of the 'Stage 1+' aircraft began to arrive at Dhahran to replace the original F.3s, which returned to the UK. As No.11 Squadron was due to relieve the original contingent, the 'S1+' machines arrived devoid of any unit

markings except for No.11 Squadron's white two-letter codes on their tail fins – ranging from DA to DZ – in deference to the fact they would be flown by other personnel. They also wore a white outlined badge on their fins, more usually found on the cap/shoulder of RAF personnel; this consisted of an eagle encircled by the legend 'Royal Air Force Desert Eagles'. This was, however, short lived and soon disappeared, as did the two-letter code to be replaced by a single letter.

Wg Cdr David Hamilton, flying ZE961/DH, led the first six S1+ aircraft (including two spares) to Saudi Arabia via Akrotiri. A second six aircraft arrived on 22 September, allowing the original twelve to return home. Aircraft accommodation at Dhahran was shared with the F.3s of No.29 Squadron RSAF, the aircraft operating from open 'sun shelters', commonly referred to a 'car ports' by the crews. However, with the imminent threat of air or missile attack from Iraq, concrete revetments began to spring up, affording more protection to the aircraft. A changeover of personnel took place on 24 November, and the the Dhahran Tornados F.3s came under the command of Wg Cdr Andy Moir, OC of No.43 Squadron, his supporting crews coming from No.29 (RAF) and No.25 Squadrons (the latter donating just one crew), and by the onset of the conflict the 'F.3 Squadron' had on charge eighteen aircraft. As diplomatic efforts faded the oper-

GEC-Marconi Ariel Towed Radar Decoy

The TRD, or 'Turd' as it is known in 'RAF-speak', is designed to present enemy SAM systems with an alternative target far behind the aircraft towing the device. The TRD is advertised as being more effective than ejected decoys such as chaff and more effective than cross-polar jamming. There are actually two derivations of the Ariel system, both designed to operate in the E–J bands: one is a high-power autonomous data-linked unit, and a second uses EW equipment in the host aircraft acting as a 'slave' jammer. Work on the TRD began in 1986, housed on a BAe Jetstream, then onboard a Buccaneer, and it made its first supersonic trials with the BAe EAP in 1989, with Tornado trials being undertaken in 1994. The TRD was used operationally for the first time during the Gulf War when it was fitted to RAF Nimrods.

**In the aftermath of the war, an F.3 overflies a burning oil well in Kuwait – Saddam's legacy
to the Coalition forces.** No.II(AC) Squadron via Mike Tomlinson

ations centre was moved to a concrete bunker, and men and machines were guarded day and night by the RAF Regiment.

The F.3s formed an integral part of the overall air defence system, and were placed as a barrier across the border routes. Take-off weights were in the order of 25 tonnes, including 9 tonnes of internal and external fuel. The F.3s launched in pairs supported by VC-10 tankers from Riyadh, each making two 'prods' during the course of their 41/2-hour CAP routine. Practice interceptions were made some 200 miles south of Dhahran, with targets being provided by Mirage F.1s from France and the Free Kuwaiti Air Force, who obligingly simulated the performance of the Iraqi F-1s.

Just prior to the onset of *Desert Storm*

Celcius Tech BOL

The Tornado F.3s also began to introduce the Celcius Tech BOL integral chaff launcher which had already been successfully fitted to the Harrier force. The BOL pylon is fitted to the inner wing missile station instead of the standard LAU-7 AAM rail, the rear of the pylon containing sheets of chaff which are then cut and dispensed, whilst the forward portion has a bulbous nose containing missile seeker coolant. BOL is a high-capacity countermeasures dispenser originally developed for installation inside a missile launcher, thus causing no reduction in weapon payload capacity or flight performance. BOL has revolutionized the dispensing of chaff and IR payloads by its ingenious design. An elongated boxed shape houses a long stack of countermeasure payload. An electromechanical drive mechanism feeds the packs towards the rear of the dispenser where one pack at a time is separated from the stack and released into the airstream. The release mechanism forces initial dispersion of the chaff or IR payload, which is then enhanced by the vortex fields behind the aircraft. If used with chaff, a large radar cross-section is generated in short time, achieving radar break-lock effectively and consistently. The high capacity of the dispensers (160 per pack) gives pilots the sustained defensive capability needed to accomplish missions successfully. If used with IR payload, the same airstream phenomenon will build up a cloud of radiation. BOL has been integrated with a range of missile launchers, including the RAF's standard LAU-7 Sidewinder launcher.

Vicon 28 Series 400 flare launchers were subsequently upgraded to Vicon 28 Series 400 for those F.3s involved in Operation *Deny Flight*. Author

the Squadron received the coded order to implement Plan Wolfpack, the liberation of Kuwait, H-Hour being defined as 0300 local on 17 January 1991. However, when the pace of *Desert Storm* operations became intense, the biggest surprise to the ADV contingent was the almost non-existent Iraqi Air Force, who presented no opposition in the F.3's patrol areas. On 18 January a little action nearly came their way, when Wg Cdr Moir and his wingman were vectored north into Kuwait as a formation of A-10 'Warthogs' were being persued by Iraqi fighters. The F.3s blew off their fuel tanks and locked onto their targets from long range. The Iraqi fighters, on seeing their RWRs light up, broke off the chase and ran. On other occasions the F.3s were fired upon by AAA guns with no

effect. The Iraqis' unwillingness to fight led to the decision to move the offensive CAP line forward, positioning the DCA CAP north of the border and overhead the Iraqi army, allowing the American F-15s greater freedom into Iraq itself.

Media reports had indicated a problem associated with silica dust from the desert coating the Tornado engine turbine blades with a layer of glass that clogged the cooling holes causing overheating. The silica only ever inconvenienced the Tornado GR.1, which is fitted with the Mk103 engines, whereas the F.3 had the improved Mk104 which has single crystal blades, resistant to the problem.

Following the cessation of hostilities, the Tornado F.3 crews were somewhat peeved that they were not called upon to engage

targets over occupied Kuwait or Iraq itself, as the constant no-show CAPs became tiring and tedious. There were many reasons floated as to why the Tornadoes were not committed, many centering around their lack of agility compared to the more capable F-15 Eagles, and their lack of suitable Have Quick equipment. The F.3s were not originally designed with dog-fighting in mind, but as very few engagements between opposing forces were, the Tornado Detachment felt that, given the opportunity, their tactics, training and weaponry would have proved their long-standing belief that the Tornado F.3 was indeed a potent interceptor.

Following their competent undertaking of some 360 missions, and acknowledging the pledge given to the Arab side of the

A Tornado F.3 from the Air Warfare Centre trials the GEC-Marconi *Aerial* Towed Radar Decoy System, housed in a modified BOZ pod.

Head-on hunter. RAF

Coalition, which allowed for no long-term presence in the Gulf, the 'Desert Eagles' were swiftly withdrawn, and all flying ceased on 8 March. On the 12th six aircraft left for home, followed on the 9th by another pair, with the remainder leaving on the 15th. Wg Cdr Roy Trotter landed his specially marked Tornado back at RAF Coningsby on the 13th, with the other five weary-looking aircraft following in short order.

Operation *Grapple* – F.3s over Bosnia

Soon after the Gulf War the RAF once again found itself thrust into a war zone; this time, however, it was a little closer to home, in the former Yugoslavia. The mechanics surrounding the politics and humanitarian issues of this conflict are outside the remit of this book, but the closed European environment within which the warring factions were set posed a very real threat to the RAF aircraft operating in the Balkans region.

Under the NATO-led Operation *Deny Flight* the RAF's 'Stage 1+' Tornado F.3s, were tasked with flying CAP patrols above Bosnia-Hercegovina, protecting not only fellow NATO warplanes and UNPROFOR (UN Protection Force) troops, but also RAF Jaguars and Harriers who were undertaking air support missions and laser designation duties, the committment coming under the UK designation of Operation *Grapple*. Operation *Grapple* itself was activated in response to the United Nations Resolution 836 which imposed an air exclusion zone over the region. Unlike in the Gulf War, the Tornado F.3s were not held back, and were therefore flying 'with their gloves off', committed to dealing with any aggressive act with deadly force. The F.3s began operations in March 1993 from Gioia del Colle in Italy, one of the AMI's Tornado operating bases, which provided an ideal location, having most of the neccessary ground support in situ. Initially it was the aircraft and crews from RAF Leeming who assumed the CAP role, with Nos11, 23 and 25 Squadrons all detaching air and ground crews to Gioia before the baton was passed to RAF Coningsby's Nos5 and 29 Squadrons.

A similar selection of stores and self protection aids were carried over Bosnia as in the Gulf, comprising initially of four Skyflash and later four Improved Skyflash medium-range AAMs, a mix of two AIM-9L and AIM-9M Sidewinder AAMs, the single Mauser cannon, plus Vinten flare and Phimat Chaff dispensers. Skyflash missile fits varied during the course of operations, the aircraft sometimes carrying only two missile, one on the forward port station and one on the starboard rear station. Similarly to the Gulf, the aircraft also carried the smaller 330gal wing tanks, allowing greater 'g' limits. The use of the

ABOVE: **The insignia of the AMI's 12° Gruppo**. Dave Stock

ABOVE: **Italian eagle/lightning tail insignia**. Dave Stock

Vinten Vicon flare dispensers fitted to the Tornado F.3s during the Gulf War had been expanded to a fleet-wide fit, though these units were subsequently upgraded to Vicon 28 Series 400 for those F.3s involved in Operation *Deny Flight*.

The 'S1+' aircraft operating over the Balkans found themselves thrust into a high-threat environment including sophisticated hostile SAMs, which revealed some serious shortcomings in the aircrafts' defensive suite, most notably after a pair of F.3s were fired upon by Serb SA-2 and SA-6 SAMs on 24 November 1995, thankfully with no effect. However, this problem had been recognized sometime earlier by the MoD, and as a result some of the RAF Leeming-based F.3s were noted carrying GR.1-style outer wing pylons, these items being reportedly first fitted during 1994, and were clearly designed to accommodate the latest item in the RAF's defensive arsenal, the GEC-Marconi Radar and Defence Systems Ariel Towed Radar Decoy System, or TRD. Housed in a modified IDS-style BOZ chaff/flare pod, the Ariel towed decoy is fitted under the port wing, with a standard BOZ or Phimat pod as a counterbalance on the starboard wing.

AMI ADV

During the early 1990s, delays with the Eurofighter 2000's service entry date began to cause considerable concern to the Italian Air Force, who found themselves in need of a cheap yet viable interceptor fill the gap between their ageing F-104S/ASAM Starfighters and the entry to service of the AMI's first batch of Eurofighters. Talks began between the governments of Italy and Great Britain in February 1993 as to the possible leasing to the AMI of up to twenty-four RAF Tornado F.3s. This was then agreed as an initial 'five year no-cost lease', with a further five-year extension option, and the deal was subsequently signed on 17 November 1993 following Italy's examination of other leasing opportunities, led by the USA with their F-16 and F-15. The possible lease of these would have been politically difficult, as they may have posed a threat to Italy's procurement of the Eurofighter. However, an MoU was signed on 18 March 1994 between the Italy and the UK, which covered the provision of

aircraft, aircrew and groundcrew training and logistic support for the term of the Tornado F.3's service life with the AMI.

The other governing factor surrounding the eventual choice of the F.3, apart from the political ramifications was the ease of integration into the AMI's existing Tornado operations and maintenance structure. The F.3 was also slated to receive the indigenous Selenia Aspide AAM, though this did not actually happen, the Italian government instead opting to lease ninety-six Skyflash missiles to arm the aircraft. The RAF was, at the time of the original proposal committed to reducing its front-line air defence strength in the light of the diminishing Cold War threat, and one visible result was the disbandment of No.23(F) Squadron at RAF Leeming in January 1994. This released some fifteen aircraft, and with a lower than expected attrition rate within the F.3 force surplus aircraft were available.

As the AMI has no experience of operating the Tornado in the air defence role the leased F.3s, known simply as ADVs in Italian parlance, are flown by two pilots, with a number being specifically trained as WSOs. The first of these backseat flyers were experienced pilots and will pilot the ADV after a three-year tour, retaining their flying currency on the MB339. Their WSO experience using the Skyflash BVR missile system will also give them an invaluable edge when they eventually convert to the Eurofighter 2000. Initial aircrew training was undertaken by the No.56(R) Squadron, the UK-based Tornado F.3 OCU at RAF Coningsby, with mostly former F-104 Starfighter pilots attending, although one or two were ex-Tornado IDS flyers.

The Italian ADVs were taken from various production batches, and all were modified to the Stage 1 standard, and before delivery they were further modified to Stage 1+ at RAF St Athan, the additional costs being met by the Italians themselves. This gave them the AA radar, NVGs, uprated RHWR, chaff/flare dispensers and Have Quick II secure voice radios. The first aircraft of the initial batch were handed over to the AMI at RAF Coningsby in July 1995, the balance being delivered to Gioia del Colle, to re-equip the 360° Stormo's 120° Gruppo, and the second beach were delivered to the 530° Stormo's 210° Gruppo at Camerai, which is also home to the 1 Centro Manutenzione Principale

Tornado, the Italian Maintenance Unit.

The first aircraft, ZE832/MM7202/36-12, set the standard for AMI camouflage and markings, being finished in RAF Air Defence Grey with small 'washed out' red/white/green roundels and white code letters, with its RAF serial on the dorsal spine. This aircraft was flown to RAF Coningsby on 23 June by St Athan test pilot Sqn Ldr Gregg Wheele for the official handover ceremony. Within the AMI, the Tornado F.3s will operate within a MFFO (Mixed Fighter Force Operation) concept with the F-104 Starfighters, flying in a 1:2 ratio, enabling the Tornados' systems, and in particular the Foxhunter radar, to act as an AEW&C aircraft, directing the Starfighters to the most suitable targets. The Starfighter, despite of its age, remains a potent weapons system.

Italian ADV Operators

36° Stormo – 12° Gruppo Caccia Intercettori

12° Gruppo continued to operate its F-104 Starfighters at its Gioia del Colle base until 1995 when it re-equipped with the Tornado F.3. The Gruppo's operations are split into four Squadrigle, these being 73a, 74a, 89a and 90a, wearing an insignia of a black prancing horse superimposed onto a red bow and arrow on a green disc. Declared 'combat ready' in February 1995, the unit began flying CAP over the Adriatic in support of Operation *Deny* Flight.

53° Stormo – 21° Gruppo Caccia Intercettori

53° Stormo's 21o Gruppo consists of 73a, 74a, 89a and 90a Squadrigle, and became the AMI's second Tornado F.3 user during 1987; based at Novara/Camerai, it was a time-served operator of the Starfighter. 21° Gruppo's markings consist of a tiger on a blue disc carried on the aircraft's intakes with the motto *Ad Hostes Rugens* along with the Stormo's traditional 'Cutlass and Ace' playing card symbol on the tail fin.

Tornado F.3 – on Display

One of the most powerful – and noisy – experiences afforded to the airshow-goer in the UK and abroad is the 'positive thunder' of the RAF Tornado F.3 display. In the past the display team for the current year was chosen from volunteers from the front-line squadrons, but since 1994, with the Tornado's increased out of area commitments, the trend has been to select a crew from No.56(R) Squadron, the Tornado F.3 OCU. Such was the choice of the 1995 Display Team of Flt Lts Matt Hawkins and Jon 'Herbie' Hancock, both instructors with the OCU. Matt Hawkins explains:

I don't think anyone will miss the F.3 display! Having an aircraft run in at 100ft, wings swept back and pulling into a tight minimum-radius turn in full afterburner is guaranteed to get the heads turning and force the faces out of the beefburgers!

As a display aircraft the F.3 is in its element. The original interceptor concept of long range patrols and extended loiter times still rings true, but now we do so much more with the aircraft than was ever conceived. Most aircrew will admit that they enjoy using the aircraft at low-level over land, where being honest, the performance is very impressive to say the least.

Being the display crew is a secondary duty for Hancock and Hawkins, who have their 'day job' rooted in aircrew training, and in these times of increased aircrew throughput, to then also be the 'public face' of the F.3 is a huge commitment. Each of the crews also has the opportunity to attempt to persuade the 'powers that be' to have a dedicated and specially painted aircraft, such as the unforgettable 'Red Zebra' ZE907 aircraft flown by the Flt Lts Fred Grundy and Martin Parker, the 1990 229 OCU display crew. Happily for the boys, a rather understated but highly original 'famous Waldo-Pepper' style scheme was approved for their 1995 display mount, ZE732/S. Hawkins continues:

We always liked to get airborne and push straight into the routine. We always lined the aircraft up so our rotate was abeam crowd centre and we pulled into our min-radius turn with lots and lots of noise. The gear came smartly in as we climbed, and we nipped back down for a nice 240kt turn back along the crowd line.

Then we pitched out to the fifty; Derry, wing over and pulled round, back along the runway and pitched to a half horizontal eight – up to gate height then nose down into a 300ft, 270-degree hard turn. Pulling around we stuck out the flaps, airbrakes and gear, and moved back onto line at 210kt. At datum the gear was selected up and I had to 'sit on my hands' while it travelled in as were getting close to the limiting speed. 'Herbie' in the back was then calling 'hold it ... hold it' ... whilst I was champing at the bit to get into the next manoeuvre. The final run came as we accelerated to 600kt – which is Mach 0.9 (any faster and a few greenhouses would be shattered) – down to 100ft, wings swept back, straight down the line, at centre pitching to the vertical and up to 20,000ft! End of show

In 1998 the privilege of providing the Royal Air Force F.3 Solo Display for the second year in succession was given to No.25(F) Squadron, based at RAF Leeming. This continues the long tradition at 25 Squadron of display flying, which started with the Hendon Pageant in 1924, flying Sopwith Snipes. Pilot for

Flt Lts Herbie Hancock (left) and Matt Hawkins. Author

The famous 'Red Zebra' ZE907 aircraft flown by the Flt Lts Fred Grundy and Martin Parker, the 1990 229OCU display crew. Author

1998 was Flt Lt Pete 'Willy' Hackett and his backseater, Flt Lt John Shields. The display jet chosen was ZE165/ZK, which and carried the code letters formerly used on No.25(F) Squadron's Mosquito night fighters during World War Two.

The 'Nearly' Machines

Luftwaffe Air Defence Tornado

Germany considered using the Tornado ADV to meet its requirements on several occasions, after initially considering re-arming its existing IDS versions for air defence. The LVJ or *Luftverteidigungs-Jäger* Tornado was another attempt to find a derivative that would meet the Germans' new fighter needs, which eventually led to their participation in the Eurofighter 2000 programme. The aircraft was again based on the ADV, but with a low-set delta wing coupled with canards to increase lift. The study was abandoned in 1980 due to its inadequate performance.

Other potential customers included Canada who showed a late interest in the production Tornado as a potential candidate for a new fighter to replace the F-104, fulfilling a primary air-to-air role and a secondary air-to-surface role. This interest was nurtured by Panavia, which put together a highly attractive package, which would have included a Canadian assembly line for aircraft engines ordered by the CAF, and manufacture of components for all Tornados. CAF aircrew flew the Tornado during January 1978, and Panavia made a formal proposal to Canada in February that year. In the end, however, the air-to-air requirement ruled out Tornado, and Canada purchased F-18 Hornets.

Oman was the first nation actually to order the Tornado, although the order for eight ADV F.2s was subsequently cancelled. Jordan also attempted to aquire Tornado ADVs via Saudi, but direct negotiations between Jordan and BAe in 1988 led to the signing of a contract for a batch of eight ADVs. Jordan was, however, forced to cancel its order in 1989 due to financial difficulties until 'more favourable circumstances prevail'. Malaysia, too, began to show a serious interest in acquiring Tornado in the late 1980s, but opted to purchase the cheaper Hawk from BAe. South Korea and Thailand had a requirement for some fifty Tornados, and a Tornado/Hawk package was also on offer. In the end the prospect drew a blank. Spain, Greece and Turkey were also courted, and indeed Turkey ordered forty Tornados, but their 'international credit' was not seen as being worthy enough and the deal was cancelled. Ironically, Iraq was also a potential customer, but their involvment in the war with Iran ruled out any export deals.

Super Tornado

The 'Tornado International', was a paper project based again on the ADV, but with an additional ground-attack capability. Although in essence remaining an ADV, it would have had provision for ALARM and Sea Eagle missiles, and at one time it was hoped it may be selected to replace Buccaneer in the RAF maritime strike role.

Appendix: Tornados in Detail

BRITISH TORNADOS

Serial	Type	Variant No.	Plane Set	Constructors No.	Further Comments
XX946	P02	P-02		Prototype	
XX947	P03	P-03		Prototype	
XX948	P06	P-06		Prototype	
XX950	P08	P-08		Prototype	w/o 12/6/79
	P10	P-10			Static Test Airframe
XZ630	GR.1	PS-12		Pre-production	
XZ631	GR.4	PS-15		Pre-production	
ZA254	F.2	AA001	003	ADV Prototype	
ZA267	F.2	AB001	018	ADV Prototype	
ZA283	F.2	AC001	033	ADV Prototype	
ZA319	GR.1	BT001	001	3001	
ZA320	GR.1	BT002	005	3002	
ZA321	GR.1	BS001	007	3003	
ZA322	GR.1	BS002	009	3004	
ZA323	GR.1	BT003	011	3005	
ZA324	GR.1	BT004	013	3006	
ZA325	GR.1	BT005	014	3007	
ZA326	GR.1P	BT006	016	3008	Low flying laser radar research
ZA327	GR.1	BS003	020	3009	
ZA328	GR.1	BS004	022	3010	
ZA329	GR.1	BS005	024	3011	w/o 9/8/88
ZA330	GR.1	BT007	025	3012	
ZA352	GR.1	BT008	027	3013	
ZA353	GR.1	BS006	028	3014	
ZA354	GR.1	BS007	030	3015	
ZA355	GR.1	BS008	032	3016	
ZA356	GR.1	BT009	035	3017	
ZA357	GR.1	BT010	037	3018	
ZA358	GR.1	BT011	038	3019	
ZA359	GR.1	BS009	040	3020	
ZA360	GR.1	BS010	041	3021	
ZA361	GR.1	BS011	042	3022	
ZA362	GR.1	BT012	043	3023	
ZA365	GR.1	BT029	156	3079	
ZA366	GR.1	BT030	159	3080	w/o 3/6/87
ZA367	GR.1	BT031	161	3081	GooseBay II 3/98
ZA368	GR.1	BT032	163	3082	w/o 19/7/94
ZA369	GR.4A	BS051	166	3083	
ZA370	GR.1A	BS052	168	3084	Al Kharj A 7/98
ZA371	GR.4A	BS053	172	3085	
ZA372	GR.1A	BS054	173	3086	Al Kharj E 7/98
ZA373	GR.1A	BS055	175	3087	
ZA374	GR.1	BS056	178	3088	
ZA375	GR.1B	BS057	180	3089	GooseBay
ZA376	GR.1	BS058	183	3090	w/o 10/5/91

Serial	Type	Variant No.	Plane Set	Constructors No.	Further Comments
ZA392	GR.1	BS059	185	3091	w/o 17/1/91
ZA393	GR.1	BS060	188	3092	
ZA394	GR.1A	BS061	190	3093	w/o 9/1/90
ZA395	GR.1A	BS062	192	3094	
ZA396	GR.1	BS063	194	3095	w/o 20/1/91
ZA397	GR.1A	BS064	197	3096	w/o 1/8/94
ZA398	GR.1A	BS065	199	3097	Ali Al Salim,Kuwait S 7/98
ZA399	GR.1B	BS066	3099		
ZA401	GR.1A	BS068	206		
ZA402	GR.1	BS069	209	3101	Incirlik R 7/98
ZA403	GR.1	BS070	211	3102	w/o 24/1/91
ZA404	GR.1A	BS071	214	3103	
ZA405	GR.1A	BS072	216	3104	Ali Al Salim Kuwait Y 7/98
ZA406	GR.1	BS073	217	3105	Ali Al Salim Kuwait CI 7/98
ZA407	GR.1B	BS074	219	3106	Ali Al Salim Kuwait AJ-G 7/98
ZA408	GR.1	BS075	222	3107	w/o 12/7/84
ZA409	GR.1B	BT033	3108		Goose Bay FQ 3/98 Country Garden
ZA410	GR.1	BT034	227	3109	
ZA411	GR.1B	BT035	229	3110	
ZA412	GR.1	BT036	232	3111	
ZA446	GR.1B	BS076	234	3112	AWC-SAOEU E 6/98
ZA447	GR.1B	BS077	235	3113	Incirlik FA 7/98
ZA448	GR.1	BS078	237	3114	w/o 30/3/88
ZA449	GR.1	BS079	240	3115	
ZA450	GR.1B	BS080	242	3116	French Onion
ZA451	GR.1	BS081	245	3117	w/o 6/2/84
ZA452	GR.1B	BS082	247	3118	Lobster Bisque
ZA453	GR.1B	BS083	249	3119	Ali Al Salim Kuwait AJ-M 7/98
ZA454	GR.1	BS084	252	3120	w/o 30/4/90
ZA455	GR.1B	BS085	254	3121	Incirlik FE 1/97
ZA456	GR.1B	BS086	257	3122	
ZA457	GR.1B	BS087	259	3123	A.Salim Kuwait AJ-J 7/98 Scotch Broth
ZA458	GR.1	BS088	262	3124	Incirlik JA 7/98
ZA459	GR.1B	BS089	264	3125	Incirlik AJ-B 7/98
ZA460	GR.1B	BS090	266	3126	
ZA461	GR.1B	BS091	269	3127	
ZA462	GR.1	BS092	271	3128	
A463	GR.1	BS093	273	3129	
ZA464	GR.1	BS094	276	3130	w/o 14/8/90
ZA465	GR.1B	BS095	278	3131	
ZA466	GR.1	BS096	281	3132	w/o 19/10/90
ZA467	GR1	BS097	283	3133	w/o 22/1/91
ZA468	GR.1	BS098	285	3134	w/o 20/7/89
ZA469	GR.1B	BS099	288	3135	
ZA470	GR.1	BS100	290	3136	
ZA471	GR.1B	BS101	293	3137	
ZA472	GR.1	BS102	295	3138	Ali Al Salim Kuwait CT 7/98
ZA473	GR.1B	BS103	298	3139	Royal Game
ZA474	GR.1B	BS104	300	3140	
ZA475	GR.1B	BS105	302	3141	
ZA490	GR.1B	BS106	305	3142	Ali Al Salim Kuwait FJ 7/98
ZA491	GR.1B	BS107	307	3143	Goose Bay FK 3/98
ZA492	GR.1B	BS108	310	3144	Ali Al Salim Kuwait FL 7/98
ZA493	GR.1	BS109	312	3145	w/o 17/6/87

Serial	Type	Variant No.	Plane Set	Constructors No.	Further Comments
ZA494	GR.1	BS110	314	3146	w/o 18/7/84
ZA540	GR.1	BT013	047	3024	w/o 12/9/91
ZA541	GR.1	BT014	048	3025	
ZA542	GR.1	BS012	050	3026	
ZA543	GR.1	BS013	052	3027	
ZA544	GR.1	BT015	054	3028	
ZA545	GR.1	BS014	057	3029	w/o 14/8/90
ZA546	GR.1	BS015	058	3030	
ZA547	GR.1	BS016	060	3031	
ZA548	GR.1	BT016	061	3032	
ZA549	GR.1	BT017	063	3033	
ZA550	GR.1	BS017	064	3034	
ZA551	GR.1	BT018	067	3035	
ZA552	GR.1	BT019	068	3036	
ZA553	GR.1	BS018	070	3037	
ZA554	GR.1	BS019	071	3038	
ZA555	GR.1	BT020	074	3039	w/o 2/12/86
ZA556	GR.1	BS020	075	3040	
ZA557	GR.4	BS021	077	3041	
ZA558	GR.1	BS022	078	3042	w/o 28/10/83
ZA559	GR.1	BS023	081	3043	
ZA560	GR.1	BS024	082	3044	
ZA561	GR.1	BS025	084	3045	w/o 16/8/90
ZA562	GR.1	BT021	085	3046	
ZA563	GR.1	BS026	088	3047	
ZA564	GR.1	BS027	090	3048	
ZA585	GR.1	BS028	091	3049	
ZA586	GR.1	BS029	093	3050	w/o 27/9/83
ZA587	GR.1	BS030	096	3051	
ZA588	GR.1	BS031	098	3052	
ZA589	GR.1	BS032	099	3053	
ZA590	GR.1	BS033	101	3054	
ZA591	GR.1	BS034	104	3055	
ZA592	GR.1	BS035	105	3056	
ZA593	GR.1	BS036	107	3057	w/o 9/8/88
ZA594	GR.1	BT022	110	3058	
ZA595	GR.1	BT023	112	3059	
ZA596	GR.1	BS037	113	3060	
ZA597	GR.1	BS038	116	3061	
ZA598	GR.1	BT024	118	3062	
ZA599	GR.1	BT025	120	3063	
ZA600	GR.1	BS039	122	3064	
ZA601	GR.1	BS040	124	3065	
ZA602	GR.1	BT026	127	3066	
ZA603	GR.1	BS041	129	3067	w/o 8/11/84
ZA604	GR.1	BT027	131	3068	
ZA605	GR.1	BS042	134	3069	w/o 10/12/86
ZA606	GR.1	BS043	136	3070	
ZA607	GR.1	BS045	141	3072	
ZA609	GR.1	BS046	143	3073	Goose Bay
ZA610	GR.1	BS047	147	3074	w/o 12/12/85
ZA611	GR.1	BS048	148	3075	
ZA612	GR.1	BT028	150	3076	
ZA613	GR.1	BS049	152	3077	

Serial	Type	Variant No.	Plane Set	Constructors No.	Further Comments
ZA614	GR.1	BS050	153	3078	
ZD707	GR.1	BS111	319	3148	
ZD708	GR.4	BS112	321	3149	
ZD709	GR.1	BS113	324	3150	
ZD710	GR.1	BS114	326	3151	w/o 14/9/89
ZD711	GR.1	BT037	329	3152	
ZD712	GR.1	BT038	331	3153	
ZD713	GR.1	BT039	334	3154	
ZD714	GR.1	BS115	336	3155	
ZD715	GR.1	BS116	339	3156	
ZD716	GR.1	BS117	341	3157	
ZD717	GR.1	BS118	344	3159	w/o 14/2/91
ZD718	GR.1	BS119	346	3160	w/o 13/1/91
ZD719	GR.1	BS120	348	3161	
ZD720	GR.1	BS121	352	3162	
ZD738	GR.1	BS122	354	3163	w/o 27/7/87
ZD739	GR.1	BS123	358	3165	
ZD740	GR.1	BS124	360	3166	
ZD741	GR.1	BT040	361	3167	
ZD742	GR.1	BT041	364	3168	
ZD743	GR.1	BT042	366	3169	
ZD744	GR.1	BS125	371	3171	Ali Al Salim Kuwait BD 8/98
ZD745	GR.1	BS126	373	3172	
D746	GR.1	BS127	376	3173	
ZD747	GR.1	BS128	379	3175	
ZD748	GR.1	BS129	382	3176	
ZD749	GR.1	BS130	384	3177	Ali Al Salim Kuwait BG 7/98
ZD788	GR.1	BS131	389	3179	
ZD789	GR.1	BS132	391	3180	Al Kharj CB/(JE) 7/98
ZD790	GR.1	BS133	394	3181	
ZD791	GR.1	BS134	400	3183	w/o 16/1/91
ZD792	GR.1	BS135	402	3184	Incirlik
ZD793	GR.1	BS136	405	3185	
ZD808	GR.1	BS137	409	3187	w/o 10/5/88
ZD809	GR.1	BS138	411	3188	
ZD810	GR.1	BS139	414	3189	
ZD811	GR.1	BS140	416	3190	
ZD812	GR.1	BT043	420	3192	
ZD842	GR.1	BT044	423	3193	
ZD843	GR.1	BS141	426	3194	
ZD844	GR.1	BS142	429	3196	
ZD845	GR.1	BS143	432	3197	w/o 26/2/96
ZD846	GR.1	BS144	434	3198	w/o 9/1/96
ZD847	GR.1	BS145	437	3199	
ZD848	GR.1	BS146	441	3201	
ZD849	GR.1	BS147	444	3202	
ZD850	GR.1	BS148	447	3204	Goose Bay DR 3/98
ZD851	GR.1	BS149	450	3205	Goose Bay AJ 3/98
ZD890	GR.1	BS150	452	3206	Goose Bay AE 3/98
ZD891	GR.1	BS151	455	3208	w/o 13/1/89
ZD892	GR.1	BS152	460	3210	Ali Al Salim Kuwait BJ 7/98
ZD893	GR.1	BS153	463	3211	w/o 20/1/91
ZD894	GR.1	BS154	471	3214	w/o 30/3/87
ZD895	GR.1	BS155	477	3216	

Serial	Type	Variant No.	Plane Set	Constructors No.	Further Comments
ZD899	F.2	AT001	318	3147	
ZD900	F.2	AT002	342	3158	to rebuild ZE343
ZD901	F.2	AT003	356	3164	to rebuild ZE154
ZD902	F.2	AT004	367	3170	TIARA
ZD903	F.2	AT005	377	3174	to rebuild ZE728
ZD904	F.2	AT006	387	3178	to rebuild ZE759
ZD905	F.2	AS001	397	3182	to rebuild ZE258
ZD906	F.2	AS002	408	3186	to rebuild ZE294
ZD932	F.2	AS003	418	3191	to rebuild ZE255
ZD933	F.2	AS004	428	3195	to rebuild ZE729
ZD934	F.2	AT007	438	3200	to rebuild ZE786
ZD935	F.2	AT008	446	3203	to rebuild ZE793
ZD936	F.2	AS005	453	3207	to rebuild ZE251
ZD937	F.2	AS006	459	3209	to rebuild ZE736
ZD938	F.2	AS007	464	3212	to rebuildZE295
ZD939	F.2	AS008	469	3213	to rebuild ZE292
ZD940	F.2	AS009	474	3215	to rebuild ZE288
ZD941	F.2	AS010	479	3217	to rebuild ZE254
ZD996	GR.1A	BS156	480	3218	
ZD997	IDS	BS157	483	3219	to RSAF as 701 then 751(CS001)
ZD998	IDS	BS158	488	3221	to RSAF as 702 then 752(CS002)
ZE114	IDS	BS159	490	3222	to RSAF as 703 then 753(CS003)
ZE115	IDS	BT045	495	3224	
ZE116	GR.4A				
ZE168	F.3	AS020	549	3247	
ZE199	F.3	AT014	552	3248	
ZE200	F.3	AS021	555	3249	
ZE201	F.3	AS022	559	3251	
ZE202	F.3	AT015	562	3253	to AMI as MM55056
ZE203	F.3	AS023	565	3254	
ZE204	F.3	AS024	569	3255	
ZE205	F.3	AT016	571	3256	to AMI as MM55061
ZE206	F.3	AS025	574	3257	
ZE207	F.3	AS026	576	3258	
ZE208	F.3	AT017	581	3260	to AMI as MM55060
ZE209	F.3	AS027	583	3261	
ZE210	F.3	AS028	586	3262	Spares Leuchars CAT 5 w/o 30/10/95
ZE250	F.3	AT018	590	3264	
ZE251	F.3	AS029	593	3265	rebuilt with F.2 ZD936
ZE252	F.3	AS030	594	3266	to AMI as MM7225
ZE253	F.3	AT019	600	3268	
ZE254	F.3	AS031	602	3269	rebuilt using F.2 ZD941
ZE255	F.3	AS032	605	3270	rebuilt with F.2 ZD932
ZE256	F.3	AT020	607	3271	
ZE257	F.3	AS033	610	3272	
ZE258	F.3	AS034	612	3273	rebuilt using F.2 ZD905
ZE287	F.3	AT021	614	3274	
ZE288	F.3	AS035	617	3275	rebuilt with F.2 ZD940
ZE289	F.3	AS036	619	3276	
ZE290	F.3	AT022	622	3277	
ZE291	F.3	AS037	624	3278	
ZE292	F.3	AS038	626	3279	rebuilt using F.2 ZD939
ZE293	F.3	AT023	629	3280	
ZE294	F.3	AS039	631	3281	rebuilt with F.2 ZD906

Serial	Type	Variant No.	Plane Set	Constructors No.	Further Comments
ZE295	F.3	AS040	633	3283	rebuilt using F.2 ZD938
ZE296	F.3	AT024	636	3285	
ZE338	F.3	AS041	638	3286	
ZE339	F.3	AS042	641	3287	
ZE340	F.3	AT025	643	3288	
ZE341	F.3	AS043	645	3289	
ZE342	F.3	AS044	647	3290	
ZE343	F.3	AT026	649	3291	rebuilt using F.2 ZD900
ZE728	F.3	AT027	652	3292	rebuilt using F.2 ZD903
ZE729	F.3	AS045	654	3293	rebuilt using F.2 ZD933
ZE730	F.3	AS046	656	3294	to AMI as mm7204
ZE731	F.3	AS047	658	3295	
ZE732	F.3	AS048	660	3296	
ZE733	F.3	AS049	662	3297	w/o 30/10/95
ZE734	F.3	AS050	664	3298	
ZE735	F.3	AT028	666	3299	
ZE736	F.3	AS051	669	3300	rebuilt using F.2 ZD937
ZE737	F.3	AS052	671	3301	
ZE755	F.3	AS053	673	3302	
ZE756	F.3	AS054	674	3303	
ZE757	F.3	AS055	676	3304	
E758	F.3	AT029	679	3306	w/o 28/9/96
ZE760	F.3	AS057	681	3307	to AMI as MM7206
ZE761	F.3	AS058	683	3308	to AMI as MM7203
ZE762	F.3	AS059	685	3309	to AMI as MM7207
ZE763	F.3	AS060	687	3310	
ZE764	F.3	AS061	689	3311	
ZE785	F.3	AS062	691	3312	
ZE786	F.3	AT030	693	3313	rebuilt using F.2 ZD934
ZE787	F.3	AS063	695	3314	to AMI as MM7205
ZE788	F.3	AS064	697	3315	
ZE789	F.3	AS065	699	3316	w/o 10/3/95
ZE790	F.3	AS066	700	3317	
ZE791	F.3	AS067	702	3318	
ZE792	F.3	AS068	704	3319	to AMI as MM7211
ZE793	F.3	AT031	705	3320	rebuilt using F.2 ZD935
ZE794	F.3	AS069	707	3321	
ZE808	F.3	AS070	709	3322	
ZE809	F.3	AS071	711	3323	w/o 8/6/94
ZE810	F.3	AS072	712	3324	
ZE811	F.3	AS073	714	3325	to AMI as MM7208
ZE812	F.3	AS074	716	3326	
ZE830	F.3	AT032	718	3327	
ZE831	F.3	AS075	719	3328	
ZE832	F.3	AS076	721	3329	to AMI as MM7202
ZE833	F.3	AS077	723	3330	w/o 21/7/89
ZE834	F.3	AS078	725	3331	
ZE835	F.3	AS079	726	3332	to AMI as MM7209
ZE836	F.3	AS080	728	3333	to AMI as MM7210
ZE837	F.3	AT033	730	3334	to AMI as MM55057
ZE838	F.3	AS081	732	3335	
ZE839	F.3	AS082	733	3336	
ZE858	F.3	AS083	735	3337	w/o 21/10/93
ZE859	ADV	AS084	737	3338	to RSAF as 2905 (DS001)

Serial	Type	Variant No.	Plane Set	Constructors No.	Further Comments
ZE860	ADV	AS085	739	3339	to RSAF as 2906 (DS002)
ZE861	ADV	AS086	740	3340	to RSAF as 2901 (DT001)
ZE862	F.3	AT034	742	3341	w/o 10/1/96
ZE884	ADV	AS089	747	3344	to RSAF as 2904 (DT004)
ZE885	ADV	AS090	749	3345	to RSAF as 2907 (DS003)
ZE886	F.3	AS091	751	3346	to RSAF as 2908 (DS004)
ZE887	F.3	AS092	753	3347	
ZE888	F.3	AT035		3348	
ZE889	F.3	AS093	757	3349	
ZE890	ADV	AS094	758	3350	to RSAF as 2909 (DS005)
ZE891	ADV	AS095	760	3351	to RSAF as 2910 (DS006)
ZE905	ADV	AS096	761	3352	to RSAF as 2911 (DS007)
ZE906	ADV	AS097	763	3353	to RSAF as 2912 (DS008)
ZE907	F.3	AS098	765	3354	
ZE908	F.3	AT036	766	3355	
ZE909	ADV	AS099	768	3356	to RSAF as 3451 (DT005)
ZE910	ADV	AS100	770	3357	to RSAF as 3452 (DT006)
ZE911	F.3	AS101	772	3358	to AMI as MM7226
ZE912	ADV	AS102	773	3359	to RSAF as 3453 (DS009)
ZE913	ADV	AS103	775	3360	to RSAF as 3454 (DS010)
ZE914	ADV	AS104	777	3361	to RSAF as 3455 (DS011)
ZE934	F.3	AT037	778	3362	
ZE935	ADV	AS105	780	3363	to RSAF as 3456 (DS012)
ZE936	F.3	AS106	781	3364	
ZE937	ADV	AS107	782	3365	to RSAF as 3457 (DS013)
ZE938	ADV	AS108	784	3366	to RSAF as 3458 (DS014)
ZE939	ADV	AS109	785	3367	to RSAF as 3459 (DS015)
ZE940	ADV	AS110	787	3368	to RSAF as 3460 (DS016)
ZE941	F.3	AT038			
ZE943	ADV	AS112	791	3371	to RSAF as 3461 (DS017)
ZE944	ADV	AS113	793	3372	to RSAF as 3462 (DS018)
ZE961	F.3	AS114	794	3373	
ZE962	F.3	AS115	796	3374	
ZE963	F.3	AT039	797	3375	
ZE964	F.3	AT040	798	3376	
ZE965	F.3	AT041	799	3377	
ZE966	F.3	AT042	800	3378	
ZE967	F.3	AT043	801	3379	
ZE968	F.3	AS120	802	3380	
ZE969	F.3	AS121	803	3381	
ZE982	F.3	AS122	804	3382	
ZE983	F.3	AS123	805	3383	
ZG705	GR.1A	BS172	811	3387	
ZG706	GR.1A	BS173	813	3389	
ZG707	GR.1A	BS174	814	3390	
ZG708	GR.1A	BS175	815	3391	w/o 1/9/94
ZG709	GR.1A	BS176	816	3392	
ZG710	GR.4A	BS177	819	3393	
ZG711	GR.1A	BS178	820	3394	
ZG712	GR.1A	BS179	822	3395	
G713	GR.1A	BS180	824	3396	
ZG714	GR.1A	BS181	825	3397	
ZG725	GR.1A	BS182	828	3399	w/o 10/9/94
ZG726	GR.1A	BS183	829	3400	

Serial	Type	Variant No.	Plane Set	Constructors No.	Further Comments
ZG727	GR.1A	BS184	832	3402	
ZG728	F.3	AS124	834	3403	to AMI as MM7229
ZG729	GR.1A	BS185	836	3405	
ZG730	F.3	AS125	838	3406	to AMI as MM7230
ZG731	F.3	AS126	841	3408	
ZG732	F.3	AS127	845	3410	to AMI as MM7227
ZG733	F.3	AS128	850	3413	to AMI as MM7228
ZG734	F.3	AS129	855	3416	to AMI as MM7231
ZG735	F.3	AS130	859	3418	to AMI as MM7232
ZG750	GR.4	BT051	862	3420	
ZG751	F.3	AS131	863	3421	
ZG752	GR.1	BT052	868	3424	
ZG753	F.3	AS132	872	3426	
ZG754	GR.1	BT053	875	3428	
ZG755	F.3	AS133	877	3429	
ZG756	GR.1	BT054	880	3431	
ZG757	F.3	AS134	882	3432	
ZG768	F.3	AS135	886	3435	to AMI as MM7233
ZG769	GR.1	BT055	889	3437	
ZG770	F.3	AS136	891	3438	
ZG771	GR.1	BT056	893	3440	
ZG772	F.3	AS137	899	3443	
ZG773	GR.	BS186	902	3445	
ZG774	F.3	AS138	904	3446	
ZG775	GR.1	BS187	907	3448	
ZG776	F.3	AS139	908	3449	
ZG777	GR.1	BS188	909	3450	
ZG778	F.3	AS140	911	3451	
ZG779	GR.1	BS189	911	3452	
ZG780	F.3	AS141	912	3453	
ZG791	GR.1	BS190	913	3454	
ZG792	GR.1		914	3455	
ZG793	F.3	AS142	915	3456	
ZG794	GR.1	BS192	916	3457	
ZG795	F.3	AS143	917	3458	
ZG796	F.3	AS144	918	3459	
ZG797	F.3	AS145	919	3460	
ZG798	F.3	AS146	920	3461	
ZG799	F.3	AS147	921	3462	
ZH552	F.3	AT044	922	3463	
ZH553	F.3	AT045	923	3464	
ZH554	F.3	AT046	924	3465	
ZH555	F.3	AT047	925	3466	
ZH556	F.3	AT048	926	3467	
ZH557	F.3	AT049	927	3468	
ZH558	F.3	AT050	928	3469	w/o 8/7/94
ZH559	F.3	AT051	929	3470	
ZH905	IDS	CT015	930	3471	to RSAF as 7501
ZH906	IDS	CT016	931	3472	to RSAF as 7502
ZH907	IDS	CT017	932	3473	to RSAF as 7503
ZH908	IDS	CT018	933	3474	to RSAF as 8301
ZH909	IDS	CT019	934	3475	to RSAF as 8302
ZH910	IDS	CT020	935	3476	to RSAF as 8303
ZH911	IDS	CT021	936	3477	to RSAF as 6625

Serial	Type	Variant No.	Plane Set	Constructors No.	Further Comments
ZH912	IDS	CT022	937	3478	to RSAF as 6626
ZH913	IDS	CT023	938	3479	to RSAF as 6627
ZH914	IDS	CT024	939	3480	to RSAF as 6628
ZH915	IDS	CS035	940	3481	to RSAF as 6629 (recce)
ZH916	IDS	CS036	941	3482	
ZH917	IDS	CS037	942	3483	to RSAF as 6631
ZH918	IDS	CS038	943	3484	to RSAF as 6632
ZH919	IDS	CS039	944	3485	
ZH920	IDS	CS040	945	3486	
ZH921	IDS	CS041	946	3487	to RSAF as 7504
ZH922	IDS	CS042	947	3488	to RSAF as 7505
ZH923	IDS	CS043	948	3489	to RSAF as 7506
ZH924	IDS	CS044	949	3490	to RSAF as 7507
ZH925	IDS	CS045	950	3491	to RSAF as 7508
ZH926	IDS	CS046	951	3492	to RSAF as 7509
ZH927	IDS	CS047	952	3493	to RSAF as 7510
ZH928	IDS	CS048	953	3494	
ZH929	IDS	CS049	954	3495	to RSAF as 7512
ZH930	IDS	CS050	955	3496	
ZH931	IDS	CS051	956	3497	to RSAF as 7514
ZH932	IDS	CS052	957	3498	
IZH933	IDS	CS053	958	3499	
ZH934	IDS	CS054	959	3500	
ZH935	IDS	CS055	960	3501	
ZH936	IDS	CS056	961	3502	
ZH937	IDS	CS057	962	3503	
ZH938	IDS	CS058	963	3504	
ZH939	IDS	CS059	964	3505	
ZH940	IDS	CS060	965	3506	
ZH941	IDS	CS061	966	3507	
ZH942	IDS	CS062	967	3508	
ZH943	IDS	CS063	968	3509	
ZH944	IDS	CS064	969	3510	
ZH945	IDS	CS065	970	3511	
ZH946	IDS	CS066	971	3512	
ZH947	IDS	CS067	972	3513	
ZH948	IDS	CS068	973	3514	
ZH949	IDS	CS069	974	3515	
ZH950	IDS	CS070	975	3516	
ZH951	IDS	CS071	976	3517	
ZH952	IDS	CS072	977	3518	

GERMAN TORNADOS

Serial	Type	Variant No.	Plane Set	Constructors No.	Further Comments
98+01	P11	PS-11		Pre-production,	wfu
98+02	P13	PS-13		Pre-production	
98+03	ECR	PS-16		Pre-production	
98+04	P01	P-01	Prototype	(D-9591),	wfu
98+05	P04	P-04	Prototype	(D-9592)	w/o 16/4/80
98+06	P07	P-07	Prototype,	wfu	
98+59	IDS	ex	43+21		
98+60	IDS	ex	43+89		
98+79	ECR	ex	45+75		
43+01	IDS	GT001	002	4001	

Serial	Type	Variant No.	Plane Set	Constructors No.	Further Comments
43+02	IDS	GT002	004		
43+03	IDS	GT003	006	4003	
43+04	IDS	GT004	008	4004	
3+05	IDS	GT005	010	4005	
43+06	IDS	GT006	012	4006	
43+07	IDS	GT007	015	4007	
43+08	IDS	GT008	017	4008	
43+09	IDS	GT009	019	4009	
43+10	IDS	GT010	021	4010	
43+11	IDS	GT011	023	4011	
43+12	IDS	GS001	026	4012	GI Erding
43+13	IDS	GS002	029	4013	
43+14	IDS	GS003	031	4014	
43+15	IDS	GT012	034	4015	
43+16	IDS	GT013	036	4016	
43+17	IDS	GT014	039	4017	
43+18	IDS	GS004	044	4018	
43+19	IDS	GS005	046	4019	w/o 10/6/97
43+20	IDS	GS006	049	4020	
43+21	IDS	GT015	051	4021	changed to 98+59
43+22	IDS	GT016	053	4022	
43+23	IDS	GT017	055	4023	
43+24	IDS	GS007	059	4024	w/o 17/6/86
43+25	IDS	GS008	062	4025	
43+26	IDS	GS009	066	4026	
43+27	IDS	GS010	069	4027	
43+28	IDS	GS011	072	4028	49FW, USA
43+29	IDS	GT018	076	4029	
43+30	IDS	GS012	079	4030	
43+31	IDS	GT019	083	4031	
43+32	IDS		089	4033	
43+34	IDS	GS014	092	4034	
43+35	IDS	GT021	095	4035	
43+36	IDS	GS015	097	4036	49FW, USA
43+37	IDS	GT022	100	4037	
43+38	IDS	GS016	103	4038	
43+39	IDS	GS017	106	4039	w/o 5/1/84
43+40	IDS	GS018	109	4040	
43+41	IDS	GS019	111	4041	
43+42	IDS	GT023	115	4042	
43+43	IDS	GT024	117	4043	
43+44	IDS	GT025	121	4044	
43+45	IDS	GT026	123	4045	
43+46	IDS	GS020	126	4046	
43+47	IDS	GS021	128	4047	
43+48	IDS	GS022	130	4048	
43+49	IDS	GS023	132	4049	w/o 24/9/85
43+50	IDS	GS024	135	4050	
43+51	IDS	GT027	137	4051	w/o 2/9/88
43+52	IDS	GS025	140	4052	
43+53	IDS	GS026	142	4053	
43+54	IDS	GS027	145	4054	
43+55	IDS	GS028	146	4055	
43+56	IDS	GS029	149	4056	w/o 16/11/89

Serial	Type	Variant No.	Plane Set	Constructors No.	Further Comments
43+57	IDS	GS030	151	4057	
43+58	IDS	GS031	155	4058	
43+59	IDS	GS032	157	4059	
43+60	IDS	GS033	160	4060	
43+61	IDS	GS034	162	4061	
43+62	IDS	GS035	165	4062	
43+63	IDS	GS036	167	4063	
43+64	IDS	GS037	169	4064	
43+65	IDS	GS038	171	4065	
43+66	IDS	GS039	174	4066	w/o 23/9/84 or 9/1/84
43+67	IDS	GS040	177	4067	
43+68	IDS	GS041	179	4068	
43+69	IDS	GS042	181	4069	
43+70	IDS	GS043	184	4070	
43+71	IDS	GS044	186	4071	
43+72	IDS	GS045	189	4072	
43+73	IDS	GS046	191	4073	
43+74	IDS	GS047	193	4074	AMARC/AY0001
43+75	IDS	GS048	196	4075	
43+76	IDS	GS049	198	4076	
43+77	IDS	GS050	200	4077	
43+78	IDS	GS051	203	4078	
43+79	IDS	GS052	205	4079	
43+80	IDS	GS053	208	4080	
43+81	IDS	GS054	210	4081	
43+82	IDS	GS055	212	4082	
43+83	IDS	GS056	215	4083	w/o 28/4/96
43+84	IDS	GS057	218	4084	w/o 31/10/91
43+85	IDS	GS058	221	4085	
43+86	IDS	GS059	223	4086	
43+87	IDS	GS060	226	4087	
43+88	IDS	GS061	228	4088	
43+89	IDS	GS062	230	4089	changed to 98+60
43+90	IDS	GT028	233	4090	
43+91	IDS	GT029	236	4091	
43+92	IDS	GT030	239	4092	
43+93	IDS	GT031	241	4093	w/o 6/7/84
43+94	IDS	GT032	243	4094	
43+95	IDS	GS063	246	4095	AMARC/AY0002
43+96	IDS	GS064	248	4096	
43+97	IDS	GT033	251	4097	
43+98	IDS	GS065	253	4098	
43+99	IDS	GS066	256	4099	
44+00	IDS	GS067	258	4100	
44+01	IDS	GT034	260	4101	
44+02	IDS	GS068	263	4102	
44+03	IDS	GS069	265	4103	
44+04	IDS	GS070	268	4104	
44+05	IDS	GT035	270	4105	
44+06	IDS	GS071	272	4106	
44+07	IDS	GS072	275	4107	
44+08	IDS	GS073	277	4108	
44+09	IDS	GS074	279	4109	
44+10	IDS	GT036	282	4110	

Serial	Type	Variant No.	Plane Set	Constructors No.	Further Comments
44+11	IDS	GS075	284	4111	
44+12	IDS	GS076	287	4112	
44+13	IDS	GS077	289	4113	
44+14	IDS	GS078	291	4114	
44+15	IDS	GT037	294	4115	
44+16	IDS	GS079	296	4116	
44+17	IDS	GS080	299	4117	
44+18	IDS	GS081	301	4118	w/o 4/12/87
44+19	IDS	GS082	304	4119	
44+20	IDS	GT038	306	4120	49FW, USA
44+21	IDS	GS083	308	4121	
44+22	IDS	GS084	311	4122	
44+23	IDS	GS085	313	4123	
44+24	IDS	GS086	316	4124	
44+25	IDS	GT039	317	4125	
44+26	IDS	GS087	320	4126	
44+27	IDS	GS088	323	4127	
44+28	IDS	GS089	325	4128	
44+29	IDS	GS090	327	4129	
44+30	IDS	GS091	330	4130	
44+31	IDS	GS092	332	4131	
44+32	IDS	GS093	335	4132	
44+33	IDS	GS094	337	4133	
44+34	IDS	GS095	340	4134	
44+35	IDS	GS096	343	4135	
44+36	IDS	GT040	347	4136	
44+37	IDS	GT041	349	4137	
44+38	IDS	GT042	351	4138	
44+39	IDS	GT043	353	4139	
44+40	IDS	GS097	355	4140	
44+41	IDS	GS098	359	4141	
44+42	IDS	GS099	362	4142	
44+43	IDS	GS100	365	4143	
44+44	IDS	GS101	368	4144	
44+45	IDS	GS102	370	4145	w/o 24/10/85
44+46	IDS	GS103	372	4146	
44+47	IDS	GS104	374	4147	w/o 21/1/86
44+48	IDS	GS105	378	4148	
44+49	IDS	GS106	380	4149	
44+50	IDS	GS107	383	4150	
44+51	IDS	GS108	385	4151	
44+52	IDS	GS109	388	4152	
44+53	IDS	GS110	390	4153	
44+54	IDS	GS111	393	4154	
44+55	IDS	GS112	395	4155	
44+56	IDS	GS113	396	4156	
44+57	IDS	GS114	398	4157	
44+58	IDS	GS115	401	4158	
4+59	IDS	GS116	403	4159	
44+60	IDS	GS117	404	4160	
44+61	IDS	GS118	407	4161	
44+62	IDS	GS119	410	4162	
44+63	IDS	GS120	412	4163	
44+64	IDS	GS121	415	4164	

Serial	Type	Variant No.	Plane Set	Constructors No.	Further Comments
44+65	IDS	GS122	417	4165	
44+66	IDS	GS123	421	4166	
44+67	IDS	GS124	422	4167	w/o 24/8/96
44+68	IDS	GS125	425	4168	
44+69	IDS	GS126	427	4169	
44+70	IDS	GS127	431	4170	49FW, USA
44+71	IDS	GS128	433	4171	
44+72	IDS	GT044	435	4172	
44+73	IDS	GT045	439	4173	
44+74	IDS	GT046	440	4174	w/o 8/8/91
44+75	IDS	GT047	443	4175	
44+76	IDS	GS129	445	4176	
44+77	IDS	GS130	448	4177	
44+78	IDS	GS131	451	4178	
44+79	IDS	GS132	454	4179	
44+80	IDS	GS133	457	4180	
44+81	IDS	GS134	458	4181	
44+82	IDS	GS135	462	4182	
44+83	IDS	GS136	465	4183	
44+84	IDS	GS137	466	4184	
44+85	IDS	GS138	468	4185	
44+86	IDS	GS139	470	4186	
44+87	IDS	GS140	472	4187	
44+88	IDS	GS141	475	4188	
44+89	IDS	GS142	476	4189	
44+90	IDS	GS143	481	4190	
44+91	IDS	GS144	482	4191	
44+92	IDS	GS145	484	4192	
44+93	IDS	GS146	487	4193	w/o 12/3/86
44+94	IDS	GS147	489	4194	
44+95	IDS	GS148	491	4195	
44+96	IDS	GS149	494	4196	
44+97	IDS	GS150	496	4197	
44+98	IDS	GS151	499	4198	
44+99	IDS	GS152	501	4199	w/o 19/1/93
45+00	IDS	GS153	504	4200	
45+01	IDS	GS154	506	4201	
45+02	IDS	GS155	508	4202	
45+03	IDS	GS156	510	4203	
45+04	IDS	GS157	512	4204	
45+05	IDS	GS158	516	4205	
5+06	IDS	GS159	518	4206	
45+07	IDS	GS160	521	4207	
45+08	IDS	GS161	523	4208	
45+09	IDS	GS162	525	4209	
45+10	IDS	GS163	528	4210	
45+11	IDS	GS164	530	4211	
45+12	IDS	GT048	533	4212	
45+13	IDS	GT049	535	4213	
45+14	IDS	GT050	539	4214	
45+15	IDS	GT051	541	4215	
45+16	IDS	GT052	543	4216	
45+17	IDS	GS165	546	4217	
45+18	IDS	GS166	548	4218	

Serial	Type	Variant No.	Plane Set	Constructors No.	Further Comments
45+19	IDS	GS167	551	4219	
45+20	IDS	GS168	553	4220	
45+21	IDS	GS169	554	4221	
45+22	IDS	GS170	558	4222	
45+23	IDS	GS171	560	4223	
45+24	IDS	GS172	564	4224	
45+25	IDS	GS173	566	4225	
45+26	IDS	GS174	568	4226	
45+27	IDS	GS175	570	4227	
45+28	IDS	GS176	572	4228	
45+29	IDS	GS177	575	4229	
45+30	IDS	GS178	577	4230	
45+31	IDS	GS179	579	4231	
45+32	IDS	GS180	582	4232	w/o 24/8/96
45+33	IDS	GS181	584	4233	
45+34	IDS	GS182	587	4234	
45+35	IDS	GS183	589	4235	
45+36	IDS	GS184	592	4236	
45+37	IDS	GS185	594	4237	
45+38	IDS	GS186	596	4238	
45+39	IDS	GS187	599	4239	
45+40	IDS	GS188	601	4240	
45+41	IDS	GS189	604	4241	
45+42	IDS	GS190	606	4242	
45+43	IDS	GS191	608	4243	
45+44	IDS	GS192	611	4244	
45+45	IDS	GS193	613	4245	
45+46	IDS	GS194	616	4246	
45+47	IDS	GS195	618	4247	
45+48	IDS	GS196	620	4248	
45+49	IDS	GS197	623	4249	
45+50	IDS	GS198	625	4250	
45+51	IDS	GS199	628	4251	
45+52	IDS	GS200	630	4252	
45+53	IDS	GS201	637	4253	
45+54	IDS	GS202	640	4254	
45+55	IDS	GS203	642	4255	
45+56	IDS	GS204	646	4256	
45+57	IDS	GS205	648	4257	
5+58	IDS	GS206	651	4258	w/o 7/9/93
45+59	IDS	GS207	653	4259	
45+60	IDS	GT053	655	4260	
45+61	IDS	GT054	657	4261	
45+62	IDS	GT055	659	4262	
5+63	IDS	GT056	661	4263	w/o 19/11/91
45+64	IDS	GS208	663	4264	
45+65	IDS	GS209	665	4265	49FW, USA
45+66	IDS	GS210	667	4266	
45+67	IDS	GS211	668	4267	
45+68	IDS	GS212	670	4268	
45+69	IDS	GS213	672	4269	
45+70	IDS	GT057	4271		
45+72	IDS	GS215	680	4272	
45+73	IDS	GT058	682	4273	

Serial	Type	Variant No.	Plane Set	Constructors No.	Further Comments
45+74	IDS	GS216	684	4274	
45+75	IDS	GS217	686	4275	changed to 98+79
45+76	IDS	GS218	688	4276	
45+77	IDS	GT059	690	4277	
45+78	IDS	GS219	692	4278	
45+79	IDS	GS220	694	4279	
45+80	IDS	GS221	696	4280	w/o 25/8/95
45+81	IDS	GS222	698	4281	
45+82	IDS	GS223	701	4282	
45+83	IDS	GS224	703	4283	49FW, USA
45+84	IDS	GS225	703	4285	
45+86	IDS	GS227	710	4286	49FW, USA
45+87	IDS	GS228	713	4287	
45+88	IDS	GS229	715	4288	
45+89	IDS	GS230	717	4289	
45+90	IDS	GS231	720	4290	
45+91	IDS	GS232	722	4291	
45+92	IDS	GS233	724	4292	
45+93	IDS	GS234	727	4293	
45+94	IDS	GS235	729	4294	
45+95	IDS	GS236	731	4295	
45+96	IDS	GS237	734	4296	
45+97	IDS	GS238	736	4297	w/o 25/8/95
45+98	IDS	GS239	738	4298	
45+99	IDS	GS240	741	4299	
46+00	IDS	GT060	743	4300	
46+01	IDS	GS241	745	4301	
46+02	IDS	GS242	748	4302	
46+03	IDS	GT061	750	4303	
46+04	IDS	GT062	752	4304	
46+05	IDS	GT063	754	4305	
46+06	IDS	GT064	756	4306	
46+07	IDS	GT065	759	4307	
46+08	IDS	GT066	762	4308	
46+09	IDS	GT067	764	4309	
46+10	IDS	GS243	767	4310	
46+11	IDS	GS244	769	4311	
46+12	IDS	GS245	771	4312	
46+13	IDS	GS246	774	4313	
46+14	IDS	GS247	776	4314	
46+15	IDS	GS248	779	4315	
46+16	IDS	GS249	783	4316	w/o 6/2/90
46+17	IDS	GS250	786	4317	w/o 31/10/91
46+18	IDS	GS251	789	4318	
46+19	IDS	GS252	792	4319	
46+20	IDS	GS253	795	4320	
46+21	IDS	GS254	806	4321	
46+22	IDS	GS255	807	4322	
46+23	ECR	GS256	817	4323	
46+24	ECR	GS257	818	4324	
46+25	ECR	GS258	821	4325	
46+26	ECR	GS259	823	4326	
46+27	ECR	GS260	827	4327	
46+28	ECR	GS261	830	4328	

Serial	Type	Variant No.	Plane Set	Constructors No.	Further Comments
46+29	ECR	GS262	833	4329	
46+30	ECR	GS263	837	4330	
46+31	ECR	GS264	839	4331	
46+32	ECR	GS265	842	4332	
46+33	ECR	GS266	844	4333	
46+34	ECR	GS267	847	4334	
46+35	ECR	GS268	848	4335	
46+36	ECR	GS269	851	4336	
46+37	ECR	GS270	854	4337	
46+38	ECR	GS271	856	4338	
46+39	ECR	GS272	858	4339	
46+40	ECR	GS273	860	4340	
46+41	ECR	GS274	864	4341	
46+42	ECR	GS275	866	4342	
46+43	ECR	GS276	869	4343	
46+44	ECR	GS277	871	4344	
46+45	ECR	GS278	873	4345	
46+46	ECR	GS279	876	4346	
46+47	ECR	GS280	879	4347	
46+48	ECR	GS281	881	4348	
46+49	ECR	GS282	884	4349	
46+50	ECR	GS283	887	4350	
46+51	ECR	GS284	890	4351	
46+52	ECR	GS285	894	4352	
46+53	ECR	GS286	896	4353	
46+54	ECR	GS287	898	4354	
46+55	ECR	GS288	900	4355	
46+56	ECR	GS289	903	4356	
46+57	ECR	GS290	906	4357	
98+02	ECR	WTD-61			
98+03	ECR	WTD-61			
98+59	ECR	WTD-61			
98+60	ECR	WTD-61			
98+79	ECR	WTD-61			
98+97	ECR	WTD-61			

ITALIAN TORNADOS

Serial	Type	Variant No.	Plane Set	Constructors No.	Further Comments
MM586	P05	P-05	ex X-586	Prototype	
MM587	P09	P-09	ex X-587	Prototype	
MM7001	P14	PS-14			
MM588				Pre-production	wfu 9/88
MM7002	IDS	IS001	065	5003	
MM7003	IDS	IS002	073	5004	
MM7004	IDS	IS003	5006		
MM7005	IDS	IS004	094	5007	
MM7006	IDS	IS005	102	5008	
MM7007	IDS	IS006	114	5010	
MM7008	IDS	IS007	119	5011	
MM7009	IDS	IS008	125	5012	
MM7010	IDS	IS009	133	5013	
MM7011	IDS	IS010	139	5014	
MM7012	IDS	IS011	154	5016	w/o 20/10/92
MM7013	IDS	IS012	158	5017	

Serial	Type	Variant No.	Plane Set	Constructors No.	Further Comments
MM7014	IDS	IS013	170	5019	
MM7015	IDS	IS014	176	5020	
MM7016	IDS	IS015	187	5022	
MM7017	IDS	IS016	195	5023	
MM7018	IDS	IS017	207	5025	
MM7019	IDS	IS018	213	5026	
MM7020	IDS	IS019	225	5028	
MM7021	IDS	IS020	231	5029	
MM7022	IDS	IS021	244	5031	
MM7023	IDS	IS022	250	5032	
MM7024	IDS	IS023	255	5033	w/o 14/12/95
MM7025	IDS	IS024	261	5034	
MM7026	IDS	IS025	267	5035	
MM7027	IDS	IS026	274	5036	
MM7028	IDS	IS027	280	5037	
MM7029	IDS	IS028	286	5038	
MM7030	IDS	IS029	292	5039	
MM7031	IDS	IS030	297	5040	
MM7033	IDS	IS032	309		
MM7034	IDS	IS033	315	5043	
MM7035	IDS	IS034	322	5044	
MM7036	IDS	IS035	328	5045	
MM7037	IDS	IS036	333	5046	
MM7038	IDS	IS037	338	5047	
MM7039	IDS	IS038	345	5048	
MM7040	IDS	IS039	350	5049	
MM7041	IDS	IS040	357	5050	
MM7042	IDS	IS041	363	5051	
MM7043	IDS	IS042	369	5052	
MM7044	IDS	IS043	375	5053	
MM7045	IDS	IS044	381	5054	w/o 26/7/84
MM7046	IDS	IS045	386	5055	
MM7047	IDS	IS046	392	5056	
MM7048	ECR	IS047	399	5057	
MM7049	IDS	IS048	406	5058	
MM7050	IDS	IS049	413	5059	
MM7051	IDS	IS050	419	5060	
MM7052	IDS	IS051	424	5061	
MM7053	IDS	IS052	430	5062	
MM7054	IDS	IS053	436	5063	
MM7055	IDS	IS054	442	5064	
MM7056	IDS	IS055	449	5065	
MM7057	IDS	IS056	456	5066	
MM7058	IDS	IS057	461	5067	
MM7059	IDS	IS058	467	5068	
MM7060	IDS	IS059	473	5069	
MM7061	IDS	IS060	478	5070	
MM7062	IDS	IS061	492	5072	
MM7063	IDS	IS062	498	5073	
MM7064	IDS	IS063	503	5074	
MM7065	IDS	IS064	514	5076	
MM7066	IDS	IS065	520	5077	
MM7067	IDS	IS066	526	5078	
MM7068	IDS	IS067	531	5079	

Serial	Type	Variant No.	Plane Set	Constructors No.	Further Comments
MM7069	IDS	IS068	537	5080	w/o 18/11/93
MM7070	IDS	IS069	544	5081	
MM7071	IDS	IS070	550	5082	
MM7072	IDS	IS071	556	5083	
MM7073	IDS	IS072	563	5084	
MM7074	IDS	IS073	567	5085	w/o 18/1/91
MM7075	IDS	IS074	573	5086	
MM7076	IDS	IS075	580	5087	w/o 31/8/95
MM7077	IDS	IS591		5089	
MM7079	ECR	IS078	597	5090	
MM7080	IDS	IS079	603	5091	
MM7081	IDS	IS080	609	5092	
MM7082	ECR	IS081	615	5093	
MM7083	IDS	IS082	621	5094	
MM7084	IDS	IS083	627	5095	
MM7085	IDS	IS084	634	5096	
MM7086	IDS	IS085	639	5097	
MM7087	IDS	IS086	644	5098	
MM7088	IDS	IS087	650	5099	
MM7202	ADV	AS076	721	3329	ex-ZE832
MM7203	ADV	AS058	683	3308	ex-ZE761
MM7204	ADV	AS046	656	3294	ex-ZE730
MM7205	ADV	AS063	695	3314	ex-ZE787
MM7206	ADV	AS057	681	3307	ex-ZE760
MM7207	ADV	AS059	685	3309	ex-ZE762
MM7208	ADV	AS073	714	3325	ex-ZE811
MM7209	ADV	AS079	726	3332	ex-ZE835
MM7210	ADV	AS080	728	3333	ex-ZE836
MM7211	ADV	AS068	704	3319	ex-ZE792
MM7225	ADV	AS030	595	3266	ex-ZE252
MM7226	ADV	AS127	845	3410	ex-ZG732
MM7228	ADV	AS128	850	3413	ex-ZG733
MM7229	ADV	AS124	834	3404	ex-ZG728
MM7230	ADV	AS125	838	3406	ex-ZG730
MM7231	ADV	AS129	855	3416	ex-ZG734
MM7232	ADV	AS130	859	3418	ex-ZG735
MM7233	ADV	AS135	886	3435	ex-ZG768
MM7234	ADV	AS019	545	3245	ex-ZE167
MM55000	IDS	IT001	045	5001	
MM55001	IDS	IT002	056	5002	
MM55002	IDS	IT003	080	5005	
MM55003	IDS	IT004	108	5009	
MM55004	IDS	IT005	144	5015	
MM55005	IDS	IT006	164	5018	
MM55006	IDS	IT007	182	5021	
MM55007	IDS	IT008	201	5024	
MM55008	IDS	IT009	220	5027	
MM55009	IDS	IT010	238	5030	
MM55010	IDS	IT011	485	5071	
MM55011	IDS	IT012	507	5075	
MM55056	ADV	AT015	562	3253	ex-ZE202
MM55057	ADV	AT033	730	3334	ex-ZE837
MM55060	ADV	AT017	581	3260	ex-ZE208
MM55061	ADV	AT016	571		ex-ZE205

SAUDI TORNADOES

Serial	Type	Variant No.	Plane Set	Constructors No.	Further comments
751	IDS	CS001	483	3219,	ex-ZD997, ex-701 (BS157)
752	IDS	CS002	488	3221,	ex-ZD998, ex-702 (BS158)
753	IDS	CS003	490	3222,	ex-ZE114, ex-703 (BS159)
754	IDS	CT001	495	3224,	ex-ZE115, ex-704 (BT045)
755	IDS	CT002	522	3235,	ex-ZE120, ex-705 (BT046)
756	IDS	CT003	547	3246	w/o 28/8/89
757	IDS	CS004	511	3230,	ex-ZE117, ex-707 (BS161)
758	IDS	CS005	515	3232,	ex-ZE118, ex-708 (BS162)
759	IDS	CT004	598	3267,	ex-ZE147 (BT048)
760	IDS	CS006	517	3233,	ex-ZE119 (BS163)
761	IDS	CS007	527	3237	
762	IDS	CS008	534	3240,	ex-ZE122 (BS165)
763	IDS	CS009	536	3241,	ex-ZE123 (BS166), w/o 25/7/94
764	IDS	CS010	540	3243,	ex-ZE124 (BS167), w/o 2/5/93
765	IDS	CS011	557	3250,	ex-ZE126 (BS168), w/o 20/1/91
766	IDS	CS012	561	3252,	ex-ZE144 (BS169)
767	IDS	CS013	578	3259,	ex-ZE145 (BS170)
768	IDS	CT005	632	3282	
769	IDS	CT006	635	3284	w/o 29/11/90
770	IDS	CS014	588	3263,	ex-ZE146 (BS171)
771	IDS	CT007	808	3384	
772	IDS	CT008	809	3385	
773	IDS	CT009	810	3386	w/o 18/7/94
774	IDS	CT010	812	3388	
2901	ADV	DT001	740	3340,	ex-ZE861 (AS086)
2902	ADV	DT002	744	3342,	ex-ZE882 (AS087)
2903	ADV	DT003	746	3343,	ex-ZE883 (AS088)
2904	ADV	DT004	747	3344,	ex-ZE884 (AS089)
2905	ADV	DS001	737	3338,	ex-ZE859 (AS084)
2906	ADV	DS002	739	3339,	ex-ZE860 (AS085)
2907	ADV	DS003	749	3345,	ex-ZE885 (AS090)
2908	ADV	DS004	751	3346,	ex-ZE886 (AS091)
2909	ADV	DS005	758	3350,	ex-ZE890 (AS094)
2910	ADV	DS006	760	3351,	ex-ZE891 (AS095)
2911	ADV	DS007	761	3352,	ex-ZE905 (AS096)
2912	ADV	DS008	763	3353,	ex-ZE906 (AS097)
2913	ADV	DT005	768	3356,	ex-ZE909, ex-3451 (AS099)
2914	ADV	DT006	770	3357,	ex-ZE910, ex-3452 (AS100)
2915	ADV	DS009	773	3359,	ex-ZE912, ex-3453 (AS102)
2916	ADV	DS010	775	3360,	ex-ZE913, ex-3454 (AS103)
2917	ADV	DS011	777	3361,	ex-ZE914, ex-3455 (AS104)
2918	ADV	DS012	780	3363,	ex-ZE935, ex-3456 (AS105)
2919	ADV	DS013	782	3365,	ex-ZE937, ex-3457 (AS107)
2920	ADV	DS014	784	3366,	ex-ZE938, ex-3458 (AS108)
2921	ADV	DS015	785	3367,	ex-ZE939, ex-3459 (AS109)
2922	ADV	DS016	787	3368,	ex-ZE940, ex-3460 (AS110)
2923	ADV	DS017	791	3371,	ex-ZE943, ex-3461 (AS112)
2924	ADV	DS018	793	3372,	ex-ZE944, ex-3462 (AS113)
6601	IDS	CS015	826	3398	
6602	IDS	CS016	831	3401	
6603	IDS	CS017	835	3404	
6604	IDS	CS018	840	3407	

Serial	Type	Variant No.	Plane Set	Constructors No.	Further Comments
6605	IDS	CS025	874	3427	
6606	IDS	CS026	878	3430	
6607	IDS	CS027	883	3433	
6608	IDS	CS028	885	3434	
6609	IDS	CS029	888	3436	
6610	IDS	CS030	892	3439	
6611	IDS	CS031	895	3441	
6612	IDS	CS032	897	3442	
6613	IDS	CS033	901	3444	
6614	IDS	CS034	905	3447	
6615	IDS	CS019	843	3409	
6616	IDS	CS020	846	3411	
6617	IDS	CS021	849	3412	
6618	IDS	CS022	852	3414	
6619	IDS	CS023	853	3415	
6620	IDS	CS024	857	3417	(recce)
6621	IDS	CT011	861	3419	
6622	IDS	CT012	865	3422	
6623	IDS	CT013	867	3423	
6625	IDS	CT021	936	3477,	ex-ZH911
6626	IDS	CT022	937	3478,	ex-ZH912
6627	IDS	CT023	938	3479,	ex-ZH913
6628	IDS	CT024	939	3480,	ex-ZH914
6629	IDS	CS035	940	3481,	ex-ZH915 (recce)
6630	IDS	CS036	941	3482,	ex-ZH916
6631	IDS	CS037	942	3483,	ex-ZH917
6632	IDS	CS038	943	3484,	ex-ZH918
7501	IDS	CT015	930	3471,	ex-ZH905
7502	IDS	CT016	931	3472,	ex-ZH906
7503	IDS	CT017	932	3473,	ex-ZH907
7504	IDS	CS041	946	3487,	ex-ZH921
7505	IDS	CS042	947	3488,	ex-ZH922
7506	IDS	CS043	948	3489,	ex-ZH923
7507	IDS	CS044	949	3490,	ex-ZH924
7508	IDS	CS045	950	3491,	ex-ZH925
7509	IDS	CS046	951	3492,	ex-ZH926
7510	IDS	CS047	952	3493,	ex-ZH927
7512	IDS	CS049	954	3495,	ex-ZH929
7514	IDS	CS051	956	3497,	ex-ZH931
8301	IDS	CT018	933	3474,	ex-ZH908
8302	IDS	CT019	934	3475,	ex-ZH909
8303	IDS	CT020	935	3476,	x-ZH910

Glossary

A&AEE	Aircraft / Armament Establishment	CAP	Combat Air Patrol	FRP	
AAA	Anti-Aircraft Artillery	CBLS	Carrier Light Bomb Stores	FTS	Flying Training School Future CA
AAM	Air-to-Air Missile	CBU	Cluster Bomb Unit	GMR	Ground Mapping Radar
AAR	Air-to-Air Refuelling	CCD	Charge-Coupled Devices	HARS	Heading Attitude Reference System
ACA	Advanced Combat Aircraft	CCIP	Continuously-Computed Impact		
ACM	Air Combat Manouvering	CDLP	Combined Laser and Designated Pod	HAS	Hardened Aircraft Shelter
ADC	Air-Data Computer			HDD	Head-Down Display
ADI	Attitude Director Indicator	CLDP	Combined Laser Designator Pod	HOTAS	Hands On Throttle And Stick
AECM	Active Electronic Countermeasures	CoG	Centre of Gravity	HUD	Head-Up Display
AEW	Aircraft Engineering Wing	CPGS	Cassette Preparation Ground Station	IAW	Imagery Analysis Workstations
AFB	Air Force Base				
AFDS	Autopilot and Flight Director System	CRT	Cathode Ray Tube	If-Rep	In-Flight Report
		CSAS	Command Stability Augumentation System	IFC	Instrument Flying Conditions
AFVG	Anglo-French Variable Geometry			IFF	Identification Friend or Foe
		CTTO	Central Trials and Tactics Organisation	IFR	In-Flight Refuelling
AI	Airborne Intercept (radar)			IIS	Infra- Red Imaging System
ALARM	Air Launched Anti-Radiation Missile	CVR	Cockpit Voice Recorder	IMC	Instrument Meteorological Conditions
		DACT	Dissimilar Air Combat Training		
AMRAAM	Medium Range Air-to-Air Missile			INS	Inertial Navigation System
		DASS	Defensive Aids Sub System	IRLS	Infra-Red Line Scan
AOA	Angle Of Attack	DERA	Defence Evaluation and Research Agency	IRST	Infra-Red Search and Track
APU	Auxiliary Power Unit			JMC	Joint Maritime Course
ARF	Aircrew Reconnaissance Facility	DRA	Defence Research Agency	JTIDS	Joint Tactical Information Distribution System
		DTEO	E-scope		
ARWE	Advanced Radar Warning Equipment	EAP	Experimental Aircraft Prototype	LGB	Laser Guided Bomb
				LIR	Low Infra-Red
ASE	Allowable Steering Error	EBW	Electron-Beam Welding	LOROP	Low Angle Oblique Photography
ASF	Aircraft Servicing Flight	ECM	Electronic Countermeasures		
AShM	Anti-Ship Missile	ECR	Electronic Combat and Reconnaissance	LRMTS	Laser Rangefinder and Marked Target Seeker
ASM	Air-to-Surface Missile				
ASM	Air-to-Surface Missile	EIAW	Enhanced Imagery Analysis Workstation	LRU	Line Replacement Unit
ASRAAM	Short Range Air-to-Air Missile			MBB	*Messerschmitt-Bolkow-Blohm*
		ELS	Emitter Locator System	MD loop	Manoeuvre/Demand loop
ATF	Automatic Terrain-Following	EO	Electro-Optical	MDTS	Mission Data Transfer System
AVM	Air Vice-Marshal	ERU	Ejector Release Unit	MEPU	Monofuel Emergency Power Unit
AVS	Advanced Vertical Strike	ETPS	Empire Test Pilots School		
AWACS	Airborne Warning / Control System	FAA	Federal Aviation Authority	MFD	Multi-Function Display
		FADEC	Full Authority Digital Electronic Control	MFFO	Mixed Fighter Force Operation
AWC	Air Warfare Centre				
AWS	Automatic Wing Sweep	FI	Fatigue Index	MLU	Mid-Life Upgrade
BAC	British Aircraft Corporation	FJTS	Fast Jet Training Squadron	MMS	Missile Management System
BDA	Bomb Damage Assessment	FLIR	Forward-Looking Infra-Red	MoD	Ministry of Defence
BDR	Battle Damage Repair	FMICW	Frequency Modulated Interrupted Continuous Wave	MPA	Maritime Patrol Aircraft
BITE	Built-In Test Equipment			MRA 75	Multi-Role Aircraft for 1975
BVR	Beyond Visual Range	FOD	Foreign Object Damage	MTU	*Motoren und Turbinen Union*

MWCS	Multiple Weapon Carrier System		Interpretation Centre		Programme
NAMMA	NATO MRCA Management Agency	ROF	Royal Ordnance Factory	TFR	Terrain-Following Radar
		RWR	Radar Warning Receiver	TIALD	Thermal Imaging Airborne Laser Designator
NAMMO	NATO MRCA Management Organization	SACEUR	Supreme Allied Command Europe	TIARA	Tornado Integrated Avionics Research Aircraft
Notam	Notice to Airmen	SAHR	Secondary Attitude and Heading Reference	TICMS	Thermal Imaging Common Module System
NVG	Night Vision Goggles	SAM	Surface-to-Air Missile		
OCA	Offensive Counter-Air	SAOEU	Strike Attack Operational Evaluation Unit	TIRRS	Tornado Infra-Red Reconnaissance System
OCU	Operational Conversion Unit				
OEU	Operational Evaluation Unit	SAP	Simulated Attack Profile	TISMT	Tornado In Service Maintenance Team
OFP	Operational Flight Programme	SARS	Secondary Attitude Reference System	TOEU	Tornado Operational Evaluation Unit
OTC	Official Test Centre	SATCOM	Satellite Communications	TOT	Time on Target
PBF	Pilot Briefing Facility	SBAC	Society of British Aircraft Companies	TRD	Towed Radar Decoy
PE	Procurement Executive			TTTE	Tri-national Tornado Training Establishment
PGM	Precision Guided Munition	SEAD	Suppression of Enemy Air Defences		
PI	Photographic Interpreter			TWCU	Tornado Weapons Conversion Unit
PINST	Proof of Installation	SLIR	Side Looking Infra-Red		
PLTK	Planned Track	SMS	Stores Management System	UK ADR	UK Air Defence Region
PRF	Pulse Repetition Frequency	SPILS	Spin Prevention and Incidence Limiting System	UKVG	
PTA	Practice Target Area			UNPROFOR	UN Protection Force
QWI	Qualified Weapons Instructor	SPRITE	Signal Processing In The Element	VASTAC	Vector Assisted Attack
RAE	Royal Aircraft Establishment			VCR	Video Cassette Recorder
RAF	Royal Air Force	STF	Special Trials Fits	VMC	Visual Meteorological Conditions
RAM	Radar Absorbent Material	SURPIC	Surface Picture		
RFC	Royal Flying Corps	SWAM	Surface Wave Absorbent Material	WSO	Weapons System Operator
RHAWS	Radar Homing and Warning Receiver	TACAN	Tactical Air Navigation		
RIC	Reconnaissance	TAP	TIALD Accelerated		

Index